D0891561

LANGUAGE, HISTORY, STYLE

LANGUAGE, HISTORY, STYLE

Leo Spitzer and the Critical Tradition

James V. Catano

UNIVERSITY OF ILLINOIS PRESS
Urbana and Chicago

© 1988 by the Board of Trustees of the University of Illinois
Manufactured in the United States of America
C   5   4   3   2   1

This book is printed on acid-free paper.

Library of Congress Cataloging-in-Publication Data

Catano, James V., 1950–
     Language, history, style.

     Includes index.
     1. Spitzer, Leo, 1887–1960—Contributions in
criticism.   2. Criticism—History—20th century.
3. Style, Literary.   I. Title.
PN75.S65C3   1988   801′.95′0924   87-35723
ISBN 0-252-01530-4

For Beth and Michelle
Thanks for all your help

Contents

Acknowledgments

I would like to thank those who read all or parts of this book in manuscript and who willingly offered suggestions and encouragement. I am especially grateful to Neil Lazarus, Richard Macksey, Michelle Massé, Gerald Mulderig, Robert Scholes, Theresa Toulouse, and Rosmarie Waldrop. I would also like to give particular thanks to Beth and Michael Goodwin and to Annette and Lucien Massé for all their support, and to Betsey Toulouse, who was of immense help to me during my stay in Seattle. I was in that city under the generous auspices of the National Endowment for the Humanities, whose summer grant allowed me to undertake part of the research that went into this text. I conducted that research in the Special Collections of the Suzzalo Library of the University of Washington—my thanks to the staff there and to the staff of the Eisenhower Library Special Collections and the Ferdinand Hamburger Jr. Archives of The Johns Hopkins University. Finally, I would like very much to thank Ann Weir, Beth Bower, and all of the other members of the University of Illinois Press, with whom it has been a pleasure to work.

Portions of the arguments from chapters 4 and 7 have appeared in earlier form in *Language and Style* 15 (1982) and *Style* 19 (1985).

Introduction

Leo Spitzer's work in literary stylistics covers the period from 1910 to 1960, fertile and formative years for both stylistics and contemporary literary theory. Stylistics, as Spitzer boldly conceived it, was to "bridge the gap between linguistics and literary history. . . . The individual stylistic deviation from the norm must represent an historical step taken by the writer. . . : it must reveal a shift of the soul of the epoch. . . ."[1] Spitzer's use of linguistic methodology has since become a commonplace of literary stylistics, just as the late nineteenth century's commitment to a scientific linguistics has been refined and furthered during the twentieth. But his related concern with "literary history" (in which a style directly reveals the intellectual context of the age) has survived in less recognizable form, often appearing simply as a canonical assumption of a text's artistic worth. It is a dangerous assumption, however, since it ignores the need to produce arguments for the critical relevance of stylistics as a discipline. These two concerns, then—scientific description and epistemological value, linguistic methodology and literary significance—continue to underlie contemporary arguments about the true nature and value of stylistic study.

It is easy to uncover that first concern within Spitzer's studies. "I had in mind," he noted often, "the more rigorously scientific definition of an individual style, the definition of a linguist which would replace the casual, impressionistic remarks of literary critics" (*Linguistics and Literary History*, 11). And in numerous essays—ranging from "Wortkunst und Sprachwissenschaft" (1925) to "Linguistics and Literary History" (1948) to the

posthumous "Les Études de style et les différents pays" (1961),[2]—Spitzer
sought to outline such a method. While shifts in linguistic method have
produced numerous variants of his particular formula, Spitzer's procedures
have continued to serve as both a foundation and a point of contention
for critics of literary style. For example, in 1957 Michael Riffaterre described his newly proposed stylistic method as an objective extension of
Spitzer's work.[3] The objective quality Spitzer sought would be obtained,
Riffaterre declared, by supplementing Spitzer's highly educated critical
readings with the formal analytical procedures of a newer linguistic science. Riffaterre's stated intentions echoed Spitzer's call for a scientific,
linguistically oriented stylistics. Yet Spitzer would have none of Riffaterre's
revision, and he fired off a blistering review of Riffaterre's book.[4] Clearly,
the literary and linguistic environment had changed in the years from
1910 to 1958, and at the heart of that change lies the second key concern
of Spitzer's stylistics: the relationship of style to its context.

To Spitzer, Riffaterre's proposed approach was a mid-century sacrifice
of the human dimensions of language and literature to the goals of scientific
method. To Riffaterre, Spitzer's denunciation was a refusal to recognize
the methodological strengths of linguistic formalism. But seen in terms
of the larger history of style and its study, the exchange simply encapsulates
the theoretical struggles of the first half century of modern stylistics.
Stylistics, caught between the interpretive goals of literary criticism and
the descriptive power of linguistic methodology, has needed to redefine
itself continually in relation to both. Continental stylistics, following the
tradition mapped out by philology, has attempted throughout this century
to produce schools of thought that pursue historical and comparative
studies of style. Yet these schools have been forced to battle constantly
against the shift toward general linguistics. That shift, while often less
than satisfying for literary analyis, has proved to be the path most often
followed both by European and Anglo-American stylistics. In order to
maintain its status as a critical discipline, a good portion of modern stylistics
has adapted itself to the rising interest in systematic analyses of language,
temporarily turning away from a socially or contextually defined stylistics.
Eager for objective methods of analysis, literary stylisticians have readily
appropriated the linguistic studies of Saussure, Bloomfield, Chomsky, and
others, as they searched for a more efficient description of the linguistic
features of the text.

By 1970, however, the increasing variety of linguistic theories fragmented the theoretical base of this stylistic hegemony, and studies of

style became ready targets in such works as Barbara H. Smith's *On the Margins of Discourse* (1978), Stanley Fish's "What Is Stylistics?" (Parts 1 and 2, 1973 and 1980), and E. D. Hirsch's *The Aims of Interpretation* (1976).[5] The central argument undertaken by these essays repeats the core tension felt in Spitzer's opening comment: while today's more objective studies efficiently produce large amounts of stylistic data, they also must struggle to relate that data to a larger literary and interpretive context. The result of such questioning has been the reawakening of stylistics to a history it has too easily forgotten and the strengthening of its desire to reevaluate its critical goals. In short, literary stylistics once again faces the task of relating its beliefs about style (as a form of historical and cultural knowledge) to the power of linguistic science (as a culturally validated descriptive method).

The importance of Spitzer to this reformation extends far beyond his early founder's role. Spitzer's ongoing struggle to match an acceptable descriptive methodology with a post-Romantic epistemology of style remains the central problem to be solved by modern stylistics. The key to resolving that struggle lies in recognizing the organicist presence that still lingers in stylistic theorizing, and replacing it with a new definition of the relationship between style, language, and knowledge. This book's major argument is that Spitzer's thinking provides primary examples of the way in which that new definition should be constructed. Spitzer's attempts to supplement empirical description with a fuller critical interpretation provides the preliminary arguments for today's attempts to adopt other descriptive models—psychoanalytic, aesthetic, historical, and rhetorical—to stylistic analysis (and to the description of linguistic and stylistic context, whether of production or interpretation). Yet because of Spitzer's own critical milieu, he was led, time and time again, to assume that many of these models lowered style's general aesthetic value, shifting the text too fully into a specific historical situation. For Spitzer, the realm of social history appeared inadequate to support the declared aesthetic value of literary style, and his uniting of historical and literary interpretation remained tenuous.

Spitzer's dilemma has resurfaced in today's debates with a new urgency. The dissatisfaction surrounding much of today's stylistic work has led us to recognize, once again, that literary style exists neither as a contextually independent aesthetic value nor as a function of particular linguistic features, but as a form of cultural activity. Simply put, the production of literary style is a part of socially expressive and constitutive behavior, and stylistics helps to reveal the linguistic and cultural frameworks that are a part of that production. As Mary Pratt and Mary Poovey tell us, style has ideological roots worth exploring.[6] This return to social and historical issues in the study of style reintroduces descriptive frameworks that Spitzer often explored, and in following his career we are led back to the basic question of stylistic analysis: How can stylistics produce a descriptive framework that remains committed to the move by Romantic and post-Romantic criticism into the heady realms of knowledge?

But if Spitzer's career offers so much to literary stylistics, why has he been overlooked of late? A simple answer lies in the nature of academic disciplines. Because the relevance of literary criticism supposedly rests in the knowledge it produces, we often think that the question we ask of our disciplines is essentially context-free: What do we know, thanks to this approach, or method, or discipline? In reality, of course, the question is really one of What do we *want* to know?, and that desire is never innocent. In the early half of this century, the answers to these questions were usually framed in terms of empirical knowledge or ahistorical interpretation. For nearly fifty years Richardsian and New Critical aesthetics provided stylistics with that second approach, but it was the growing power of linguistics as an academic discipline that really provided the underpinning for the study of style. Linguistic efficiency, presented as a way of attaining scientific knowledge, seemed to engage a primary descriptive procedure upon which all other aspects of stylistics could stand. But while the goal of efficient descriptive power may exist as an ideological current influencing many contemporary stylistic methods, it represents only one movement among others, and it has no primary claim to truth value. Indeed, recognition of the reductionism caused by an excessively efficient linguistics has renewed the interest of linguists in the pragmatic issues of discourse. Stylistic method, in matching this shift, has begun again to look beyond the boundaries of strict linguistic description, hoping to use related disciplines to explain literary style. As was apparent to Spitzer at the outset of his career, adequate stylistic methodology can only be constructed by incorporating into stylistic theory a variety of descriptive models concerned with describing language as a complex, culturally centered activity, of which style is a productive component.

Because social desires and pressures affect academic pursuits, this book—and its particular historical glance at Spitzer—contains a second argument for the value of his career to modern stylistic interpretation. It demonstrates how Spitzer's stylistics was affected (as stylistics still is) by its historical relation to other academic disciplines and intellectual values, and thus displays the underlying tensions that now lead us to embrace, or still reject, those very disciplines that seemed so important to stylistic interpretation in the past. The consequences of academic bias are thus both a part of Spitzer's career and an argument for reevaluating his thinking. Historical context—when redefined to include the ideological frameworks governing a particular historical moment—can be recognized as important, then, not only to the production and interpretation of literary style, but to the advancement of literary stylistics as well.[7]

The first chapter of this book discusses the historical debates and dilemmas behind the formation of twentieth-century stylistics. Spitzer's own early attempts at resolving some of these dilemmas are analyzed in chapters 2 and 3. Until now, René Wellek's 1960 eulogy, "Leo Spitzer (1887–1960)," has provided the quickest overview of the early period. But Wellek clearly prefers those parts of Spitzer's literary criticism that operate in the aesthetic mode, and he focuses on the multicultural, panhistorical aspect of Spitzer's criticism to resolve arguments between Spitzer and other critics, such as Bruneau and Hytier.[8] I will follow a different approach. Chapters 2 and 3 will focus less on Spitzer's aesthetics and more on his desire to describe author and history in a form adequate to both his linguistic training and his critical desires. Three articles—"Wortkunst und Sprachwissenchaft" (1925), "Zur Sprachlichen Interpretationen von Wortkunstwerken" (1930), and "Linguistics and Literary History" (1948)— form the backbone of these chapters.[9]

The last of these three articles was composed after Spitzer's flight from Nazi persecution and his subsequent move to the United States. That emigration removed Spitzer from the source of his training and thought, and it was accompanied by an increasing reliance upon personal authority in Spitzer's readings, a reliance that coupled only too readily with the assertion of beauty and truth that often accompanies a general aestheticism. It is a tendency that would prove to fit reasonably well, as we will see in chapter 4, with the New Critical trends that dominated Anglo-American critical thinking at this time. My own basic belief—that external descriptive models of language and behavior are necessary for the adequate description of style—must eventually come into direct conflict with this aspect of Spitzer's later thinking and its vision of the proper aesthetic reading. Faced with an ongoing academic drift toward positivism, Spitzer tended to overprotect his position by retreating into a hierarchical representation of aesthetic value as the key to literary history—a form of argument present most clearly in his disagreements with Lovejoy and Burke (1941–1948) over history and rhetoric (chapter 4), and with Hytier, Bruneau, and Riffaterre (1950–1960) over literary and linguistic methods (chapter 5).

Spitzer's death brought an end to these exchanges, although there was a burst of discussion on Spitzer from 1960 to 1970 in essays by Wellek, Starobinski, Gray, and Dupriez, among others. That era itself came to a neat end in 1970, when Starobinski revised his initial study and reissued it in two different texts, one of them the first French-language edition of essays by Spitzer. Not surprisingly, the high tide of formal linguistic stylistics from 1970 to 1980 matches a low ebb in the discussion of Spitzer. But formalism has faced its own detractors of late, and Geoffrey Green's book on Auerbach and Spitzer (1982), David Bellos's edition of translations (1983), and the Stanford collection of essays (1988)[10] have declared the silence of the 1970s to be no more than a brief lacuna in English-language studies of Spitzer. In continental Europe Starobinski's essay "La Stylistique et ses méthodes: Leo Spitzer" has renewed interest in Spitzer by glancing more closely at the critical desires behind his thinking. Starobinski portrays—and champions—the uncertainties arising from Spitzer's opposing drives for a scientific criticism and a fuller literary history, while Starobinski's own interest in the open-ended nature of critical points of view leads him to praise Spitzer's distaste for positivistic analysis (580). Starobinski also rightly notes that Spitzer's interest in a psychology or sociology of style would have benefited from a more rigorous psychological, sociological, or philosophical framework. At the same time, David Bellos has continued to stress the literary history addressed in all of Spitzer's works (*Leo Spitzer: Essays on Seventeenth-Century French Literature*) by noting the more direct link between language and behavior in Spitzer's "politico-linguistic tracts" (xv).[11]

Still, the tenor of Spitzer's later career is captured in his gradual establishment of critical boundaries, and Bellos notes Spitzer's move away from the systematic integration of history into his procedures. This tendency to shift away from particular psychological explanations as the key to stylistic analysis and toward interpretations defined by a general historical context is extended by Spitzer's later movement away from history itself toward a wider-ranging cultural sensibility. Social issues, specific events, or the ideologies behind them thus defer to aesthetic, moral, and spiritual explanations of the literary work. This tendency has been well illustrated in Green's discussion of Spitzer and Auerbach (*Literary Crit-*

icism and the Structures of History), a study that clarifies Spitzer's sense
of the moral nature and purpose of the critical life and underlines his
continual thinking on the critic's position in the larger social framework.
The importance of the social status of critical thinking to Spitzer, as well
as its moral imperatives, can be found in another portrait of him and his
general philosophy of criticism—Starobinski's translation of five "aphorisms" from Spitzer's *Stilstudien*. Together they define Spitzer's sense of
the critic's proper position in relation to the text and, as Bellos also has
noted, they are useful in categorizing the various facets of Spitzer's scholarly activity. The aphorisms propose five scholarly areas as the components
of all academic activity: scientific specialization, methodological enrich-
ment, philosophical orientation, social engagement, and metaphysical
questioning. The last four areas are actively pursued by Spitzer, and the
latter three are clearly visible as a part of his authoritative critical stance.
The one area that Spitzer continually struggles with is the second one—
the methodological—and in the resolution of that struggle lies the bridge
between the specialist's descriptive role and the interpretive stance of
the literary critic.

The way in which stylistic theory finally can build that bridge is the
focus of the last chapter of this book. What *would* a Spitzerian stylistics
look like, Starobinski has mused, if it addressed "Freudian or Marxist
inferences," "intentional antecedents, affective or socio-economic infra-
structures" (*Études*, 20)? The answer is that such an ideologically alert
framework, designed and strengthened to support Spitzer's critical goals,
would produce a stylistics that grants literary style its desired critical
relevance while meeting the requirements for an adequate description of
literary discourse.

NOTES

1. Leo Spitzer, *Linguistics and Literary History* (Princeton, N.J.:
Princeton University Press, 1948; rpt. New York: Russell & Russell, 1962).
2. Leo Spitzer, "Wortkunst und Sprachwissenchaft," *Germanisch-romanisch Monatsschrift*, 13 (1925), 169–86; "Linguistics and Literary History," *Linguistics and Literary History*, 1–39; and "Les Études de style
et les différents pays," *Langue et Littérature, Actes de la Fédération
Internationale des Langues et Littératures Modernes* (Paris: Société d'Édition « Les Belles Lettres », 1961), 23–39.
3. Michael Riffaterre, *Le Style des Pléiades de Gobineau: essai d'ap-*

plication d'une méthode stylistique (New York: Columbia University Press, 1957), 20.

4. Leo Spitzer, "Review of *Le Style des Pléiades de Gobineau: essai d'application d'une méthode stylistique* by Michael Riffaterre," *Modern Language Notes,* 73 (1958), 68–74.

5. Barbara H. Smith, *On the Margins of Discourse* (Chicago: University of Chicago Press, 1978); Stanley Fish, *Is There a Text in This Class?* (Cambridge, Mass.: Harvard University Press, 1980); E. D. Hirsch, *The Aims of Interpretation* (Chicago: University of Chicago Press, 1976).

6. Mary Poovey, *The Proper Lady and the Woman Writer: Ideology as Style in the Works of Mary Wollstonecraft, Mary Shelley, and Jane Austen* (Chicago: University of Chicago Press, 1984); Mary Pratt, "The Ideology of Speech-Act Theory," *Centrum,* 1, no. 1 (Spring, 1981), 5–18 and "Conventions of Representation: Where Discourse and Ideology Meet," in *Contemporary Perceptions of Language: Interdisciplinary Dimensions, Georgetown University Round Table on Languages and Linguistics 1982* (Washington, D.C.: Georgetown University Press, 1982), 139–55. Poovey holds to a general and wide-ranging sense of ideology: "Ideology, as I use the term, governs not just political and economic relations but social and even psychological stresses as well" (xiv). Eagleton both admits and exempts some of these areas from ideology in his definition: "By ideology I mean, roughly, the ways in which what we say and believe connects with the power structure and power relations of the society we live in. It follows from such a rough definition of ideology that not all of our underlying judgments and categories can usefully be said to be ideological" (Terry Eagleton, *Literary Theory: an Introduction* [Minneapolis: University of Minnesota Press, 1983], 14–15). I will adhere to Poovey's more general definition.

7. The work of M.M. Bakhtin provides a remarkably similar case of the vagaries of the critical marketplace. Currently seen as a growing force in critical thought, until recently Bakhtin's work was virtually unknown in the English-speaking critical world—an oversight that ignores his position in relation to the imposing figures of Continental philology. As Michael Holquist notes in discussing the incredible range of his work, Bakhtin "belongs to the tradition that produced Spitzer, Curtius, Auerbach and . . . Wellek" (M.M. Bakhtin, *The Dialogic Imagination,* ed. Michael Holquist [Austin: University of Texas Press, 1981], xvii). It is a tradition that insists upon the inclusion of cultural interpretation in language study. Not surprisingly, then, Bakhtin's work contains the same desire to resolve the critical tensions between linguistic form and cultural discourse that we will find in Spitzer. (See especially Bakhtin's essay "Discourse in the Novel" in Holquist.)

8. René Wellek, "Leo Spitzer (1887–1960)," *Comparative Literature*, 12 (1960), 310–34. Wellek's article and its bibliography constitute one of the better English-language introductions to Spitzer's work. The article is necessary reading for anyone analyzing Spitzer's work. Sister Eileen Craddock's dissertation, *Style Theories as Found in Stylistic Studies of Romance Scholars (1900–1950)*, vol. 43 of *Studies in Romance Languages and Literatures* (Washington, D.C.: Catholic University of America, 1952), contains a large amount of theoretical material gleaned from various sources. Although the major portion of the study consists of translations, there are some short summaries at the end of each chapter as well.

9. Leo Spitzer, "Zur Sprachlichen Interpretationen von Wortkunstwerken," *Neue Jahrbucher für Wissenschaft und Jugendbildung*, 6 (1930), 632–51; rpt. *Romanische Stil- und Literaturstudien* (Marburg: Elwert, 1931), 4–53. Wellek argues that these articles only narrowly define Spitzer's literary theory. But Wellek himself uses them specifically for the purpose of discussing Spitzer's early career, and they remain important in understanding the struggles that faced Spitzer as he pursued his stylistic goals. As we will see later, those goals are not just a part of his early career; they are central to Spitzer's thinking as a whole.

10. Jean Starobinski, "La Stylistique et ses méthodes: Leo Spitzer," *Critique* (July, 1964), 579–97; rev. and rpt. as "Leo Spitzer et la lecture stylistique," in Leo Spitzer, *Études de style*, ed. J. Starobinski (Paris: Gallimard, 1970), 7–42 (page references are to this work); and Starobinski, *La relation critique* (Paris: Gallimard, 1970), 34–81; Bennison Gray, "The Lesson of Leo Spitzer," *Modern Language Review*, 71, no. 4 (October, 1966), 547–55; B. Dupriez, "Jalons pour une stylistique littéraire," *Le Français Moderne*, 32 (1964), 45–53 (Dupriez discusses Spitzer very briefly); Geoffrey Green, *Literary Criticism and the Structures of History: Erich Auerbach and Leo Spitzer* (Lincoln: University of Nebraska Press, 1982); David Bellos, ed., *Leo Spitzer: Essays on Seventeenth-Century French Literature* (Cambridge: Cambridge University Press, 1983); Alban K. Forcione *et al.*, eds., *Leo Spitzer: Representative Essays* (Stanford, Cal.: Stanford University Press, 1988).

11. Leo Spitzer, *Betrachtungen eines Linguisten über Houston Stewart Chamberlains Kriegaufsätze und die Sprachbewertung im allgemeinen* (Leipzig, 1918); *Fremdwörterhatz und Fremdvölkerhass, eine Streitschrift gegen Sprachreinigung* (Vienna, 1918). These contextually based concerns are further demonstrated by Spitzer's use of contemporary writers to teach linguistics following World War I to soldiers, who—not surprisingly—rejected any disjunction between the academic and the social, between style and history.

1 The Historical Background
Rhetoric, Linguistics, and Literary Criticism

The rise of literary stylistics as an academic discipline is primarily a twentieth-century phenomenon, its arrival linked to the related appearance of literary criticism and linguistics as independent academic pursuits. Charles Bally's *Précis de stylistique* (1905)[1] is regularly used to mark the beginning of *stylistique*, that is, the linguistic analysis of a language's stylistic possibilities. Modern literary theory announces its presence twelve years later, according to Terry Eagleton,[2] through Viktor Shklovsky's 1917 Formalist essay "Art as Device." The beginning of modern literary stylistics, or *Stilforschung*, can be placed neatly between those other two milestones by tying it to the start, in 1910, of Leo Spitzer's career.[3]

The concerns of modern stylistics thus rest, both temporally and theoretically, between the concerns of modern linguistics and modern literary theory, sharing the analytical and interpretive goals of each in varying proportions. At the same time, stylistics continues to have close ties with the third major influence on thinking about style: rhetoric. Through these ties, modern stylistics maintains the tradition of relating its own status to the status accorded to other descriptive methods within the culture's intellectual and social framework—the most important of them continuing to be rhetoric, linguistics, and literary criticism. To this disciplinary tangle must be added a further complication, which all three areas depend upon in turn—the Romantic and post-Romantic view of language as a component of knowledge, and style as an epistemologically significant use of language. Thus, to the methodological and disciplinary issues surrounding

the description of style, we must add the further "philosophical" issu
how to define the knowledge that literary style supposedly captures.

The modern concept of literary style, like that of literature itself, has
been heavily qualified by Romanticist ideas of literature as acontextual,
or at least as floating in the cleaner aesthetic air found above any particular
social context. This attitude permeates early Romantic views of style and
later is subsidized by twentieth-century concerns with formally objective
definitions of language. These Romantic and post-Romantic attitudes differ
markedly from much of the long-standing, pre-Romantic rhetorical concern with style as a contextually dependent form of social interaction. Yet
Romantic attitudes have gradually been accepted as a natural historical
development away from the concerns of rhetoric. That easy historical
judgment has come under scrutiny of late, however, as the deep-seated
ideological considerations underlying Romantic and post-Romantic intellectual frameworks have been brought to light.[4] These arguments have
begun to have a profound effect on contemporary stylistic theory, for in
demonstrating that literary and linguistic *theory* do not operate in a contextual vacuum, such arguments also demonstrate that the *production* of
literature and language must be influenced by historical context. That
may be a commonsense view of writing, but it has been downplayed in
Anglo-American criticism for over seventy-five years.

The renewed interest in discussing historical contexts and ideological
constraints goes to the heart of modern stylistic theorizing, which has
tended to rest its claims for critical validity on a combination of the
methodological power ascribed to a context-free scientific formalism in
linguistics and the post-Romantic importance of organicist aesthetics in
literature. The combined influence of these attitudes has led to the rejection of a stylistics rooted in the functional contextuality offered by earlier
rhetorical traditions, whether of a classical or an eighteenth-century stamp,
and to the acceptance of a stylistics rooted in literary and linguistic formalism.

Leo Spitzer's attempt to provide a stylistic method from within these
strictures presents the essential goals—and difficulties—at the core of
modern stylistics. He began as early as 1910 to conceive of a literary
stylistics founded on the descriptive power of linguistic analysis. Despite
his later antagonism toward neo-grammarian linguistics, Spitzer never
denied the importance of his formal training in historical linguistics. In
fact, he was to state a preference for such work if the only other option
were an open-ended and amorphous response to literature.[5] His difficulties

arose when he attempted to match the descriptive goals of linguistic stylistics with the larger literary significance granted to style by Romantic and post-Romantic definitions of literature. Formal linguistic description could be rooted in the historical methods of Meyer-Lübke, but such methods did not lead naturally to literary-critical discussions of the high aesthetic value of literary language.

The high cultural significance accorded to literature and literary style rests, for Spitzer (as it does ultimately for many critics), on the foundation established by Romantic organicism. The desire to define linguistic usage as the embodiment of a neo-Humboldtian intellectual development pairs readily with Spitzer's interest in a stylistics that defines literary expression as the highest form of knowledge. But this desire to see literature as the cultural product *par excellence* threatens to place style beyond the descriptive reach of most linguistic models, as well as most models of behavior, since psychology, sociology, and history may be too rooted in the factual to address the intellectual grandeur sought for literature. The refinements that Spitzer provided for his stylistic method arose from his attempts to resolve the tension between his aesthetic vision and the opposing reductionism he found within the various methodologies through which he searched, looking for interpretive support. Spitzer's strongest desire was to define literature in terms of factual linguistic data, an organic literary experience, and a historical analysis of literary expression. His attempts to do so define the basic issue facing stylistics today: How can one maintain the complex intellectual significance accorded to literary style while making use of historical, linguistic, and other descriptive models, especially when those models are often structured around an opposing value of descriptive efficiency?

The tensions surrounding that question have not been as evident in recent stylistic work as they are in the work of Spitzer. The neat match between formalism in literary theory and descriptive objectivity in linguistic methodology has suppressed the differences between their separate goals. But that union has become somewhat strained since 1975, primarily because the intellectual value attached to formalism in linguistic description has dropped within both linguistics and literary criticism. At the same time, there has been a related rise in the importance of rhetorical models of language, mainly because of their adaptability to contextual and situational description. Yet all of these shifts have not altered the post-Romantic critical desire to forge epistemological links between the use of language and the creation of and response to literary style. Nor have the changes led to a significant reduction in the basic value still attached to scientific methodology in general.

What has been added lately to this critical mélange is a desire to root these values (literary and otherwise) not in essentialist soil alone, but in the more banal—yet crucial—ground of social and historical activity as well. Mary Poovey's definition of style—"'ideology' as it has been internalized and articulated by the individual"—retreats not one step from assigning high intellectual significance to language and style, but it does investigate their importance in terms of the socially constitutive and regulative power of ideology. Her uniting of ideology and style—"ideology as style suggests the lived experience of cultural values"—defines literary style as *productive* of values rooted in historical and social behavior, and not simply as expressive of contextually independent aesthetic values.[6] Such a shift is not to be easily blended with traditional critical values, however, since it requires radical changes in the theory and description of literature as well as of style.

Style, as we noted previously, has always been defined through other disciplines, and stylistics has followed that tradition, depending heavily upon related disciplines for descriptive power and validity. This search for external support is visible in a proliferation of unions between stylistics and other descriptive systems, some judged more holy than others, some more historically established than others, some simply more useful than others. Bennison Gray, who in 1966 held up Spitzer as a singular lesson for all stylistic sinners, nevertheless provided an excellent list of possible forms and models for analysis: style as behavior (psychology), style as the speaker (rhetoric), style as the latent (philology), style as the individual (literary criticism), style as the implicit speaker (philosophy), and style as language (linguistics). Seymour Chatman's 1971 list provided a less elegant but numerically equal set of related disciplines (poetics and criticism, rhetoric, structuralism, philology, and semantics), while Richard Ohmann in 1964 had already provided a somewhat hectic enumeration of twelve "approaches." Gray's own list—in combination with his subsequent argument against the possibility of a scientific or logical explanation of style—underscores two "facts" about style that are not a part of his study. The first implication is that style continued to maintain its significance in literary-critical thinking, even in the face of Gray's self-described empirical and logical attack. The second unintended consequence of Gray's list is its demonstration of the inherent complexity of the issues involved. Gray's taxonomy covers the full historical range of disciplines related to style—

from classical rhetoric to contemporary linguistics—and serves to stress the needs of stylistics more strongly than it manages to dismiss the entire concept.[7]

Modern literary stylistics thus faces the end of its first century in the midst of reevaluating itself and its methods. One primary motivation behind that reevaluation consists of a renewed desire to tie epistemology and literary style together by describing social motivations behind language use—a contextual orientation that Romanticism downplayed both in literature (where the teaching of *belles-lettres* overtook and replaced that of rhetoric in the first quarter of the nineteenth century) and in linguistics (where scientific procedures led to an increasing interest in context-free analysis). The driving force behind a newer, socially framed criticism lies in the growing critical tendency to uncover not only the institutional biases surrounding any academic discipline such as stylistics, but also to reveal the ideological roots of literary production and of style itself. According to this orientation, artistic intention involves more than simple discourse rules or a desire for personal expression. Literary style enacts and reproduces the writer's sense of the constraints that are imposed by any culture's boundaries. This introduction of an ideologically alert analysis has become increasingly important to stylistic theory and has renewed the stylistic tradition of using those external theories—in this case historical, psychological, sociological, and political methods of analysis—that provide the field with the descriptive strength it needs as an academic discipline and the critical relevance it desires. The reformation of modern stylistic theory thus involves not only the introduction of new methods, but also a reorientation of stylistics to its own complex history, a history that (as we will see) proves to be the source of many of stylistics's inherent self-contradictions.

The Rhetorical Background

A useful, three-part taxonomy of Western rhetoric—technical, sophistic, and philosophical—displays the effects of such contradictions very well. The breakdown provides both a historical categorization and a framework for evaluation. Technical rhetorics, broadly defined, encompass those pragmatic handbooks that teach the proper means of arguing in a public forum (usually the law courts), and they are saddled with the negative weight carried by most pedagogical tools. Such rhetorics often are condemned as reductive by post-Romantic critics, who see them as resolving complex issues with simplistic methods. The next category, that of sophistic rhetoric, overcomes the taint of technical functionality through its broad concern with human convention. The ideal orator, defined by sophistic rhetoric in terms of the speaker's manner of presentation and role as civic leader, is to be imitated on both counts. Within a framework such as that established by Isocrates, the study of style (as the imitation of achieved orators) bolsters the simple listing of techniques and rule-based precepts with the study of exemplary oratorical activity (or texts, the territory of the literary critic).

When these two approaches are combined, they produce the rhetorical tradition that is centered in Cicero's *De Inventione* and the *Rhetorica ad Herennium*, the most important current within rhetorical thought up to the Renaissance and beyond. The influence of this tradition on literary criticism has been extensive, due in part to the process that George Kennedy refers to as *letteraturizzazione:* "the tendency of rhetoric to shift its focus from persuasion to narration, from civic to personal contexts, and from discourse to literature, including poetry."[8] As a result of that tendency, the most recognizable features of rhetorical texts (other than their presentation of commonplaces or the parts of an argument) are the equally recognizable features of many stylistic handbooks: schemes and tropes. The ready availability of such features leads, quite naturally, to the production of literary rhetorics in which the idea of style is paramount, such as Demetrius's *On Style*, Hermogenes's *On Ideas of Style*, and Longinus's *On the Sublime*.

Those texts are part of one major current in the stylistic tradition, but their place in modern critical thinking is indicative of rhetoric's post-Romantic drop in value. Modern criticism has preferred to place more literary works, such as Aristotle's *Poetics* or Horace's *Ars Poetica*, ahead of rhetorical descriptions, seeing them as more important because of their primary concern with the issue of literary expression.[9] Rhetoric is portrayed as a context-bound model for communication skills and deemed to be of lesser significance than the aesthetically framed model of literary knowledge offered after the eighteenth century. The rising tide of Romantic organicism easily overwhelms the functionally framed discourse model of rhetoric, a victory eventually institutionalized in the academies of Britain and the United States with the replacement of rhetoric by *belles-lettres* after 1850. Style, as presented by rhetoric, is seen as smacking of the banal and tasteless world of everyday politics, an approach that appears demeaning to a post-Romantic world where literature has become a primary center of cultural values.

The implications of that shift in values are clear in Kennedy's own preference for philosophical rhetoric—the third and historically the slimmest strand in the rhetorical tradition. What Aristotle's rhetoric allows the user to do, in Kennedy's words, is "to discover [*theoresai*] the available means of persuasion. It is thus a theoretical activity and discovers knowledge" (Kennedy, *Classical Rhetoric*, 63). Rhetoric, in this format, escapes from the supposedly functional teaching of social behavior or verbal and literary skills and becomes, instead, an intellectual exploration, an epistemological activity. The greater acceptability of that format to a modern viewpoint is clear. Rhetoric, as a method of describing discourse, is believed to offer more when it engages the question of philosophical knowledge than when it teaches forms of social, civic, or political activity.

Kennedy's analysis underscores the requirement that rhetoric be engaged in the production or analysis of knowledge if it is to maintain intellectual validity. The dangers of not doing so are visible in the regular attempts to shift invention (rhetoric's supposed philosophical heart) into logic, leaving rhetoric to gather about itself the supposedly thin and shabby garments of arrangement and style (along with the even less warming tatters of memory and delivery). Until the Romantic redefinition of style, the intellectual difficulties of a rhetoric without philosophical invention are those of a stylistics without the guardian angel of literary aesthetics. As Kennedy knows, such a rhetoric is as defenseless as a homeless child: "With the end of Book 2 Aristotle's philosophical art of rhetoric is complete. The last sentence, however, states that we must now consider style and arrangement, and in Book 3 Aristotle proceeds to do so with no further reference to his abandonment of his original concept of philosophical rhetoric" (76). Kennedy's concerns are clear. Without a philosophical component, rhetoric loses its intellectual power; it becomes (as it did so clearly within Ramistic revisions) nothing but the technical presentation of style. Without a claim to the formation of knowledge or a sustaining pedagogical environment, rhetoric must come to be seen not as art but as rote; and style, operating within this model, finds its role defined as ornamentation rather than intellectually productive activity.

It must be said that rhetoric, despite its separation from philosophy until the twentieth century, did not suffer prior to the Romantic period. Its place within the pedagogical world remained solid. But from the modern perspective, that pedagogical strength carries little weight. The social power provided by the trivium has long since faded, and no discipline is foolish enough to abandon any ideologically powerful position already achieved by it in the rather nasty world of academic infighting. Following its rise to a position of intellectual prominence, English Literature has rarely laid claim to only a functional value, and stylistics has taken its cue from literary theory. The rise of modern stylistics thus follows the trajectory defined by literature's rise as a premier humanistic discipline—a rise measurable, on the one hand, in the increased post-Romantic interest in ahistorical aesthetics, and on the other, in the mid-nineteenth-century decline of a socially defined rhetoric. That set of opposing curves matches well with another arc that cuts across this particular Romantic and post-Romantic academic sky: linguistics.

The Linguistic Background—Classical and Medieval

As was true with rhetoric, the use of linguistic theory in modern stylistics grows out of a long-standing relation that is both intimate and strained, often supportive, and not infrequently antagonistic—depending upon the particular values of the time. The early relationship between style and linguistics is colored by two opposing issues that are still operating today: the desire to establish linguistic study as a nonapplied, contextually independent analysis of language constituents versus the interest in studying language as a mirror (or formative cause) for a plethora of social paradigms. These desires may overlap, yet the traditional dichotomy between analytic description and functional application remains. And it is the second, less "pure" version of linguistic study that regularly couples with literary stylistics prior to the Romantic period.

The work of the Alexandrian literary critics displays the classical interest in discussing language as a social determinant and a literary vehicle, while the work of the Stoics produces the classical format of an analytical approach, albeit one that is influenced by philosophical and logical categories. In describing these two traditions—and their differences—R. H. Robins deftly displays his own modern sense of literary style's unwanted intrusion into the pursuits of linguistic science:

> Up to this period, the context in which linguistics had developed had been philosophical, and in particular logical, enquiries; the linguistic science of the Stoics formed a part, though a distinct and articulated part, of their general philosophical system. But from this time on

another motivation made itself felt in ancient linguistics, the study
of literary style; firstly, there was a concern for "correct" Greek
pronunciation and grammar, that is classical Greek . . . ; and sec-
ondly, in the widespread study of classical literature and of the works
of Homer, commentaries on the language and the content were required by many readers within the newly Hellenized world.[10]

Robins's explanation carries overtones not unlike those heard in discussions of rhetoric. He implies that the concern with analyzing and describing literary style contains the seeds of a later flowering of prescription
rather than description, along with a subsequent drop in the descriptive
power of linguistic "science." The tensions produced by that division
between social interpretation and scientific description, already present
in the classical era, do not fade over time. Instead, they become formalized
within academic disciplines as early as the thirteenth century.[11] The relationship between literary style and linguistics thus has a long and strained
tradition, and one that is complicated (as was true in rhetoric) by a deep
separation between analytical and aesthetic goals.

The history of linguistic study and its relation to style thus displays a
set of intellectual and institutional tensions similar to those involving
rhetoric and style. The difference between the modern academic success
of linguistics and the fading of rhetoric lies in the degree to which linguistics managed to shift from philosophical and pedagogical explanations
to those of scientific description.[12] Seen in this light, Robins's division of
the grammatical/linguistic tradition is based upon the same sense of current values in the intellectual marketplace as that displayed by Kennedy
when he discusses nonphilosophical rhetoric. Both men know only too
well that when their disciplines approach literary study, they also move
away from the modern interest in nonapplied descriptive analysis. Kennedy has no intention of condemning the classical blend of literature and
rhetoric, but only wants to offer his preference for a model that best
accommodates the modern sense of intellectual, epistemological validity.
The same feeling leads Robins to imply that the study of language, when
shifted from analytical to evaluative description, too often lapses into
unfortunate pedagogical prescription.

The modern desire to establish linguistics as a self-sufficient, scientific
discipline has led historians to the discovery of theoretical precursors in
schools such as that of the modistae, the speculative grammarians of the
thirteenth and fourteenth centuries. The modistae's embrace of Aristotle

as the champion of logic served to reintroduce philosophy into linguistic analysis, while their rejection of the medieval Priscian and Donatus (on the grounds that they inadequately addressed the real nature of language) helped the modistae to downgrade the role of literature, the then-dominant partner in grammatical study.[13] Like many of today's prominent linguistic models, speculative grammar relied heavily upon its ability to present grammatical studies as a near-scientific endeavor— rational, universal, and nonhistorical—rather than as a pedagogical or literary discipline. The locus of power for such an approach lies in the descriptive capacity of its methodology. "By applying to their very specializing Latin their revised Aristotelian method, the speculative grammarians attempted to utilize the ideas expressed by Bacon in order to found a science of grammar—a coherent set of rules—according to which pure thought could be channeled most effectively into highly formalized expression" (Uitti, *Linguistics and Literary Theory*, 55). When realized through a supposedly universal set of logical rules, this undertaking takes on an abstracting cast, a description of language independent of actual patterns of use. The concern with language as a social or literary product fades before the desire for a universal grammar.

The methodological tug-of-war established by these differing goals can be found throughout the history of linguistics. For its part, Renaissance language study is best described as eclectic, its stage populated by figures interested both in the classical texts and in describing the living vernaculars. Not surprisingly, that interest led to a reintroduction of the literary/linguistic union that had been sundered in arguments such as those of the modistae. The generalizing tendencies of the speculative grammarians were strongly attacked by Renaissance grammarians, who saw the work as "philosophically pretentious, educationally undesirable, and couched in a barbarous degeneration of the Latin language" (Robins, *Short History of Linguistics*, 109). In essence, the Renaissance reintroduced issues of use to linguistic methodology. The universalistic goals of speculative grammarians did not disappear completely, however, and discussions such as the *Grammaire générale et raisonnée* of Port Royal (1660) provided new versions of the search for the universal in language. But neoclassical literary interests, as well as the linguistic needs brought on by cross-cultural commerce and trade, lent increased ideological weight to good and correct usage, as can be seen in essays by Swift ("A Proposal for Correcting, Improving, and Ascertaining the English Tongue," 1712),

Johnson (*Dictionary*, 1755), and Voltaire ("Langues," 1769). Such arguments are obviously problematic, and they were to be quickly overshadowed by the looming presence of the Romantic Period.

The Romantic Period

The issues that surround the formation of modern stylistics make their first complete appearance during the Romantic Period, when aesthetic expression gained the upper hand in literary thinking and the stage was set for a new vision of linguistic epistemology. Linguistic work in this period demonstrates, once more, the long-standing desire to root the description of language in human behavior, and the universal, acontextual logic of a speculative grammar shrinks before the interest in describing the historical development and variability of individual languages. Pioneering linguists, such as Bopp (1791–1867), Rask (1787–1832), and Grimm (1785–1863), depart from the anaerobic confines of logical grammar for the more sustaining environs of actual languages and historical comparativism. At the same time, these linguists abandon the logical machinery constructed for nonhistorical general grammars and strike out in search of new methods more adequate to an empirical description of particular languages.

The influential growth of nineteenth-century linguistics testifies to the success of the program. But by introducing new scientific methods and goals, nineteenth-century linguists paradoxically limited their own movement back toward the actual user of language. Their search for the historical background of language and its changing forms eventually led not to social history but to a cause-and-effect brand of historicism. The victory of a linguistics devoted to temporal progression rather than to social development is readily visible in the subsequent valorization of the law-oriented portion of Grimm's or Verner's work. But it is the less scientifically structured work of Wilhelm von Humboldt that best displays the underlying tensions of the period, those internal contradictions that were to prove so influential in the early formation of stylistics. Humboldt's *Über die Verschiedenheit des menslichen Sprächbaues und ihren Einfluss auf die geistige Entwicklung des Menschengeschlechts* (*Linguistic Variability and Intellectual Development*, 1836) provides the Romantic version of the modern linguist's (and stylist's) recurring dilemma: How is one to resolve the conflict between a desire for descriptive, analytic strength and a concern for language as a socially and intellectually productive activity?

The central theme of Humboldt's work lies in its description of language use as a dynamic tension between the given elements of a language and the user's creative synthesis of those elements into a functioning and intellectually progressive whole. Within the Humboldtian framework, language is not an object, it is "an activity, and an unbroken activity, even when it is fixed in writing, where its, so to speak, dead parts have to undergo anew a process of spiritual elaboration."[14] Language change and development depend upon individual intellectual development, which depends, in turn, upon the progress of language: "Observation of the connection between linguistic variation and the distribution of tribes on the one hand, and the production of human intellectual power on the other, as a relationship developing progressively in varying degree and in new configurations, is the theme with which [*Linguistic Variability*] will be concerned, insofar as these two phenomena are capable of clarifying each other."[15]

For Humboldt, the nature of language lies not simply in its material aspect but also in the intellectual activity of the user. His attempt to include that activity leads to what Aarsleff describes as Humboldt's paired concerns with "the ultimate subjectivity of language" and with humanity's "désir irrésistable de sociabilité," the need to communicate and be understood.[16] Language becomes the cultural activity of sharing and creating both the language itself and the society of which it is the premier aspect. In a direct rejection of language as object or material alone, Humboldt produces the statement that Spitzer later will seize upon: "Language is not *ergon* but *energeia*," not an object but a knowledge-producing activity; "the real language lies in the act of its physical production" (27).[17]

But the motif of language as an activity centered in dynamic intellectual growth sets Humboldt's theoretical beliefs in direct opposition to the developing methodological requirements of nineteenth-century comparative historical linguistics. Humboldt's vision of language as an activity productive of intellect clearly strains any descriptive system. Changes in a word's sound pattern can be documented to a reasonable degree; changes in an individual's or nation's intellectual capacity are much more difficult to define, let alone measure. The basic issue of what constitutes an adequate description of language is thus intensified by Humboldt's definition and the Romantic individualism that colors it. By framing language behavior as primary intellectual activity, Humboldt achieves three results, two of which are desired, one not. First, he portrays language—and, consequently, linguistic study—as central to epistemology. Second, he removes language from its abstract home in logic and rationalism and places it back among its users. The unfortunate third result is that the vagueness of his general method makes it difficult for his arguments to coexist with more formalistic visions of historical description. "Comparative linguistics," Humboldt declares, "or the precise investigation of the diversity through which innumerable peoples resolve the problem of linguistic structure imposed upon them as human beings, fails to attract serious interest unless its relationship to the pattern of national intellectual power is made clear" (xix). The beauty of these epistemological visions cannot mask the problem of matching the intellectual development assumed by Humboldt with that other nineteenth-century goal of the "precise investigation" of the facts of historical linguistics. There is no efficient synthesis of the two available within Humboldt's own work, certainly none available within the descriptive historical models growing in importance at the time, and thus no possibility of providing a specific methodological procedure to validate Humboldt's larger vision. The complex role he envisions for the user is destined to fall before the rising power of nineteenth-century linguistic methodology.

The increasing importance of scientific procedures only widened the rift between those scholars interested primarily in the description of temporal change and those devoted to a social history of language. Jesperson, encapsulating the response of later linguists more concerned with repeatable scientific methods than with intellectual variability, wryly declares that Humboldt "lifts us to a higher plane where the air may be purer, but where it is also thinner and not seldom cloudier as well."[18] In like fashion, Holger Pedersen quickly notes Humboldt's study of the Javanese language, "in which the kinship between Indonesian and Polynesian is clearly proved," and then goes on to other linguists, choosing not to discuss the philosophical issues that Humboldt saw as central to his work.[19]

Ernst Cassirer's neo-Kantian outlook, on the other hand, leads him to stress Humboldt's distaste for "this empirical-realist approach which obstructs the extension of our knowledge of language, and makes what knowledge we have dead and barren."[20] Cassirer's judgment is indebted to Romantic aesthetics, and he structures his reading of Humboldt around three particular oppositions:

1. Humboldt's vision of language contains a primary opposition between "the individual and the 'objective' spirit" (*Philosophy of Symbolic Forms*, 156).

2. "Any inquiry into language must proceed 'genetically'"; it does not need to be pursued in terms of its temporal genesis, "but we must recognize the finished structure of language as something derived and mediated" (159).

3. "In every complete and thoroughly formed language the act of designating a concept by definite material characteristics must be augmented by a specific endeavor . . . which place[s] the concept in a definite category of thought" (161–62).

Uniting these oppositions offers manifest difficulties, and Humboldt provides no specific social or psychological middle ground between the territories of intellect and language. While Humboldt's work obviously raises some of the issues needed to sustain language's key role in any epistemology, his discussion provides no strong external criteria (objective or speculative) concerning the nature of intellectual growth, beyond the evidence of the languages themselves and the assumption of a unifying organicism.[21] The idea of mind as a form of behavior—or society as an organized system—usually fades as Humboldt's discussion of language as a social need leaps quickly from describing linguistic features to speculating on spiritual motives, with too little of the social texture that really constitutes most linguistic usage.[22] The activity of language users, although definable within a rhetorical, social, or psychological framework, instead comes to rest upon Humboldt's Romantic belief in the dynamism of mental creativity.

The intellectual status of nineteenth-century organicism was sufficient to validate Humboldt's particular vision. But organic dynamism soon retreated before the organism as described within the increasingly powerful ideological framework of scientific method. The importance and prestige of biology among the natural sciences—and of those sciences within the general intellectual framework of the time—led many linguists to define themselves as fellow natural scientists. Their goal was to adopt the biological approach not only as a metaphor but as a set of repeatable procedures. In the process, they provided a renewed separation between aesthetic and scientific, mentalist and objective approaches to linguistic description. Jesperson states the separation succinctly: "While the philologist looked upon language as part of the culture of some nation, the linguist looked upon it as a natural object; and when in the beginning of the nineteenth century philosophers began to divide all sciences into the two sharply separated classes of mental and natural sciences (*geistes- und naturwissenschaften*), linguists would often reckon their science among the latter" (Jespersen, *Language*, 65).

The simplest example of that new attitude can be found in Schleicher's *Stammbaum* model of language change. No simple analogy, these linguistic family trees were seen as natural growths—a view that lent itself to the discussion of language change in terms of physical laws. Organic creativity was replaced by organic limitation and regulation, with appeals to Darwin to support this biological view of language. The description of historical change as an aspect of society and culture was left to the philologist, who studied language in terms of the vagaries of human motivation. The hard facts of linguistic change—the actual, verifiable material changes undergone by language—were studied by the linguist in terms of natural physical laws.

This drift toward scientific abstraction naturally met with a reaction of its own. The methodological purity of the biological model could not be sustained in the face of other clearly important factors of change such as social prestige and political power. Once more an attempt was undertaken to define language within the sphere of human behavior. A middle ground between the expressive *Sprachgeist* of the early Romantics and the subsequent "science" of the biological model was sought by the neo-grammarians. While these linguists are best known for their eventual concern with immutable sound laws, they also argued for including social and psychological factors as determinants of linguistic change. According to Osthoff and Brugmann, "language is not a thing, standing outside and above men and leading its own life, but has its true existence only in the individual . . . all changes in the life of a language can originate only with individual speakers."[23]

The neo-grammarian school and its attitudes dominated the linguistic arena during the late nineteenth century and into the twentieth, and its influence carries us to the intellectual milieu surrounding the formation of modern stylistics. The strong social and pedagogical importance of rhetoric had enabled it to maintain its vision of style and its role in the teaching of language skills up to the eighteenth century. But the rise of science and its descriptive methods ensured the importance of linguistics in the nineteenth century, and this newly found scientific value would be immensely attractive to modern stylistics as it began its own formation as an academic discipline. Rhetoric and linguistics thus underwent a relatively complementary fall and rise, with linguistics basking in the reflected glow offered to any new science in the nineteenth century. At the same time, the still-sweet odor of Romantic organicism and its arguments about language and epistemology continued to affect the twentieth-century stylistician's desire to blend comparative linguistic science and literary style. When Spitzer thus describes his new literary stylistics as "the more rigorously scientific definition of an individual style" (*Linguistics and Literary History*, 11), he is repeating the goals outlined by Romantic linguistic and critical history. What has yet to be achieved at the outset of the twentieth century is agreement between linguists and stylisticians over what constitutes an adequate scientific definition of language—and even what constitutes an adequate science—an argument that is key to the development of modern stylistics.

That Spitzer would reenact the central tension of stylistic and linguistic thinking is to be expected, given his own training by two of the premier Romance linguists of the late nineteenth century: Wilhelm Meyer-Lübke and Hugo Schuchardt. The work of Meyer-Lübke, the dominant comparatist at the turn of the century, is characterized by the neo-grammarian search for scientific precision. Through his influence, neo-grammatical attitudes colored much of the historical description provided by Romance linguistics from 1890 to 1910. Although the neo-grammarians began by attempting to draw linguistics back to the realm of behavior and usage, their real concern remained one of defining linguistic change according to internal (formal) rather than external (social, psychological, political, geographical) factors. The attractiveness of this scientific "disinterestedness," especially between the World Wars, cannot be overestimated. Having escaped the onset of the Holocaust, Spitzer would write in 1938 that his young soul envisioned Meyer-Lübke as "the great man of German science, liberal, without prejudice," whose science was not grim, but disciplined, precise, and rigorous.[24]

Unfortunately, as the neo-grammarian linguists supposedly prepared an approach that operated above the plane of social history, they also produced a model of accurate linguistic description that sharply reduced the need—and the desire—to discuss mental activity as a part of language. While concerned with cognition, neo-grammarian linguistic study often downplayed its importance, or offered portraits colored by the associational psychology of the previous era or the behaviorism of the upcoming decades. That attitude is not surprising, since the neo-grammarians' greatest successes lay in phonological description and historical reconstruction,

a success that argued for avoiding speculative areas of language and mind. Yet the neo-grammarian rejection of mentalistic orientations similar to that of Cassirer is somewhat ironic, as Cassirer himself notes. The neo-grammarians' early interest in reviving the role of the user within linguistic description—an interest that grew out of a rejection of biological positivism—was only replaced by a new form of linguistic positivism: "the whole development of the philosophy of language . . . ha[d] from the purely methodological point of view, moved in a circle" (Cassirer, *Philosophy of Symbolic Forms*, 173). The neo-grammarians initially may have rejected the excessive determination of the strict biological framework, but their own attempt to achieve a scientific level of description precluded the full study of linguistic behavior. In effect, the neo-grammarian avoidance of the user ensured a return to an abstracting historicism in which language change was described in terms of habit or chance, and the descriptive model used to validate this position became psychophysical, "the various physiological mechanisms of sound production on the one hand and the psychological mechanism of associations on the other" (Cassirer, *Philosophy of Symbolic Forms*, 172).

Because the descriptive precision of Meyer-Lübke's approach precluded any extensive move into the social or the literary aspects of actual use, a scholar such as Hugo Schuchardt provided a welcome counterbalance to Meyer-Lübke's influence both upon Romance linguistics and Leo Spitzer. Schuchardt's early rejection of the neo-grammarian approach, presented in his *Über die Lautgesetze: Gegen die Junggrammatiker* (1885), appears as the first entry in the *Hugo Schuchardt-Brevier*, a volume edited by Spitzer for Schuchardt's eightieth birthday.[25] The essay rejects the positivist tendencies of the neo-grammarians and reaffirms the psychology of the speaker as the key to linguistic description. As Kurt Jankowsky has pointed out, Schuchardt insists on starting from an initial assumption that language is an intellectual activity, thus immediately setting his descriptive goals apart from those of the neo-grammarians. From that position Schuchardt announces his belief that the neo-grammarians, "by their insistence on blindly and mechanically functioning sound laws, introduced into the research procedure mechanization where it does not belong, thereby reducing thought to a minimum and barring the progress of linguistic science. . . ."[26] The statement is not completely accurate, but the general attitude it displays toward the issue of descriptive adequacy had a profound effect on Spitzer's thinking and on Romance linguistics as a whole. Schuchardt's vision of linguistic change provides for individual influence over the language, a view that would be attractive to a literary criticism heavily indebted to Romanticism. If linguistic creativity and change affect the social and intellectual environment, then literary creativity can arguably be said to occupy a powerful position in the formation of knowledge.

These issues, as contained in the work of Meyer-Lübke and Schuchardt and addressed within Spitzer's stylistic arguments, constitute the modern version of the tensions between Romantic epistemology and scientific methodology that dictate the nature of contemporary stylistics. Spitzer's own attempts to synthesize these oppositions are captured by his emblematic travels back and forth between Vienna and Graz, between Meyer-Lübke and Schuchardt. His overarching concern is to construct a stylistics founded on a dual interest in style as individual literary expression and style as cultural expression, the latter a function of both the individual and the cultural psyche, as embodied by the language. Style is to be read as "a web of interrelations between the language and the soul of the speaker" (*Linguistics and Literary History*, 10), as the central component of a literary work, whose "life-giving center" (19) must be uncovered by the stylistician. To achieve these goals Spitzer attempts to balance the issue of linguistic objectivity with a description that encompasses the historical vision of Humboldt and Schuchardt. His primary task thus is one of finding a methodology capable of defining style as an historically significant activity, without sacrificing either the newly found scientific value of linguistics or the continuing organicist visions of *belles-lettres*. As we follow Spitzer's assumption of that task in the next chapter, we begin to uncover the foundations of modern stylistics.

NOTES

1. Charles Bally, *Précis de stylistique* (Geneva: Eggimann, 1905).

2. Terry Eagleton, *Literary Theory: An Introduction* (Minneapolis: University of Minnesota Press, 1983), vii.

3. Oswald Ducrot and Tzvetan Todorov do just that, announcing Bally and Spitzer as the two key figures in the origin of modern stylistic theory. See their *Encyclopedic Dictionary of the Sciences of Language*, trans. Catherine Porter (Baltimore, Md.: Johns Hopkins University Press, 1979).

4. Terry Eagleton, Robert Scholes (*Textual Power*), and others have provided us with a portrait of the ideological underpinning of modern critical theory; Mary Pratt has done the same for linguistics in "The Ideology of Speech-Act Theory" and "Interpretive Strategies/Strategic Interpretations: On Anglo-American Reader Response Criticism," *Bound-*

ary 2, vols. 11 and 12, no. 2 (1982/83), 210–31. See chapter 7 for a discussion of her work.

5. "If I must choose between any old-fashioned, but first-rate positivist whose aesthetic creed may be unsophisticated and crude, but who knows the exact meaning of his technical terminology, is able to handle textual, historical, and linguistic questions and to focus his undivided attention on a particular problem at the time, and a contemporary ambitious creator of new bold *aperçus* and a new terminology behind which vagueness of thought, hazy associations and verbalism are hidden, I definitely would prefer today the former." When the choices are drawn so broadly, it would be hard to choose any other way (Spitzer, "A New Book on the Art of *The Celestina*," review of *The Art of "La Celestina*," by Stephen Gilman, *Hispanic Review*, 25 [January, 1957], 1–25). The statement appears on page 23.

6. Mary Poovey, *The Proper Lady and the Woman Writer: Ideology as Style in the Works of Mary Wollstonecraft, Mary Shelley, and Jane Austen* (Chicago: University of Chicago Press, 1984), xiii.

7. Bennison Gray, "The Lesson of Leo Spitzer," *Modern Language Review*, 61, no. 4 (October, 1966), 547–55, and *Style: The Problem and Its Solution* (The Hague: Mouton, 1969). The list is taken from the chapter headings in the table of contents of the 1969 volume. Gray's solution to "The Problem" is euthanasia. Seymour Chatman, ed., *Stylistics: A Symposium* (London: Oxford University Press, 1971). The list is, again, from the table of contents. Richard Ohmann, "Generative Grammars and the Concept of Literary Style," *Word*, 20 (1964), 424–39; rpt. in *Linguistics and Literary Style*, Donald Freeman, ed. (New York: Holt, Rinehart and Winston, 1970), 258–78. See chapter 7 for a full discussion of these issues.

8. George Kennedy, *Classical Rhetoric and Its Christian and Secular Tradition from Ancient to Modern Times* (Chapel Hill: University of North Carolina Press, 1980), 5.

9. We tend to ignore the fact that, according to the classical definition of the *Poetics* or the *Ars Poetica*, they were secondary arts—not secondary in terms of importance, but secondary because they grew out of the primary arts. The influence of grammar and rhetoric upon poetics is thus extensive, with the concept of literary style being deeply rooted in these two areas of study. Nevertheless, contemporary reactions to this, the most influential of the rhetorical traditions, remains negative within much of post-Romantic literary stylistics.

10. R. H. Robins, *A Short History of Linguistics* (Bloomington: Indiana University Press, 1967), 16.

11. Karl Uitti, *Linguistics and Literary Theory* (Englewood Cliffs, N.J.: Prentice Hall, 1969), 60 (hereinafter referred to as *LLT*).

12. The emphasis on pedagogy in classical language study is visible in texts such as the *Technē Grammatikē* of Dionysius Thrax (c. 100 B.C.) and the *Institutiones Grammaticae* of Priscian (c. A.D. 500). These texts, while descriptive after the fashion of the time, are also intended to fit within a larger pedagogical scheme influenced by Alexandrian attitudes toward literature. The study of such grammars is to be accompanied by the study of literary style as an exemplary use of the language. "In the strict sense," Robins notes, such a grammar "was part of a wider scheme of propaedeutic studies leading to a proper appreciation of classical Greek literature" (Robins, *Short History of Linguistics*, 31). The *Technē* of Thrax opens with the Alexandrian portrait of grammatical ability as "the practical knowledge of the general usages of poets and prose writers," a knowledge whose strength rests in "the appreciation of literary compositions, which is the noblest part of grammar." The ultimate frame for this uniting of grammar, literature, and rhetoric in the education of the ideal orator is contained within Quintilian's ideal pedagogical system. The aspiring student, "as soon as he has learned to read and write easily, . . . should be delivered to the *grammaticus*, or teacher of literature, who will teach him correctness and the interpretation of the poets. . . . For the art of writing is combined with the art of speaking, both depending upon a study of literature, and the student should read every kind of writer, both for content and for vocabulary" (James J. Murphy, *Rhetoric in the Middle Ages* [Berkeley: University of California Press, 1974], 22–23).

It is within this pedagogical framework that Murphy places such texts as Horace's *Ars Poetica*, leaving them to be interpreted squarely in the grammatical and rhetorical tradition as "an extension of that part of grammar known as *ennartio poetarum*, the analysis of literary texts" (22–23). The study of rhetoric is one of the end goals (and supporting frameworks) for this form of linguistic study, with additional literary coloration added by that tendency toward *letteratturizzazione*. The worth of these subjects is defined according to a social framework, whose ultimate goal—recognizable in the enumeration of and presentation of rules for the correct use of figures—is the promulgation of an ideal form of discourse behavior.

13. Robins notes that it is "ironical that Priscian, who in method owed much to Aristotelian methods and whose Latin grammar was the foundation of medieval grammatical theory, is now, as champion of the *auctores* [students of classical literature] from Orleans, matched in allegorical combat with Aristotle, who had been made responsible for the assumed logical basis of grammatical rules and concepts and, as the inspiration of scholastic philosophy, had become a leader of the *artes*" (Robins, *Short History of Linguistics*, 89–90).

14. Iordan-Orr (Iorgue Iordan and John Orr), *An Introduction to Ro-*

mance Linguistics: Its Schools and Scholars, rev. by R. Posner (Oxford: Basil Blackwell, 1970), 113.

15. Wilhelm von Humboldt, *Linguistic Variability and Intellectual Development*, trans. George C. Buck and Frithjof A. Raven (Philadelphia: University of Pennsylvania Press, 1972), xx.

16. Humboldt, *Gesammelte Schriften*, vol. 3, 323. Quoted in Hans Aarsleff, *From Locke to Saussure: Essays on the Study of Language and Intellectual History* (Minneapolis: University of Minnesota Press, 1982), 343.

17. Deeply historical in its realization, Humboldt's vision takes the intellectual and linguistic interplay of the individual's language behavior and extends it outward to the progressive unfolding of individual languages as well, seeing linguistic change as genetic progression or decay. As individuals develop, providing self-growth through language change, they also alter the language, thus providing new possibilities and subtly eliminating others. This intellect-forming *energeia* is defined according to the dominant framework of the day: organisms develop not only along the lines established by their species, but along lines that also promote change and alteration in the species. Nevertheless, the structure of language is neither absolutely deterministic nor absolutely relativistic; it describes an arena of tendencies rather than necessities. "It should . . . be recognized," Robert Miller notes, "that by the term 'diversity of world perspectives,' Humboldt is espousing a linguistic, and not a philosophical relativism." Language is "the human being approaching the objective idea" (Robert L. Miller, *The Linguistic Relativity Principle and Humboldtian Ethnolinguistics* [The Hague: Mouton, 1968], 31).

18. Otto Jesperson, *Language: Its Nature, Development, and Origin* (New York: Henry Holt and Company, 1924), 57.

19. Holger Pedersen, *Linguistic Science in the Nineteenth Century: Methods and Results*, trans. John W. Spargo (Cambridge, Mass.: Harvard University Press, 1931), 130. Pedersen thus demonstrates that Humboldt is aware of the methodological needs of comparative linguistics (as could be expected from his extensive work with Javanese). His separation of language study into linguistics (general description) and philology (textual analysis) is based upon an awareness of the differing goals and procedural needs of each. But Humboldt's personal desire is for a language analysis formed around a unifying vision of high individual creativity and historical linguistic change. The motivating force behind that view is a belief in the necessary interplay between individual expression and social exchange, coupled with a disinterest in purely logical presentation or scientific measurement. Humboldt's linguistic model thus pairs fairly readily with literary models of language use and their focus on individual expression and

response. The parallel literary model for this linguistic design is provided by Coleridge's Romantic leap beyond the material and mechanical aspects of poetic language and into the transcendant imagination (See Uitti, *LLT*, 102–3).

20. Ernst Cassirer, *The Philosophy of Symbolic Forms*, vol. 1 of *Language*, trans. Ralph Mannheim (New Haven, Conn.: Yale University Press, 1955), 158 (hereinafter referred to as *PSF*). The English titles of the texts provide all the information that anyone needs in order to recognize their differing viewpoints. Lest the reader mistake the issues at hand, Pedersen's subtitle—"Methods and Results"—sets the no-nonsense tone that announces that he will not be pursuing the speculative issues to be found in Cassirer's *Philosophy of Symbolic Forms*.

This separation between linguistic science and linguistic philosophy, each with its own sense of what constitutes a legitimate description of language, will continue to repeat itself in what have become standing arguments with regular appearances in texts and journals. Spitzer's own comment in 1943 on Bloomfield's methods—"a linguistic treatise based on this anti-philosophic philosophy is bound to be a mentalistic philosophy (of the Leonard Bloomfield brand of mentalism, of course)" (*Modern Language Quarterly*, 4 [1943], 430n)—is a direct echo of Cassirer on nineteenth-century positivism in linguistics, which "remained a philosophy precisely in its rejection of metaphysics" (*PSF*, 167–68).

21. The ensuing difficulties are extended by Humboldt's related concern with the primary causes of language, a necessary adjunct to his developmental model—from which his twentieth-century translators are anxious to dissociate themselves. The source of their discomfort is clear—Humboldt's speculations lack the possibility of methodological verifiability: "His groping about for what are now familiar terms is often painful, but his constant philosophizing about matters which can now be factually ascertained or should be rejected out of hand since they do not admit of proof would certainly be anathema to the modern linguist" (Translators' Foreword, *Linguistic Variability and Intellectual Development* by Humboldt, trans. Buck and Raven, ix).

22. Cassirer rightly notes Humboldt's Kantian preoccupation with "the terrible bathos of experience" (*PSF*, 157), but the tie between the everyday use of language and the vision of mind also involves a terrific leap from the bathetic to the aesthetic.

23. Herman Osthoff and Karl Brugmann, *Morphologische Untersuchungen*, quoted by Geoffrey Sampson, *Schools of Linguistics* (Stanford, Cal.: Stanford University Press, 1980), 27.

24. Leo Spitzer, "Mes Souvenirs de Meyer-Lübke," *Le Français Moderne*, 6 (1938), 216.

25. Hugo Schuchardt, *Hugo Schuchardt-Brevier: Ein Vademekum der allgemeinen Sprachwissenschaft,* ed. Leo Spitzer (Halle: Max Niemeyer, 1922).

26. Kurt Jankowsky, *The Neogrammarians* (The Hague: Mouton, 1972), 214.

2 Linguistic Training and Critical Desire
Spitzer, Freud, and Stylistic Creativity

The previous chapter noted how attitudes toward style and its study have been tied historically to literary, rhetorical, and linguistic methods for studying language. As a result, stylistics has found itself linked not only to the methods of these particular disciplines, but also to the academic status granted to them at various historical moments. By the opening of the twentieth century, rhetoric had dramatized the workings of the academic value system by falling victim to a Romantic epistemology that placed great emphasis on the aesthetic power of expression in language. Linguistics, on the other hand, was enjoying a rise in stature as a central component of the "human sciences," and literary criticism was trying to keep pace by following that lead. But while literary criticism was struggling to blend its Romantic heritage with the descriptive formalism that characterized the new general linguistics, linguistics was also at war with itself over the positivism being tied to its scientific status.

The result of these multiple tensions was a varied offering of stylistic approaches. Vossler, Spitzer, and Bally, the field of Romance literature in general, and the later neo-linguistic school centered in Italy all contributed to the hectic growth of stylistics on the Continent during this period. Yet, even as Spitzer attempted to create a discipline in which literary style was the highest form of discourse (*Stilforschung*), Bally would reverse Spitzer's hierarchy, defining linguistic stylistics as the enumeration of a language's available stylistic features (*stylistique*)—and pointedly excluding literature from the discussion. In the midst of this fruitful chaos the basic disciplinary attraction of linguistic science remained strong, since it offered literary stylistics the lure of objective description. While Romantic organicist models had placed style high in the pantheon of creative linguistic activities, they had left it there only vaguely defined, and stronger analytical methods seemed necessary to finish the critical task. The supposedly antiliterary tinge of this linguistic approach was overcome by the general post–World War I desire for stability in all activities, and the idea of objectivity in stylistics matched well with the general desire within criticism to rest quietly in the underlying form of the textual object.

In England, meanwhile, "practical criticism" became a watchword, and the phrase signaled, as Eagleton notes, "the beginnings of a 'reification' of the literary work, the treatment of it as an object in itself, which was to be triumphantly consummated in the American New Criticism" (Eagleton, *Literary Theory*, 44). That postwar reification and isolation of the text required a new set of analytical criteria, and linguistic science was a natural starting point. But Continental linguistics and Romance philology had long since become problematic for Anglo-American work. As Linda Dowling has demonstrated, the scientific qualities of the neo-grammarian linguistics had been recognized before the turn of the century as a threat to the Victorian ideals of high literature. The "great fear" of fin-de-siècle Britain was that a scientific philology divorced from literature "would cut itself off from the moral and spiritual values Victorians looked to literature to instill."[1] Yet even as they geared up to battle this linguistic threat to English Literature, early twentieth-century critics were coming under the general influence of other scientific methods. Previous blends of linguistic and literary theory might be rejected by critics such as I. A. Richards, for example, but he and others like him would remain interested in the general descriptive power offered by scientific analysis and behavioral models of mind. At the same time, the diminution of philology's influence within Anglo-American criticism was further diminished by a shift in political attitudes. By the end of the First World War, it was possible to portray classical philology as a form of "ponderous Teutonic nonsense with which no self-respecting Englishman should be caught associating" (Eagleton, *Literary Theory*, 29). Work in language moved away from historical concerns with individual languages toward the synchronic methods of general linguistics.

In the United States, New Critical literary concerns soon would begin to assert their influence, featuring textual approaches similar to those fostered by British scholarly interests. The particular task New Criticism would undertake was to achieve academic validity, not only as a conceptual opponent of excessive scientism, but as an equally powerful analytic discipline. "New Criticism," Eagleton tells us, "evolved in the years when literary criticism in North America was struggling to become 'professionalized,' acceptable as a respective academic discipline. Its battery of critical instruments was a way of competing with the hard sciences on their own terms, in a society where such science was the dominant criterion of knowledge" (49). The ideological influence of scientific description thus somewhat paradoxically underwrote the New Criticism's drift toward objectivity in literary description, a methodological drift that easily embraced the practical criticism of scholars such as Richards. The result was a clear separation in the goals of Anglo-American writers and those of Continental critics such as Spitzer.

The Anglo-American jettisoning of rhetorical and philological methods of analysis left stylistic criticism with relatively few analytical procedures, and the resulting Anglo-American stylistic study—often characterized by its labeling practices ("masculine," "feminine," "flowing," "driving," "limpid," "rushing")—had few descriptive tools and little self-governance. "This new kind of stylistic criticism," Graham Hough declares, "developed a somewhat cavalier attitude towards both historical and linguistic considerations":

> [T]his whole school of Anglo-American stylistic analysis, lively and invigorating as it often was, was also an extremely undisciplined affair, and strangely innocent of scholarship. It was not based on any positive body of knowledge. In effect it disdained the appeal to knowledge of any kind, and rejoiced in an intuitive free-for-all. To be impartially disrespectful to both sides, we may say that if the vice of the Continental stylistics was pedantry, that of the Anglo-American school was irresponsibility.[2]

Hough's own interest in a rebirth of organicism lies behind his slighting reference to Continental work. Yet it was the Continental tradition that provided stylistics with its only real disciplinary structure during these years, and it is to the early stages of Spitzer's career that we must turn in order to map the critical tensions that dominated the attempts to make stylistics a modern academic discipline during the first half of this century.

As we turn to Spitzer, we need to recognize that in addition to the difficulties of theory and academic status surrounding the birth of stylistics, we must address those related to Spitzer's own position as a young and untested literary critic. Spitzer began his career in 1910 faced with the necessity of establishing both the validity of his arguments and his authority to make them. Whether or not we agree on the importance of his need to achieve that authoritative status, it is unlikely that Spitzer felt wholly free of the academic hierarchy that produced such a need, any more than stylistics was free to escape the need to justify its own disciplinary and intellectual validity. The academic setting of 1910 thus provided Spitzer with individual restrictions on, as well options for, his pursuit of stylistics. Whatever the response within literary circles might be, Spitzer's training in historical and comparative Romance Philology gave him a base in one of the more prestigious Continental disciplines of the period; there could be little challenge to the language training he had received from Meyer-Lübke (non-Continental beliefs notwithstanding). But Spitzer felt constrained by neo-grammarian attitudes, and he began his career by seeking an approach to language that would allow him to address literary as well as linguistic concerns. It was out of this desire that his *Stilforschung* was to be born, and at its inception Spitzer followed a time-honored pattern in the study of style: he searched for a related discipline to support his interpretive framework. His subsequent attempts to define stylistics are encapsulated in three related movements that characterize Spitzer's thinking during the period from 1910 to 1936:

1. the combined use of linguistics and psychoanalysis to provide a descriptive method that addressed the issues of science and individual creativity required by modern stylistics at this stage of its formation;

2. the attempt to replace the restrictions supposedly found in psychoanalytic and linguistic descriptive procedures with a view of general cultural expression;

3. the achievement of a personal authority that would form the final argument for Spitzer's "philological circle."

In *Linguistics and Literary History* (1948), Spitzer retrospectively portrayed his initial stylistic desires from this early period by portraying the author whom he pursued as "sensuous, witty, disciplined," and, unfortunately, disinherited by contemporary studies—"left out in the cold while we [linguists] talked about his language." Banished from linguistics by the formalism that had begun consolidating its hold over comparative/historical linguistics, Spitzer's author was no more visible in the literary training that Spitzer received from Philip August Becker. Literary study provided only a welter of "dates and historical data"[3] that buried whatever small stirrings of life the aspiring critic might glimpse. Spitzer's fellow language students, finding themselves confined within the walls of these established descriptive frameworks, were drawn by the "almost inexorable force," as Malkiel describes it, of less positivistic methods. Dialect geography or "lexically oriented 'Kulturforschung'" studies (the latter using *Wörter und Sachen* methods to study the palpable if mundane materials of a civilization) became increasingly popular. To these specifically linguistic studies one could also add, Malkiel notes, a growing number of humanistic studies that concentrated on "styles of individual authors or pleiads."[4] It was in the midst of this critical and disciplinary movement toward the culture and users of the language that Spitzer established his program for stylistic research.

The specific analysis of literary style that Spitzer proposes bears all the marks of Romantic organicism. The overall goal of the analysis is to uncover the particular stylistic feature that can be used to interpret both the center of a work's expressive structure and its particular place in the cultural sensibility. This stylistic feature may be syntactic, semantic, or phonological, but it will always reveal itself against the broader usage patterns that philology has demonstrated as current for the period in question. Spitzer's stylistics remains inherently linguistic, then, and almost always historical, while the stylistic interpretation adds a final interpretive value to these otherwise material observations.[5] Clearly, this vision of stylistics is fueled by the intellectual climate of the time as well as by the regular urge of the young critic to escape from the mentor's field. Malkiel's portrait of Spitzer and the other "angry young dissenters" who were eager to "rebel against [Meyer-Lübke's]—until then undisputed—authority" (Malkiel, "Comparative Romance Linguistics," 837), matches nicely with the nickname ("the red rooster") that Spitzer acquired at the time.[6] Such quick glimpses of the critical setting give a sense of the intellectual ferment that Spitzer himself enjoyed depicting in his descriptions of that early rebellion against linguistic and critical positivism, and Bellos echoes both men in calling Spitzer's move to literary criticism "an act of revolt" against Meyer-Lübke (Bellos, *Essays*, xii). But while Spitzer undoubtedly took pleasure in the extra flavor of personal and professional rebellion that went with experimentation, the real motive behind his move to stylistics lay, as Bellos also notes, in Spitzer's need to justify the relevance of his pursuit both to himself and to the larger academic community.

The search for that justification is apparent in Spitzer's choice of early analytical subjects and methods. "It is perhaps hard now to imagine," Bellos tells us, "just how revolutionary it was for a German academic linguist to turn his attention in 1919–20 to the study of up-to-the-minute

novelists like Barbusse or Charles-Louise Philippe" (xv), but it is not hard
to imagine some of the reasons for doing so. The study of such figures
(undertaken by students who had already received an education in the
trenches) satisfied Spitzer's need to study linguistic creativity as a function
of linguistic innovation while providing him the opportunity to root his
stylistic analyses in the social reality of the moment. The academic importance of the stylistic approach was to be matched by its immediate
social significance. But such an argument requires more than temporal
immediacy to sustain its significance; it requires an adequate model of
mind to fully define the creativity that it places at the heart of cultural
expression. The potential success of Spitzer's model thus depended upon
his successful forging of a solid link between the larger cultural vision he
proposed for style and the actual use of the language itself. Given the
larger intellectual environment of the time and Spitzer's own interest in
the question of literary creativity, it is not surprising that the figure of
Freud should have appeared as the key to the door that Spitzer was
opening between literary aesthetics and linguistic methodology. Thus, it
was "not Croce or Vossler" who influenced Spitzer in this cultural reading
of style—it was "the great Viennese Sigmund Freud," whose work on the
unconscious "revealed . . . a new doorway to the literary work."[7]

The nature and purpose of Spitzer's use of Freud has been commented
upon regularly by those interested in early work in stylistics. Much of
the commentary tries to undercut Spitzer's application of psychoanalysis
to literary criticism, arguing over the degree to which Spitzer directly
used Freudian analytical methods rather than addressing the general
influence of Freud within the academic milieu. At the same time, the
argument over application suffers from contradictory views of what a
Freudian reading should be. Wellek, for instance, limits the influence of
Freud on Spitzer by denying that the readings are "orthodox." He argues
that "Spitzer strongly emphasized the influence of Freud. Freud 'taught
the idea of a constancy of certain motifs in the psyche of poets and their
external manifestations.' But surely the use of Freud even by the early
Spitzer is far from orthodox. Freud is rather used as a justification of a
search for 'latency,' for a hidden key, a recurrent motif, a basic *Erlebnis*,
and even the world view of the author."[8] Wellek argues that "[o]nly a few
papers in Spitzer's extensive work infer sexual or pathological motivation"
(thereby establishing that at least some papers—those on Barbusse and
Diderot, for example—do demonstrate an "orthodox" Freudian reading
under this interpretation [Wellek, "Leo Spitzer," 317]). Bellos, on the

other hand, denies that Spitzer searches for hidden meanings at all: "Language is *opaque* for Freud, but for Spitzer it is—at least in those works on which he spent his creative and critical time—always, and absolutely, *transparent*" (Bellos, *Essays*, xiii). Lionel Trilling, in the meantime, adds to the controversy over what constitutes the Freudian reading by denying any similarity between latent and hidden meanings: "[T]he whole notion of rich ambiguity in literature, of the interplay between the apparent meaning and the latent—not 'hidden'—meaning, has been reinforced by Freudian concepts, perhaps even received its first impetus from them."[9]

When placed within the context of these conflicting viewpoints, the orthodoxy of Spitzer's use of Freud becomes less important an issue than the general nature of Freud's influence. Any questions about Spitzer's use of Freud need to be prefaced by asking what Spitzer intended to achieve by moving toward a psychoanalytic model in the first place. What did Freud and psychoanalysis provide that made them more influential for Spitzer than Vossler or Croce? What were the critical issues and the critical environment that led to Spitzer's initial attempt to define modern stylistics through the auspices of psychoanalysis? Part of the answer lies in the search for critical relevance and authority that the young Spitzer was pursuing on a personal as well as a disciplinary level. Another part rests on the ready exchange of ideas occurring between philological and psychoanalytic thinking at this point in time.

As a student of literary wordplay in search of ways to justify his readings, Spitzer naturally would have been attracted to Freudian views of linguistic creativity, praxis, and parapraxis. But the exchange of ideas and of influence was not one-sided, nor was it pioneered by Spitzer; it grew naturally out of the two disciplines' shared concern with language and discourse. Freud, like almost all his students, made heavy use of philological arguments and literary issues to establish the validity of his psychoanalytic readings. The exchange between the still-respected field of traditional philology and the growing science of psychoanalysis was already heavy when Spitzer began casting about for a way to describe style, and it flowed in both directions, producing an atmosphere in which issues central to the discussion of language use and mental behavior were actively pursued.[10]

On Spitzer's side, the attraction of psychoanalysis can be related to his desire to study literary language rather than the vernacular (in opposition to an approach such as Bally's) and his subsequent need to justify literary stylistics as a central component of linguistic study. Although Romanticism had provided literary criticism with arguments for the significance of literary expression, Spitzer was still working primarily as a linguist. A psychological model that offered center stage to individual linguistic word-play provided Spitzer with a descriptive framework in symmetry with the larger vision of *Sprachpsychologie* that eighteenth-century historical linguists such as Humboldt had seen as the focal point of linguistic discussion.[11] Psychoanalysis thus represented a psychological reference point to which Spitzer could attach those linguistic issues currently floating around him: Meyer-Lübke's neo-grammarian methods, Schuchardt's interest in language and culture, Humboldt's Romantic belief in language study as the key to epistemology, and Spitzer's own desire to define language change in terms of individual creative activity. It was more satisfying to address *parole* than *langue*, as Spitzer would note later, and most satisfying of all was the study of the literary text as cultural *parole* in its highest— that is, its aesthetic— form.

But arguing for these literary studies required justifying them to a skeptical linguistic audience increasingly devoted to scientific principles, an audience to whom the wordplay of novelists seemed arbitrary rather than historically influential. Freud's importance to Spitzer thus lay in Freud's use of "the logic of the unconscious" to eliminate "the arbitrariness" that had previously been attached to explanations of "dreams, tics, irrational acts, and even the appearance of neologisms" (Spitzer, "Les Études," 26). In simple terms, Freud helped to justify the fusion of a descriptive linguistics with the study of individual literary style, a fusion achieved in a form that no other linguistic or aesthetic model could match at the time. Spitzer's use of Freud thus follows the stylistic tradition of attaching language-based interpretive models to a basic descriptive framework in order to explain the nature of style.[12]

As we have noted, however, the support Spitzer could count on from psychoanalysis was far from one-sided. Philology still enjoyed (at least within the Continental academic arena) its position as a bastion of humanistic study. In the face of a rising positivism within the biological and other natural sciences (as well as the rapidly growing positivism of linguistic study), philology offered a high degree of intellectual status to any discipline that could become associated with it. The attraction of that established academic validity for psychoanalysis was bolstered by the general purposes shared by both studies. Many of the early members of Freud's circle were also trained philologists,[13] and they helped to foster two distinct areas of shared interest within each field: the study of the origins and nature of symbols and the study of general relations between linguistic and mental activity. The first area rests upon each discipline's interest in the mythic, religious, and sexual sources of particular linguistic forms. Unfortunately, the vast historical and cross-historical range addressed by this area of study and its pursuit of universal origins for language and behavior lent it an air of significance more dependent upon the range of the issues it covered than upon its actual success. The second area of shared interest, although more mundane, was more immediately applicable to specific analytic situations. The comparative procedures and studies undertaken by philology could be used to support a staple of psychoanalytic theory: the orderly nature of such historical changes offered secondary proof for the psychologically orderly nature of linguistic behavior such as parapraxes, wordplay, and general meaning shifts.

Freud was well aware of the benefits that psychoanalysis could gain from an exchange of interpretations and methods with other established disciplines, as he noted in describing the birth of *Imago*. From psychoanalysis would come interpretive possibilities for other fields, based upon the psychoanalytic theory of mind; to psychoanalyis would come the greater respectability provided by association with other, accepted fields of study (or at least the refutation of charges that the field might be esoteric—or, among the less charitable, even disreputable). Not surprisingly, Freud chose to discuss these connections by defining psychoanalysis in terms of its scientific nature, a definition that already carried its own cachet:

> In the work of psycho-analysis links are formed with numbers of other mental sciences, the investigation of which promises results of the greatest value: links with mythology and philology, with folklore, with social psychology and the theory of religion. You will not be surprised to hear that a periodical has grown up on psycho-analytical soil whose sole aim is to foster these links. This periodical is known as *Imago*, founded in 1912 and edited by Hans Sachs and Otto Rank. In all these links the share of psycho-analysis is in the first instance that of giver and only to a less extent that of receiver. It is true that this brings it an advantage in the fact that its strange findings become more familiar when they are met with again in other fields; but on the whole it is psycho-analysis which provides the technical methods and the points of view whose application in these other fields should prove fruitful.[14]

Freud had already seen the benefits of such an exchange with philology in an essay appearing in the first issue of *Imago* (1912).[15] "Über den Einfluss sexueller Momente auf Entstehung und Entwicklung der Sprache," written by Hans Sperber (Spitzer's friend and eventual coauthor), was used by Freud in the *Introductory Lectures* as philological evidence for a link between sexuality and the origins of language. He describes Sperber's essay in detail, later repeating its argument in *The Interpretation of Dreams*. Having stated the same belief in both works—"Things that are symbolically connected today were probably united in the prehistoric times by conceptual and linguistic identity"—Freud adds a note to the 1925 edition of *The Interpretation of Dreams:* "This view would be powerfully supported by a theory put forward by Dr. Hans Sperber (1912). He is of the opinion that all primal words referred to sexual things but afterwards lost their sexual meaning through being applied to other things and activities which were compared with the sexual ones" (*Standard Edition*, vol. 5, 352n). Freud's purpose here is to use philology to support that first area of shared interest: the search for the ultimate (sexual) source of all language behavior.

For Spitzer, however, the real attraction of Freud lay in their second shared area of interest. Spitzer was not concerned with Freud and Sperber's claims about the origin of language but with the possibilities revealed in Freud's reliance upon philological science to support the study of parapraxes and wordplay.[16] The techniques employed by philology to resuscitate previous word forms, based as they are upon repeatable descriptive procedures of comparison and reformation, provided psychoanalysis with the argument that there were logical processes at work behind the assumed "illogicality" of everyday language use. The influence of etymological technique shines through texts such as *Jokes and Their Relation to the Unconscious, The Psychopathology of Everyday Life*, and "The Antithetical Sense of Primal Words." Such psychoanalytic arguments in turn provided Spitzer with a ready-made claim for the validity of studying literary wordplay in particular and literary style in general. Serious human motivation, it could be argued, lay behind even the most outrageous neologisms of Rabelais, the most comic formations of Christian Morgenstern.

Psychoanalysis thus offered the young Spitzer a legitimate framework for moving beyond the simple description of material historical changes and into the arena of motivated play. The mutual interests of both disciplines served to revive the connection between critical interpretion and scientific description that Spitzer sought for modern stylistics—a connection that Spitzer believed was fading from language study in the face of the rising importance attached to the scientific alone, and it was in that context that Spitzer brought forth works such as the studies of Morgenstern, Philippe, Péguy, Romains, and Proust that are indicative of his thinking on stylistics from 1910 to 1925.

The study of Christian Morgenstern, "Die groteske Gestaltungs- und Sprachkunst Christian Morgensterns" (1918), is Spitzer's half of *Motiv und Wort: Studien zur Literatur- und Sprachpsychologie*, coauthored by Hans Sperber. A self-described psychoanalytic study,[17] its title captures the blend of linguistic and contextual description sought by Spitzer. *Motiv und Wort* is a reworking of *Wörter und Sachen*, the *Kulturforschung* method which marks cultural change through a language's acquisition of terms and names for everyday objects.[18] But Spitzer and Sperber wanted to stress emotional rather than commercial, agricultural, or other material factors in change and acquisition; the substitution of *Motiv* (motif) for *Sachen* (things) characterized the shift in the descriptive procedure. The interpretation, still concerned with a contextual and historical analysis, is not to be based upon the material objects present in the culture (a kind of anthropological vocabulary search), but upon those emotional motifs whose influence is great enough to attract sets of related linguistic materials into their orbit.

By 1921 Rudolf Meringer would declare that the method could pursue ideas as easily as objects (Iordan–Orr, *Romance Linguistics*, 64), but by this time Spitzer already had extended that interpretation one step further. Intent upon pursuing literary style as the highest form of cultural expression, Spitzer simply defined the aesthetic elements of a vocabulary as more indicative of a culture's inner workings than its material elements. The move from cultural objects to cultural emotions and ideas thus guarantees, in Spitzer's eyes, the intellectual significance of modern stylistics, while the *Motiv und Wort* procedure provides the necessary linguistic framework. The larger intellectual significance required by post-Romantic views of style is addressed by the Humboldtian interest in individual and cultural development; the scientific or descriptive validity required by the new human sciences is assured through the linguistics of Meyer-Lübke and Schuchardt, each theorist providing his separate argument for descriptive adequacy, historical development, and *Sprachpsychologie*. *Motiv und Wort* thus signals Spitzer's breaking out of the traditional cloisters of linguistic study, while it announces the modern belief that rigorous linguistic analysis should be the objective heart of any intellectually significant study of literary style.

Spitzer affirmed that these were his goals seven years later in "Wortkunst und Sprachwissenschaft" (1925), explaining that his critical procedures were designed to seek out parallels between the words of the text and its motifs, which consisted of "everything other than words: the invention of action, of characters, etc. . . ."[19] The significance of the stylistic study does not rest simply in the description of parallels between word choices and emotional motifs, however, but in rooting these parallels in the writer's psyche, which has to deal with both the subject and the words. Spitzer's justification for this claim in *Motiv und Wort* appears in a flurry of references and cross-references to various linguistic and psychological discussions. Sperber's half of the text obviously provided one area of support, since it was undoubtedly influenced by Freud. To further establish the procedure's validity, Spitzer goes on to note that Sperber's essay, which postulated an emotional core for the motifs of Meyrink, has also proved to be "biographically" correct, thus providing proof positive of the psychoanalytic interpretation. As for Spitzer's study within *Motiv und Wort,* a reference to the fabulous, mythic form of Morgenstern's word creations invokes the aegis of philology, with its long-standing tradition of using myths for investigating linguistic and cultural linguistic formation. Finally, the book's dedication—to Meyer-Lübke, the mentor of both men—provides the reference to descriptive linguistics that is needed as the final argument for the study's validity. Clustered within this discussion, then, are all the support disciplines and procedures that Spitzer invokes in his stylistic undertaking: the neo-grammarian linguistics of his training, the *Wörter und Sachen* method of Shuchardt, psychoanalysis, and the larger mythic and cultural interests of Romantic philology. Spitzer's critical task is to control all these supportive frameworks while defining literary creativity and, ultimately, a modern stylistics.

The arena that Spitzer has chosen at the moment is that of Christian Morgenstern's poetic wordplay. Morgenstern's opening to the *Galgenlieder* volume, an epigram by Nietschze ("Within every true man there is hidden a child who wants to play"), establishes the theme of artistic creativity and play that had already been raised by Spitzer in his dissertation on Rabelais.[20] This early belief in wordplay and word formation as exemplars of poetic creativity grows naturally enough out of Spitzer's interest in defining stylistics as a primary creative process amenable to linguistic analysis. The study of neologisms appeals to Spitzer as a linguist trained in historical and comparative linguistics, while the addition of the element of linguistic play allows him to introduce overtones of literary creativity—a creativity that only requires the addition of a proper intellectual weight to the admitted play of Morgenstern. Spitzer's own version of Morgenstern's epigram thus carefully balances the sheer "fun and games" of neologisms with the necessity that they be taken seriously: "[Morgenstern's] grotesque art searches for reality in the conditions of pure language, and constructs a physics of the irrational which demands to be taken seriously. It is true that his neologisms are meant for fun and games, but they are deeply anchored in the general life of the language, as well as in the writer's imagination" (*Motiv und Wort*, 90).

The influence of the Romantic and scientific traditions in post-Romantic linguistics—and the subsequent tensions in Spitzer's early struggle to define an adequate stylistics—rest quietly in this comment. Morgenstern's neologisms are open to analysis through linguistic methods: they are not random; they are (in another allusion to the scientific) a "physics of the irrational." But Spitzer has no interest in a simple materialism. He also provides, through Humboldtian phrasing, the second characteristic of his stylistic method, the one that sets his work apart from the general trends in linguistics: each historical shift will be described by Spitzer as the result of a creative mind in action, an action that alters and expands the general life of the language.

This combined set of desires reenacts the basic oppositions that exist within linguistic study: complexity versus efficiency, historical versus synchronic, mentalistic versus positivistic, individual versus general, interpretive versus descriptive. In each opposition, the complexity demanded by the first term is an unacceptable burden for the second. For Spitzer, however, efficiency of description holds no great attraction if it requires a reduction of the overall intellectual scope of stylistic study. His definition of language and linguistic creativity is an intentional response to the growing drive toward generality of description, while his use of psychoanalysis provides scientific support for the complex web of creative motivation that he insists upon as the underlying structure of language use. Spitzer's declared aim is "a kind of psychoanalysis of literary expression," an analysis in which he "tries to justify even the seemingly arbitrary constructions from the writer's particular character" (91).

Morgenstern's work certainly provides innumerable examples of what initially appear to be arbitrary "etymologies." The poems are rife with neologisms formed around wordplay and soundplay. But Spitzer uses these formations to argue for a controlling artistic sensibility, a personal conceptual framework that derives its strength from creating the peculiarities of its wordplay out of the general possibilities offered by the language. Poetic wordplay is not irrational or purely personal Spitzer argues; it depends upon the shared communal sensibility that the language embodies. In Morgenstern's work, as read by Spitzer, there are "imponderable latencies, dimly felt by many Germans in their language, which the poet elaborates" (71).

This call for a shared linguistic and cultural mythology is rather formidable, raising images of a vast panhistorical, pancultural linguistic latency. But most of the particular stylistic features that Spitzer puts on display are banal in the best sense of the term, validated by everyday linguistic behavior. The uncovered latencies often are used only to underwrite simple plays on grammatical forms and endings. Spitzer's analysis of Morgenstern's "Der Werwolf" is a case in point. "The germ of this poem," Spitzer declares, "is the reinterpretation of *Werwolf* as the nominative case of *wer* [man] and the neologisms like *Weswolf* which follow from it—a grammatical monstrosity which can only be hatched in dreams or madness. . . ." The importance of the formation lies in Morgenstern's creative ability to move this latent connotation out of the irrational and into the light of day. His creative talent rests upon his ability to express the "secret latencies, word combinations that may be slumbering in our etymological subconscious" (65).

Spitzer thus moves both style and the stylistic reading beyond the realm of secondary play by interweaving traditional philology and psychoanalytic thinking. The individual stylistic wordplay first is given linguistic validity by defining its formation in terms of the latent structural possibilities of the language—a structural possibility certainly far beyond that envisioned by Bally's stylistics. This preestablished creative value then is extended further by envisioning a shared, unconscious linguistic legacy as the full motivation for the stylistic expression. Spitzer's two-stage analysis weaves a theoretical tapestry that blends the synchronic and the diachronic, the syntagmatic and the paradigmatic. The creative sensibility of the poet is woven in by using one set of analytical threads; the historical background of the language, by using another. The poet is neither mad nor dreaming, a claim justified on two grounds: (1) the language system provides for this particular form of stylistic play, and (2) such play is part of the creative activity of mind. What Spitzer must provide in order to unify all these threads is an ultimate motivation that can serve to define the authorial sensibility producing the text.

The pursuit of that unifying sensibility is justified through psychology, while the actual analytical procedure comes very close to the method later defined as the "philological circle." First, a pattern of usage is uncovered, "the steady grooves in which [the poet's] verbal creation moves" (91). From these motifs a psychological "etymon" or "radix" is postulated. That radix is used, in turn, to further elaborate and explain the personal, particular style of the writer. This exploration of motif and word "comes closest to stylistics" (94) because it begins with established linguistic methods (here the popular *Wörter und Sachen*) and then moves beyond that method's explanatory power, substituting the mental construct or motif for the simple natural object. It does not search for an object but for the emotional *radix* which explains both literary motif and word—the psychological experience of the writer.

For Spitzer, it is this last step that extends the analysis into the creative mind and thus beyond the then-current realm of linguistic stylistics. He states as much when he differentiates his work from Martin Beutler's. Beutler's starting point "is always grammar rather than the writer's psyche." Spitzer's concern, on the other hand, "is not to sort the writer's words into grammatical pigeon holes, but to find the mainspring which all at once makes the whole fan of words jump out and open" (95). Here Spitzer winds Morgenstern's work around its expression of the relativity and individual separateness of each human life. The world reveals its basic nature through the ease with which it is molded and manipulated by language, an ease that denies the possibility of maintaining a stable, referential world of meaning. The style of Morgenstern both informs and depends upon this conceptual frame and is to be defined in relation to it.

The use of a personal conceptual framework to define a particular language use may go beyond the more empirically defined borders of linguistic analysis, but it flows directly from the tradition of Romantic stylistics. It even fits quite easily within modern literary criticism, provided that Spitzer's declared use of psychoanalysis can be rendered more innocuous, and the Romantic idealism of his linguistic theory reduced. Wellek has done both, stating that Spitzer's investigation into the author's psyche is actually just the discussion of worldview or *Weltanschauung*. Questioning Spitzer's own reference to the early Freudian influence in his work, Wellek describes the Morgenstern piece as an example of Spitzer's "weak" use of psychoanalysis: "Only a few papers in Spitzer's extensive work infer sexual or pathological motivation. . . . The bulk of the psychological papers attempts to establish connections between style and world view. . . . [A]nalyzing the word myths of Christian Morgenstern, Spitzer interprets his view of language as 'swathing further veils over an impenetrably dark world.' " (Wellek, "Leo Spitzer," 317).

Wellek's argument very clearly displays its own resolution of the tensions provided by a post-Romantic aesthetics of literature. The presentation of pathological motivations for literary expression clearly interferes with an ahistorical orientation, since such arguments imply that a literary text may be partially determined by the individual life of the author, and that determinism lowers the supposedly universal expressive significance of any artwork. A worldview, however, suggests a larger vision, implying a level of motivated creativity that extends beyond historically determined behavior, and Wellek moves to attach such an approach to Spitzer's work. Wellek's sketch thus admits the influence of psychoanalysis on Spitzer but works to mediate its importance. The strict pathological reading, seen as the true psychoanalytic reading, is to be dismissed. Such vulgar psychoanalytic criticism is assumed to lose interpretive usefulness through its attachment to what also is assumed to be the deterministic pathological behavior of a single historical figure. More acceptable to Wellek is the reading that describes an authorial worldview. On the surface, such a reading is less historically restrictive, since it implies a larger philosophical (if not fully aesthetic) attitude, and the escape from pathological determinism can be equated with a move toward a fully valid reading: the interpretation of the text in terms of its ahistorical aesthetic significance.

But the reading that studies an author's worldview still occupies the important historical territory that lies between the deterministic reading and the aesthetic response. The possibility always exists that an adequate bridge can be built between this larger philosophical view and the specific historical moment that gives rise to it. What is needed to validate such a vision is a model that attaches an epistemological link between the individual, the social moment, and the larger cultural history of that "worldview." With that goal in mind in 1918, Spitzer could justifiably propose that psychoanalytic applications were not a narrowing of the linguistic and critical sphere; they were a scientific widening of Romantic attitudes toward linguistic development, a step out into intellectual and cultural formation. Style seen as a worldview is more than a chosen means of expression; it is an epistemological activity. "The experience of language is part of experience. . . . Morgenstern writes in thoughts and thinks in language" (*Motiv und Wort*, 93). His style is not chosen simply because of its suitability to his beliefs; it is an expression of Morgenstern's psychological framework, an outgrowth of his emotional and intellectual viewpoint. In partial support of this belief Spitzer refers to a letter in which Morgenstern outlines the relation between childhood and adult play. "Why," Morgenstern speculates, "should an imaginative boy not invent, say, an Indian tribe with all its paraphernalia, including language and national anthem? And why should artistic playfulness not repeat such an act for the fun of it?" (107). Out of the malleable material of language and childhood imagination will come a world, and with it a feeling of duality, even plurality, which Spitzer sees as a central motif within the poetry. Words, as creatures in the world, mutate and regroup; they change sex via their grammatical forms; whole phrases become living families on the basis of an intentional misreading of their meaning. All this activity, occurring within a self-enclosed linguistic system that supposedly refers to the external world of reality, produces a split vision of the real and the unreal, the actual and the created.

Spitzer treats this motif of duality extensively in his discussion of the poetry (especially while analyzing Morgenstern's numerical wordplay) and uses the theme to link the playful horror of Morgenstern's poetic creations to the author's memories of childhood games. Commenting on Morgenstern's use of the *-lf* ending, Spitzer develops the motif at length. "The sound combination *-lf* (as in *Elefant, Wolf, Elf*) apparently became a symbol of horror for our author. At the same time the double meaning of *Elf* (1. elf, goblin, 2. the number 'eleven') must have fascinated him." Spitzer is even willing to speculate on the childhood origins of such a sensibility. "No doubt, Morgenstern as a child was moved and terrified on hearing the mystical counting at New Year's or at any witching hour. The name of the spirit crept into the numerical concept" (*Motiv und Wort*, 66). This blend of childhood fear and adult awareness becomes, in Spitzer's reading, a central creative motif informing Morgenstern's style. The further analysis of "Das Gebet" provides Spitzer with an opportunity to display the stylistic process for which he is arguing.

"Das Gebet"	"The Does' Prayer"
Die Rehlein beten	The does, as the hour
zur Nacht,	grows late
halb acht!	med-it-ate;
Halb neun!	med-it-nine;
Halb zehn!	med-it-ten;
Halb elf!	med-eleven;
Halb-zwölf	med-twelve;
Zwölf!	mednight!
Die Rehlein beten	The does, as the hour
zur Nacht,	grows late,
halb acht!	meditate.
Sie falten die	They fold their
kleinen Zehlein,	little toesies,
die Rehlein.	the doesies.[21]

The ritual chant of the poem/prayer, the sound-play, and the apparent pun on "Zwölf" are seen as products of Morgenstern's macabre sense of "nature" and the efficacy of the "doesies's" prayer. It is a motif that Spitzer continues to uncover, finding it "small wonder" (66) that the quickly succeeding poem is the "Zwölf-Elf"—another play on numbers accompanied by a similar sense of nocturnal malaise: "The *Zwölf-Elf* is the 'elf of twelve o'clock,' but the numerals associated with horror come into play also. When finally 'raven Ralf' enters the poem crying: 'Kra! / The end is here! The end is here!' we have the whole -*lf*-family gathered."

Spitzer engages in his own wordplay in this interpretation. As members of an elf family within the poems, these words are all names of nocturnal creatures, actors in the shadow world with which Morgenstern plays. Linguistically, however, these words are also members of the same etymological word-family—they all share the -*lf* ending. Spitzer thus lays claim to having discovered a created yet grammatically valid etymological pattern that unites both sound and meaning within a stylistic motif of numerology and horror.

All of this interpretation still rests lightly on the notion of linguistic play, however, and Spitzer's analysis must reach a higher level of interpretive seriousness in order for it to assume the critical significance that he has claimed for such stylistic manipulation. He moves toward this level by describing Morgenstern's specific playing on the number 2 as linked to "[t]he problem of the double personality slumbering in every man [that] has intrigued every thinker." For Morgenstern, Spitzer argues, this stylistic motif arises both from Morgenstern's personal emotional framework and from the language itself. There is "a linguistic stimulus" for the relativity expressed by Morgenstern. "[F]rom *zweifach* (two-fold, double), *Zweilicht* (twilight), he abstracts a *Zwi*, a man with two brains who reads double, feels double." (67), and Spitzer presents this duality as a central characteristic of Morgenstern's poetry, finding variant forms of it in the I/You question (the title of one of Morgenstern's volumes is *Ich und Du*), in mirror imagery, and in a general awareness of a gulf between the centering I and the world which it perceives outside of itself. The motive force behind playing with one's powers of perception—and the language that supposedly refers to the objects of these perceptions— is declared to be a distrust of both activities. In Spitzer's words, "A skeptical world-view shows through the purely verbal inventions" (*Motiv und Wort*, 70).

The interpretive steps necessary to tie style to author are completed by this point. Spitzer takes the child's holiday play with numbers and uses it to build a bridge toward a stylistic vision capable of carrying the significance that he seeks. He postulates an adult awareness of duality and separation in Morgenstern and uncovers a world in which the childish fear has lost its pleasurable aspects and become anxiety-ridden. Following that line of interpretation, Spitzer reads *Melancholie*, one of Morgenstern's serious volumes, as the adult expression of this anxiety of separation and enforced duality. "In *Fiesolaner Ritornellen*," Spitzer tells us, "Morgenstern returns again to the world's sorrow that two cannot be one, that the union of lovers is never complete like the union of mother and child in birth" (68). And he notes that the same collection "laments" the child's separation from the mother: " 'Will you never come back, not even in spirit? Are you dead forever? / And yet there was a time your heart blood flowed through you and me' " (69).

Spitzer goes on to propose that the metaphor of mother/child separation captures some of the major elements of Morgenstern's individual psyche: the sense of separation and consequent lack of self-definition, the related awareness of the relativity and changeable nature of life, the need to destroy the boundaries of "Ich" and "Du," of "Zwi" in an attempt to conquer the anxiety attached to these aspects of life. The validity of this interpretation is supported by the fact that Morgenstern's mother died when he was nine years old. Michael Bauer's biography of Morgenstern and the latter's own *Stufen* give an impression of the effect this loss had upon

Morgenstern. Bauer notes that Morgenstern's mother "wrote serious and comic verse with obvious literary talent," and he argues that Morgenstern had inherited from her all his "inward strength."[22] Morgenstern himself provides a third-person description of the loss. Not long after the death of his mother when he was ten, "the assault of hostile forces from without and within began":

> The boy who, cherished and spoiled, had simply played alone at home and outdoors (my playing is a sunny chapter all by itself) proved much less up to the outside world he encountered at school. It seemed as if he had even then taken over his mother's suffering although it was only twelve years later that it led to actual illness. For while there were many fresh impulses which drove him on, he was more and more subject to vague inhibitions which might not have let him reach the age he did if there had not also been some counter-forces which struggled toughly for him and always got him through the worst.[23]

The biographical material thus offers full support for the psychic portrait that Spitzer has been sketching. The process of following the patterns of Morgenstern's writing, searching for motifs with which to explain the patterns, and positing a psychological radix for the author has proved successful; moreover, the actual biographical facts support the interpretation.

Spitzer, however, makes no strong effort to develop any of these biographical facts,[24] and his determined lack of interest in the biography is often read simply as one more indication of Spitzer's avoidance of a full psychoanalytic procedure. But the belief that true psychoanalytic readings must be always and everywhere a form of psychobiography is a stereotype that has by now breathed its last.[25] For his part, Spitzer's stylistic readings from this period are undertaken in the belief that the critic can best interpret those styles produced during his own time period, and he assumes that the biographical material concerning such authors will be either fragmentary or nonexistent. The psychic portrait that Spitzer pursues is, admittedly, a construct of the investigation, even as he declares that his study is psychoanalytic. Yet Spitzer's avoidance of any speculation about, let alone any research into, the events of Morgenstern's life tells a great deal about the pressures of the critical moment and his own subsequent critical leanings. The aesthetic elevation of the text will not benefit from an inclusion of the facts of Morgenstern's life, at least in this study, and it is Spitzer's tendency to avoid such consequential biographical facts in developing his psychological "radix" that demonstrates his uncertain attitude toward the link between art and author, literary style and production. The escape from the "lower" social focus of *Wörter und Sachen* cannot be achieved if the everyday detritus of life intrudes too heavily into the portrait of the psyche.

The Romantic tension between the social individual and the individual cultural hero operates fully in Spitzer's blend of psychoanalysis and aesthetics. In disagreeing with another critic of Morgenstern, Spitzer rejects the psychologically more tame description of the artist as "only intending, not as compelled." After all, he declares, "the artistic temper is a biological reality" (*Motiv und Wort*, 99). Such a belief in a compelling creativity draws both impetus and support from arguments available not only in Freud's psychology, but also in the lingering status accorded to biology as the nineteenth century's premier science and from the comparatist's desire to emulate scientific procedure. Yet Spitzer's avoidance of biographical data underscores the Romantic commandment that the all-too-prosaic factuality of literary production must be secondary to the aesthetic value of artistic achievement. Seen in these terms, the hesitation that Wellek and Bellos note in Spitzer's use of the specifically sexual components of psychoanalytic interpretation, which is visible in the avoidance of biographical elements in the Morgenstern study, is a critical decision born of the tension of choosing between a description of the psyche as a biographical entity or as a cultural sensibility. Spitzer's interest in psychoanalysis highlights his general desire that stylistics should establish a correlation between the stylistic properties of a text and the psyche of the author—and that it should do so in terms of a science that describes both human behavior and linguistic creativity. If that interest reveals itself more often "in the world-view of the writer than in the details of his biography,"[26] it does so because Spitzer can find no adequate middle ground between the individual's history and the nonhistorical values being attached to literature at this time.

The core of Spitzer's difficulty thus rests in the Romantic era's own uncertain division of the poet as individual and as supra-individualistic. The most obvious indication of this transformation of the individual—who moves out of the activities of the *sans culottes* and into the activities of the individual artist—lies in the Romantic definition of the imagination. Faced with the option of becoming only one more individual swimming in the stream of society, Romantic poets such as Shelley could define the poetic self and the poetic imagination as operating above and beyond the plane of the merely social. Literature was not to be social practice alone, or even primarily social practice, but an expression of the individual poetic imagination that leapt beyond daily banality. The difficulties produced by this Romantic reification of the artist are manifest. Literature becomes a product of the authentic artist who, paradoxically, cannot be related to the social context at all. The resulting tension for the critic interested in the relation between style and history dominates Spitzer's work from this period, and its impact can still be found, thirty years later, in his reinterpretation of the purposes and procedures that lay behind his work in *Motiv und Wort*. The interpretive procedure, as Spitzer explains in the *Essays in Historical Semantics* (1948),[27] follows established philological methods (the "mass-strategy" of Schuchardt [5]), while it extends the approach through the use of the "less naturalistic," more emotional collecting device offered by Sperber's work. These emotional "fixing factors" serve, to use an analogy of which Spitzer was fond, as the center of a constellation of linguistic changes. At the innermost center of this constellation lies a particular "obsession," an obsession that Spitzer refers to in the same sentence as a "cultural" fixing factor.

This blending by Spitzer of concept and emotion, personal obsession and cultural determination, once again points to Spitzer's desire to unite individual intention and cultural expression into a single model of style and language. Referring to his "Puxi" study as an analysis of a "pathological . . . semantic expansion," Spitzer unites both ends of the stylistic spectrum:

> Again, in my study 'Puxi,' (1927), I treated the semantic radiation of a less pathological but no less passionate feeling, that of mother love— showing how, in one individual case, this passion succeeded in attracting a world into the orbit of the pet name given a child by its mother. Can we, then, imagine that religious and philosophical currents, which have spread over vast areas of civilization and have completely transformed the lives of their followers (as have Pythagoreanism or Christianity), should not also have been highly powerful forces for linguistic transformation, though less varied in a whimsical and arbitrary way, even more firmly established and enduringly effective, because of the momentum given by the unanimity and extent of religious passion? [*Essays*, 6]

Spitzer's easy linkage of the sensibility of the individual to a change in the philosophical and ideological sensibility of a culture reiterates his willingness to find a bridge between the language style of the single individual and that of the cultural milieu. But no method for adequately designing that bridge had made itself apparent at the time of the "Puxi" study, and this retrospective glance tells us why. Even in the Morgenstern essay (a study described by Spitzer as a psychoanalytic reading and one in which he is making use of the advantages offered by psychoanalysis) Spitzer does not assume that the gap between the individual and the cultural can be crossed by studying the middle ground of the social. Working from within the post-Romantic framework of his time, Spitzer's critical interpretation leaps over the sociological and ideological, choosing to describe a larger shared cultural awareness rather than look to the "mental constellation" as a feature of the psychopathology of everyday life or the sociohistorical milieu of the writer.

Yet Spitzer also continues to reject a full-fledged aestheticism. Having established creative wordplay as a legitimate mental activity, Spitzer does not wish to find its ultimate description outside history. The Morgenstern study demonstrates a continued concern with context, while stopping short of describing the actual life or the factuality of the historical situation. The Spitzerian psychoanalytic reading hints at establishing the source of the stylistic interpretation in human behavior, and it justifies Spitzer's move away from a positivistic study of the linguistic material alone. But for Spitzer to go further into the specific motives for this particular stylistic behavior would be to introduce two related issues that he cannot accept at this time: (1) a view of the individual author as a social construct rather than a cultural phenomenon and (2) an implication that stylistic activity might be determined by social as well as intellectual and aesthetic concerns.

As these difficulties become more apparent to Spitzer, the movement toward a new method for justifying his readings begins. These changes, culminating eventually in the philological circle so readily endorsed in his later career, are signaled by several theoretical statements written during the period from 1925 to 1931. At the same time, ongoing shifts in the critical and linguistic environment encourage a drift toward the self-sufficient text and a value-free linguistic description. Spitzer will continue to describe the studies of this period as undertaken during a period of Freudian interest. But the reference to *"eine Art Psychoanalyse"* of the text will fade: *Psyche*, itself problematic as a term, will be replaced by *Seele*, emotional complexes by intellectual/spiritual contexts. Indeed, in the later "Wortkunst und Sprachwissenschaft," Spitzer will go so far as to suggest that *Seele und Wort* might have been a better description of his methods than *Motiv und Wort* (111). Discussing that shift is the business of the next chapter.

NOTES

1. Linda Dowling, *Language and Decadence in the Victorian Fin de Siècle* (Princeton, N.J.: Princeton University Press, 1986), 105.
2. Graham Hough, *Style and Stylistics* (London: Routledge & Kegan Paul, 1969), 18–19.
3. Leo Spitzer, *Linguistics and Literary History* (Princeton, N.J.: Princeton University Press, 1948, rpt. New York: Russell & Russell, 1962), 3.
4. Yakov Malkiel, "Comparative Romance Linguistics," in *Current Trends in Linguistics*, ed. Thomas A. Sebeok, vol. 9 (The Hague: Mouton, 1972), 858.
5. Spitzer's work in historical semantics is based on a similar uniting of linguistic description and cultural significance: change in language illustrates a change in sensibility. This historical focus clearly raises problems in an age increasingly devoted to synchronic study. The particular arguments that Spitzer makes—or refuses to make—in support of his vision of literary history will prove to be central to his interpretation of style, since all of Spitzer's literary work grows out of his initial training in historical linguistics. That work is realized in two discrete but related areas of investigation: literary stylistics (and general criticism) and historical semantics. The studies differ somewhat in their material and purpose, but they are united by that underlying Romantic epistemology which ties language growth to the intellectual and spiritual development of the individual and the culture.
6. David Bellos, ed., *Leo Spitzer: Essays on Seventeenth-Century French Literature* (Cambridge: Cambridge University Press, 1983), xiii.
7. "Les Études de Style et les différent pays," *Langue et Littérature, Actes du VIII Congrès de la Fédération Internationale des Langues et Littératures Modernes*, 23–39. (The statement is from page 26.) The reference is significant, since Vossler and Croce are influential figures in the twentieth-century separation of the field of Romance linguistics from that of general linguistics. That separation has led some to see the former as a bastion of humanism, while others, such as Robert Hall, have excoriated this so-called mentalistic trend. The idealism of Vossler and Croce has constituted, according to Hall, "an antiscientific element which has been at work undermining the essential base of linguistics itself" (*Idealism*

in Romance Linguistics [Ithaca, N.Y.: Cornell University Press, 1963], 3).

8. René Wellek, "Leo Spitzer (1887–1960)," *Comparative Literature*, 12 (1960), 317. The quotation from Spitzer cited by Wellek is from "Risposta a una critica," *Convivium*, n.s., 5 (1957), 597–603.

9. Lionel Trilling, "Freud and Literature," *The Liberal Imagination* (New York: The Viking Press, Doubleday Anchor Books, 1950), 48.

10. Jameson finds the psychoanalytic model saturated with analogies to writing. (*The Prison-House of Language* [Princeton, N.J.: Princeton University Press, 1972). The specific link between philology and psychoanalysis is made by Forrester, Foucault, and others.

11. It was not Humboldt alone who had these interests, as Kurt Jankowsky notes in describing Grimm's concern with "uncovering the spiritual riches of his nation" (*The Neogrammarians: A Re-evaluation of Their Place in the Development of Linguistic Science* [The Hague: Mouton, 1972], 78). Grimm's Law tends to be better remembered than Grimm's interest in the cultural purposes behind language study.

12. The same needs motivate John Searle's use of Freud to support the thinking of Noam Chomsky:

"Throughout the history of the study of man there has been a fundamental opposition between those who believe that progress is to be made by a rigorous observation of man's actual behavior and those who believe that such observations are interesting only in so far as they reveal to us hidden and possibly fairly mysterious underlying laws that only partially and in distorted form reveal themselves to us in behavior. Freud, for example, is in the latter class, most of American social science in the former. . . . Noam Chomsky is unashamedly with the searchers after hidden laws."

Searle's general theoretical reasoning may be flawed, but his purpose is clear, and it is the same as Spitzer's: to establish the validity of a shift in linguistic thinking by relating that shift to a valued psychological method (John Searle, "Chomsky's Revolution in Linguistics," *New York Review of Books* [1972; rpt. in *On Noam Chomsky: Critical Essays*, ed. Gilbert Harman, New York: Anchor Press, 1974], 2–33). The statement is from page 2.

13. John Forrester, *Language and the Origins of Psychoanalysis* (New York: Columbia University Press, 1980), 193. Forrester discusses the links between Freud and philology at length, noting in detail the support that Freud found for his discipline in philological study.

14. Sigmund Freud, *Introductory Lectures on Psychoanalysis*, Standard Edition, 15 (London: Hogarth Press, 1963), 167–68.

15. Hans Sperber, "Über den Einfluss sexueller Momente auf Entstehung und Entwicklung der Sprach," *Imago*, 1, (1912). The book jointly published by Sperber and Spitzer, *Motiv and Wort: Studien zur Literatur- und Sprachpsychologie*, is discussed later in this chapter.

16. Although Forrester may overstress the nature of the shared interests, he does note the mutual support and the reasons why it was sought: "It was the field of the philological sciences that acted as a source and inspiration for Freud's and psychoanalysis's preoccupation with language . . . they offered him a support in external reality to which he could turn when plagued with doubt as to the value of the discoveries that he was making in mental reality" (167–68).

17. Leo Spitzer and Hans Sperber, *Motiv und Wort: Studien zur Literatur- und Sprachpsychologie* (Leipzig, 1918). Spitzer's portion of the study is not "orthodox" according to any of the previous definitions. Nor does Wellek list it as one of the "pathological" studies. This essay thus has the double merit of avoiding full contamination by that controversy and still providing a clear portrait of the underlying purposes and tensions in Spitzer's critical thinking at the time and its effects on the formation of stylistics.

18. The origin of the method has been disputed: some grant the honor of its creation to Rudolf Meringer (1859–1931), and some to Hugo Schuchardt. Spitzer himself tried to settle the question by granting the honor to both men. See Iordan–Orr, (Iorgue Iordan and John Orr), *An Introduction to Romance Linguistics: Its Schools and Scholars*, rev. by R. Posner (Oxford: Basil Blackwell, 1970), 67–68.

19. Leo Spitzer, "Wortkunst und Sprachwissenschaft," *Germanisch-romanisch Monatsschrift*, 13 (1925), 173–74.

20. Christian Morgenstern, *Galgenlieder* (Berlin: Bruno Cassirer, 1926; originally published in Berlin, 1905). Freud had already provided his own well-known version of the same idea, although that description proceeded from the other side of the equation: "Perhaps we may say that every child at play behaves like an imaginative writer, in that he creates a world of his own or, more truly, he rearranges the things of his world and orders it in a new way that pleases him better" (Sigmund Freud, "The Relation of the Poet to Day-Dreaming," in *On Creativity and the Unconscious*, ed. Benjamin Nelson [New York: Harper & Row, 1958], 44–54). The article originally appeared in 1914.

21. The translation is from Max Knight's *Christian Morgenstern's Galgenlieder* (Berkeley: University of California Press, 1963), 22–23. According to Morgenstern the poem is intended to be chanted by successive members of the gallows cult (presumably in the dark) and is "an expression of phonetics and an impression of nature" (Morgenstern, *Über die Gal-*

genlieder, 12; in Knight, 4). For more information about Morgenstern's "Club of the Gallows Gang" see Knight's introduction in which he summarizes a meeting of the group: "They . . . met in a room equipped with the abstruse paraphernalia of a fraternity devoted to the cult of the gallows—a dark light from which dangled a crimson 'life thread' (a noose?), a table covered with a black cloth, an hour glass, a rusty 'blood-spattered' sword, a burning candle, phosphorescent symbols" (Knight, 2). The club was devoted to writing and reading the humorously macabre poetry that characterizes the *Galgenlieder.*

22. Michael Bauer, *Christian Morgensterns Leben und Werk,* (Munich: R. Piper & Co., 1938), 17–18.

23. Christian Morgenstern, *Stufen,* (Munich: R. Piper & Co., 1922), 10.

24. Bauer's biography had yet to be written at this time, of course, but Spitzer mentions the recent appearance of *Stufen* in the appendix to his essay. And the poem cited above from *Melancholie* is entitled "Vor dem Bilde meiner verstorbenen Mutter." The biographical material is more ignored than unknown.

25. Although the issue ought to be a red herring by now, it is still worth noting that the role of biography in Freud's own contemporaneous literary analyses does not always fit the usual preconceived notions. "Leonardo da Vinci" is one of Freud's more thoroughgoing psychohistories, yet he admits to dissatisfaction with the results because of a lack of actual biographical facts—a position which Spitzer assumes as a given. In addition, those artistic studies which are most satisfying, such as "The Moses of Michaelangelo," often move away from a direct analysis of biography. The concern with artistic intention in that essay requires a total approach to art that investigates the art work, the response brought about by the work, and the author. Yet the emphasis is still strongly on the discovery of the author's "emotional attitude" or "mental constellation." The psychic biography is a form of critical interpretation that only covers a small band in the wider spectrum of psychoanalytic criticism.

26. Todorov and Ducrot, *Encyclopedic Dictionary of the Sciences of Language* (Baltimore, Md.: Johns Hopkins University Press, 1979), 76.

27. Leo Spitzer, *Essays in Historical Semantics* (Princeton, N.J.: Princeton University Press, 1948).

3 Broadening the Foundations of the Method
History, Culture, and Science

Between 1925 and 1931 Spitzer wrote two essays in particular that display his unfolding critical goals as well as the shifting academic pressures that were at least partially responsible for them. The general lowering of critical interest in the contextual reading is undoubtedly the most significant feature of this period, and, immersed in that milieu, Spitzer produces a description of the narrative process that shifts critical interest from the author as historical entity to the author as a function of the cultural spirit embodied by the style of the text. To achieve this shift, Spitzer begins to emphasize the textual reading both through a focus on the characters as psychic spokespersons and, perhaps more notably, by describing what would eventually come to be formalized as Wayne Booth's implied author. The intent is to define the controlling voice behind the style in terms of the context that produces it, while staying abreast of the ongoing drift toward the autonomous and autotelic text as defined by objective critical methods.

To the pressures brought about by these critical trends we need to offer one more: the continuing, growing influence of a context-free, scientific linguistics. All these forces can be seen at work in Spitzer's fight to maintain some aspect of historical interpretation in his stylistics. We need only look at his forced flight from Nazi Germany to Istanbul and the United States in 1933 and 1936 to find a fit emblem of the forces working against his success—as well as the clear need to recognize the validity of the historical reading. The first essay of this changing period, "Wortkunst und Sprachwissenschaft" (1925), appeared while Spitzer was teaching at the

University of Marburg, a position that he accepted as his relationship with Meyer-Lübke in Bonn continued to deteriorate. The second, "Zur sprachlichen Interpretation von Wortkunstwerken" (1931), appeared during the prewar chaos of Europe, three years before the Nazis removed him from his position at Cologne. From there, Spitzer subsequently moved to Istanbul, and then in 1936 made his way to Johns Hopkins in Baltimore.[1]

In these essays, Spitzer continues to champion the place of mentalistic descriptions of language and literature, as he would throughout his career. But his methods for describing, justifying, and supporting his beliefs are reworked according to his own needs and the current critical trends. At the same time, the alteration and rejection of his earlier views bear witness to Spitzer's continuing effort to provide a freestanding methodological support system for his work, a support initially sought in Spitzer's blend of Freudian theory and post-Romantic philology. Noting these shifts within Spitzer's thinking, Wellek has tried to gently place both these articles into the background of Spitzer's career, along with the well-known "Linguistics and Literary History" of 1948:[2]

> Three papers in particular, from different years, have been taken as the sum of Spitzer's theoretical wisdom. I myself in *Theory of Literature* based my comments on the two early German papers then known to me. . . . But it seems a mistake to single out these statements. They do not define his literary theory very fully, especially as it developed in his later years; they emphasize only one question and that somewhat excessively. ["Leo Spitzer," 312–13]

That one question is never fully clarified by Wellek, but it appears to be Spitzer's interest in tying author to text, a procedure that Wellek, writing in 1960, tries to dismiss in order to grant Spitzer admission to the critical center. But in the critical milieu of today, Spitzer's attempt at "justifying a method of psychological stylistics" ("Linguistics and Literary History") appears less problematic. Analysis of the articles thus remains central to our understanding of Spitzer's thinking, the historical issues surrounding it, and the importance of both to current questions.

The key issue in all these pieces remains the same: providing some means to verify the stylistic bridge that Spitzer wished to throw between the work itself and its situation of production—whether the latter is the psyche of the particular author or " 'ideological patterns,' as these are present in the history of the human mind" ("Linguistics and Literary History," 32n). Seen in that light, "Wortkunst und Sprachwissenschaft" is clearly a manifesto of sorts for Spitzer's stylistics. "Zur Sprachlichen

Interpretation," on the other hand, demonstrates Spitzer's continuing displeasure with noninterpretive linguistic stylistics and provides a rather defiant Spitzer with the chance to align himself more closely with literary and aesthetic concerns. Both essays remain similar, however, in their display of Spitzer's stylistic beliefs—and of his desire to find a descriptive methodology adequate both to those beliefs and to the critical environment of the time.

The lack of any useful ties between the methodological rigor demanded by linguists and the humanistic sensibilities sought by literary theorists forms the opening theme of "Wortkunst und Sprachwissenschaft." It is a situation that, despite all its discussion, still defines the central problem of twentieth-century stylistics:

> The light, floating effects of literary structures have made little impression on the grammatical and historical armor of the linguists . . . perhaps [the linguist] considers the necessary playfulness of art as irreconcilable with serious scholarship. . . . The literary theorists, on the other hand, rarely lack the ability to characterize a writer's personal style, but most are not sufficiently trained in linguistic details to offer more than general impressions supported by specific examples. Thus the literary theorists have too little linguistic training, the linguists too little aesthetic training for stylistics to flourish at the boundary of the two disciplines. [169]

Spitzer's stylistics, in resolving that opposition, is to operate precisely along the boundary between literary criticism and linguistics, drawing upon literary concerns to justify its search into the aesthetics of language, while finding its primary descriptive strength within linguistics. What he has yet to provide is an analytical framework acceptable to both.

By the late twenties Spitzer's original enthusiasm for psychoanalytic methods was undercut by his growing apprehension that psychoanalytic descriptions threatened the aesthetic values necessary to contemporary criticism. In place of Freud, Spitzer now invokes Vossler, describing his own efforts as "a realization of Vossler's theoretical endeavors" ("Wortkunst und Sprachwissenschaft," 171). Like Spitzer, Vossler has stepped away from linguistics in order to address literature as well. And while both Freud's psychology and Vossler's theory provide an external validation of Spitzer's study of literary creativity, Vossler's stature yields a bonus by providing support from within Romance linguistics. If his stature rests upon "a far better record among connoisseurs of literature than among linguists" (Malkiel, "Comparative Romance Linguistics," 839), so much the better, given Spitzer's dislike of linguistics' positivistic trends. A concentration on the aesthetic and humanistic aspects of language offers the necessary counterpoint to the "natural-science procedure of the linguists" ("Wortkunst und Sprachwissenschaft," 170), thus providing Spitzer's stylistics with both a competing linguistic approach and a safe niche within the discipline of Romance comparatism.

That safety is relative, however, and the clouds of an intralinguistic storm are evident in Spitzer's outline of the intellectual and historical progression of literary and linguistic study during the nineteenth and early twentieth centuries. According to Spitzer's history, modern linguistics, like literary criticism, began with an interest in the creative individual. But linguistic stylistics drifted toward a stylistics of the material alone, while linguistics proper moved from a concern with the intellectual ties between language and culture to the issues of everyday speech. Vossler's approach reverses this separation by seeing speech as expression, art as communication. The shift toward a functional description of art thus is balanced by an opposing drive toward the aestheticization of speech. Vossler would strive to maintain the historical analysis while avoiding the social determinism that Spitzer fears by "arguing for the explication of an author from his language environment, which is at least as pregnant with meaning as his other biographical environment" (170). It is this sense of a linguistically defined cultural history to which Spitzer now turns in order to resolve the tensions in his own theory between individual and culture, social determinism and cultural expressivity.

The reasons why Vossler's arguments prove attractive to Spitzer's thinking are obvious. Both men are alike in their skepticism regarding the ability of positivistic historical linguistics to deal with the aesthetic half of their interpretive program. Empirical philology "gives no answer" to Vossler's query about expressive motives in speech; its strength is that of a positivistic science that defines the causes of language change as "something arbitrary," an explanation whose universalism "can be either nothing or all possible things."[3] The strength of such a science lies in abstract description, and Spitzer moves away from it toward Vossler to find the antimechanistic attitude he wants for his stylistics. But Spitzer's sympathy for Vossler's ideas never constitutes a full agreement with Vossler's approach. Vossler replaces the empiricism of early twentieth-century linguistics with an opposing cultural interpretation, but like Croce he reaches too quickly beyond the historical for the spiritual to satisfy Spitzer's tastes.[4] Spitzer's description of his own work as a "realization" of Vossler's goals

is a declaration of difference as well as allegiance; Spitzer's avowal of
Vossler's influence presages his movement away from Vossler even as it
declares the similarity of their intentions.

Both Vossler and Croce thus help to foster an atmosphere conducive
to literary and cultural interpretation, but their importance to Spitzer is
weakened by their tendency toward non-linguistic speculation. To Spitzer,
this tendency is damaging to the formation of a scientific stylistics, and
his attitude toward Vossler remains, as Wellek notes, ambivalent: "He
without doubt admired Vossler and agreed with his general aims, but
criticized as premature his attempt to write a history of French culture
in the mirror of language. He speaks of Vossler's 'psychological impro-
visations,' of 'something autodidactic' in his work, and calls him even a
'dilettante' in linguistics" ("Leo Spitzer," 316). Jean Starobinski has echoed
Wellek's views, choosing at the same time to stress Humboldt's influence
as the primary source for all such thinking.[5] But rather than being viewed
as ultimate sources, these figures, including Freud, are best seen as
guideposts in Spitzer's search for a contextually based critical analysis and
not as all-determining father figures or mentors.

For example, Vossler's importance can be seen in the two critical concerns Spitzer ascribes to him: (1) an overarching humanistic awareness of
the aesthetic qualities of language and (2) a coupling of this awareness
with the technical ability to recreate the specific language environment
of the text. Although Spitzer draws upon Vossler's work regarding these
features, his belief in a close linguistic analysis of the text's features separates him from Vossler's wider-ranging cultural and aesthetic speculations, and certainly from those of Croce. As Bellos has made clear, Spitzer's
own Romantic idealism is "far more solidly grounded in linguistic knowledge and far more empirically oriented than those of [Vossler and Croce]"
(*Essays*, xxi). During the late twenties, Spitzer's linguistic training continued to place him in the mainstream of modern stylistic thought, even
as his historical readings forced him to swim against the current. "[B]y
his patient empiricism," Starobinski argues, "his extreme attention to the
details of composition, his respect for the literary artisan, Spitzer from
the first has brought an interest to the verbal material that the idealist
school did not willingly accord it, pressed as it was to define and to judge
the text's spiritual 'contents' " (*Études*, 18). In his own words, Spitzer is
to remain a linguist searching amidst competing models of literary criticism, a "linguistically oriented, would-be hunter" who has "crept into the
artistic realm," safe in the knowledge that he is protected by the "sys-

tematic seriousness" with which he applies his methods ("Wortkunst und Sprachwissenschaft," 172).

The importance that Spitzer attached to achieving scientific validity for his methods need not be seen solely as a product of his Continental linguistic training. Similar methodological goals appear within I. A. Richards's objective criticism and New Criticism's aesthetics of the text. In 1925 the time was right for a reification of the literary work, and the belief that literature should be studied for its inherent meaning potential rather than its social function allowed for an unusual yoking of scientific procedures and the beliefs of aesthetic organicism, a unification paradoxically achieved under the aegis of critical objectivity. Spitzer's call for a science of literary style, and his early use of psychoanalysis as a support for that new critical approach, match well with Richards's own concern for blending psychology with literary criticism. But Richards's psychology is behaviorist at base, and the difference between the psychology chosen by each man offers a quick sketch of the deeper differences that run beneath their separate developments of a formal literary criticism. Like Spitzer, Richards questions the usefulness of psychoanalytic criticism; unlike Spitzer, he does so not on the grounds of its supposed historical determinism, but on the grounds of its scientific usefulness. "Had I wished to plumb the depths of these writers' unconscious," Richards announces in *Practical Criticism*, "I should have devised something like a branch of psychoanalytic technique for the purpose."[6] Richards is not interested in describing that kind of motivation, however, but in uncovering the "ideologies" that lead to misreading, an interesting starting point that quickly shifts into finding ways to guarantee the correct reading of a text.

The differences between each critic's intentions are crucial. Working from the behaviorist psychology that was increasingly popular within linguistic circles, Richards assumed that he could avoid the issues of individual pathology or psychological determinism that troubled Spitzer's historical vision of style. The model of mind that Richards proposed was already adapted to general (if not universal) response, and with that generality available, Richards could use the power of scientific procedure to outline his ultimate arguments for the intellectual validity of literary criticism and its pursuit, not of interpretation, but of the nature of things:

> For in order to show how poetry is important it is first necessary to discover to some extent what it is. Until recently this preliminary task could only be very incompletely carried out; the psychology of instinct and emotion was too little advanced; and moreover, the wild

speculations natural in pre-scientific enquiry definitely stood in the way. . . . Both a passionate knowledge of poetry and a capacity for dispassionate psychological analysis are required if it is to be satis-factorily prosecuted.[7]

For Spitzer, such a focus on the text as a nonhistorical object was clearly unacceptable, no matter what the degree of scientific validity or the chosen version of psychology. Literary analysis remained historical at base.

The burdens produced when that historical focus is colored by a Ro-mantic heritage repeat themselves in the question Spitzer poses for himself midway through "Wortkunst und Sprachwissenschaft." "How," he asks himself, "should one proceed practically in order to prove the reflection of the individual spirit in the individual style, the stylistic personality amidst the style of the language?" (180). The commitment to a linguistic stylistics remains firm in that question; the critical task is to provide this stylistic plan with a historical or cultural link between language and stylistic intention strong enough to replace the psychoanalytic bridge from which Spitzer is now moving away. He remains certain that significant stylistic study must take notice of the "cerebral atlas" of the writer (170). Without that feature, *Stilforschung* reverts to *Stilistik*, a positivistic enumeration of stylistic features lacking any motivational purpose or contextual ground-ing. Such a collation "would only cover up the different intellectual and spiritual impulses" that lead up to a particular stylistic feature (174–75). Style remains for Spitzer "the psychic locus, the linguistic-geographical magnet or pole around which a number of significant verbal traits . . . converge, crystallize and form a personal language system within French." This "linguistic-geographical" note, "already sounded in the expression '*atlas cerebral,*' is indeed what is most essential" for Spitzer's approach to the study of literature (178).

The productive psyche thus remains the key to stylistics, and with this perspective on the individual writer, Spitzer maps out an analytical ter-ritory that stands apart from the historical study of his training: "For, as we know, the general language is nothing but an average of individual languages, a grammaticalization of various speech acts—and the act of creation is but a speech act. All innovation comes from creative individuals: *nihil est in syntaxi quod non fuerit in stylo.* Syntax and even grammar are nothing but frozen stylistics. . ." (179). The reference to "creative individuals" tells us clearly that we are dealing with a sense of language and language activity that has its ultimate roots in Humboldtian and Romantic thinking about language development. There, and within these arguments of Spitzer as well, individual innovation and change are presented as the focal points of linguistic and literary study, although that emphasis also admits that creativity is molded by the language within which the innovation takes place. Unfortunately, Spitzer is no longer relying upon a psychoanalytic sense of wordplay or general behavior to justify the discussion, and, by avoiding any other model of motivation, he sets himself a large task. His definition of style now rests upon a particular view of language behavior for which there are few analytical procedures, a fact only partially hidden in the mottoes for his work: "*[I]ndividuum non est ineffabile'*—the language of an individual style can be described precisely with linguistic methods—and *'oratio vultus animi'*—this language is the biologically necessary product of the individual spirit" (179–80).

Spitzer's conception of style as the result of a biologically necessary connection between expression and author is a repetition of the statement he made seven years previously during the Morgenstern study. But there the phrase was embedded in the self-described psychoanalytic study of Morgenstern. Here the phrase "individual spirit" signals the beginning of a shift toward the cultural—a shift made more apparent, oddly enough, through its attachment to the nineteenth-century vision of a linguistics modeled after the science of biology. Spitzer's "biologically necessary" definition of style emphasizes the unresolved blend of Romantic organicism and scientific validity that is his linguistic and critical heritage, even as it points to the prevailing winds that are shifting the critical attitudes of the moment.

Having sensed the critical environment of the time and sifted through his own stylistic concerns, Spitzer is left with the undeniable need to provide some set of analytic procedures that will serve as an underpinning for the claims he is hoping to make. But he remains unwilling to sacrifice any of his beliefs to the call for procedural accuracy. The particulars of his critical method, proposed in "Wortkunst und Sprachwissenschaft" and subsequently defined as the "philological circle," are argued (as they are in almost all his subsequent discussions) not simply in terms of their systematic efficiency or formal objectivity, but in terms of the complexity of the stylistic features they address.

Spitzer's stylistic procedures are adapted, in other words, to his beliefs about the cultural significance of style, and he candidly accepts the possibility of misinterpretation that such an approach risks. The relationship between stylistic features and the authorial psyche is never a given, he notes, never a function of the language—either solely or even primarily. As a result, there is every possibility of overinterpreting, of reading every minor feature of the work as a central facet of its style.[8] But Spitzer dismisses any attempt to increase the objectivity of the reading by addressing only the linguistic material of the text: "the possibility that there are sources of error is no criticism of the validity of a method. All that needs to be done to eliminate the possibility of error is to provide backup methods that can be used to check the initial reading" ("Wortkunst und Sprachwissenschaft," 181).

There will never be any retreat from this position. The critical reading is to be verified through those further critical arguments that can be brought to bear on the interpretation, which proceeds along admittedly nonempirical grounds. The only real question is what form the supporting arguments will take. Spitzer offers two possibilities: (1) to repeat the movement from the linguistic to the literary and back again while relating the critical response to the progressive unfolding of further details, or (2) to compare the features of the individual style with others of the same basic type. Of these two methods, the first contains the basic elements of a procedure that Spitzer claims to have followed even in the early psychological essays:

> You mark a particular use of language as I did, for instance, with Philippe's *à cause de*—with any writer you can be certain that behind the verbal peculiarity there lies a particular psychic experience. Further, you can be certain that one observation will lead to other related ones . . . so that you find a structural context, an emotionally significant complex of ideas for the writer's soul. Now you consult the literary histories on the psychic make-up of the author in question. . . . [181]

As outlined here, Spitzer's basic critical procedure is circular, as he admits, since the sole internal check on the interpretation is the interpretation itself. But the process should not be seen as sophistic as long as secondary arguments are brought to bear on the interpretation.

In 1949 Helmut Hatzfeld would readily affirm the objectivity of Spitzer's procedures, declaring them sufficient "to establish the new stylistics as an exact, controllable method." The consequences of achieving such control for criticism could be "immense," Hatzfeld declared, providing criticism with "a *science of style* [that] has haunted scholars since 1915, when Edward P. Morris vaguely anticipated Spitzer's program in a sketchy form."[9] But Hatzfeld's statements grow out of a Romance tradition still interested in contextual readings. David Lodge's 1966 comments portray the attitudes that arise from fifty-five years of Anglo-American formalism:

> In the general idea of a movement of critical response from particular example to a hypothetical general interpretation, and back again to further examples which confirm or modify the hypothesis, Spitzer provides a sound model for critical procedure, its novelty inhering mainly in its application to linguistic usage. What is unsatisfactory about Spitzer's method—to an English critic, at least—is its orientation to psychological explanation and interpretation of the artist, and to the formulation of those grand schematic theories about cultural change and the history of ideas so dear to the German scholarly mind.[10]

Lodge's critical attitude is hardly shocking; it embodies the mid-century dominance of noncontextual analysis within both linguistics and literary criticism. That dominance accounts for the ease with which he dismisses the extratextual portrait of the artist (including any discussion of the author as an extension of the culture at large) and his assumption (fully justified) that he has the backing of mainstream Anglo-American thinking. Mainstream attitudes have a way of changing, however, and the specific focus of Lodge's rejection is worth noting. Spitzer's actual procedures are accepted, since they focus attention on the formal features of the text. The method, in other words, contains what Lodge judges to be adequate provisions for self-evaluation and reinterpretation. What he rejects, however, are the larger interpretive claims with which Spitzer defends the relevance of his theory of style and which separate his interpretive scheme from strict formal analyses. To be stylistic in Spitzer's eyes, the study must move from the text to its larger context of production. It is a position Spitzer will never abandon, whatever the current trends might be.

There are three contexts that Spitzer uses to construct his stylistic framework: (1) the literary corpus, (2) the author's mental framework, and (3) the larger history of the text and its situation of production. The first context is almost always assumed, and few have bothered to argue its usefulness. More important are the the last two external contexts, those of the author's psyche and its relation to the historical situation. We have already seen Spitzer hesitate over using any actual biographical material, even though his goal has been to work within the immediate significance provided by the contemporary text with the tools offered by psychological science. But that purpose has been shaken by charges of determinism and parochialism, and, in order to justify his reading, Spitzer now shifts to a more general intellectual biography based upon a shared cultural milieu. The need to surround the literary work with high aesthetic significance, to which Spitzer is bound by his Romantic tendencies, and the growing promotion of Literature as a premier academic study, lead Spitzer to avoid any specific psychological detail that hints at socially motivated behavior.

At the same time, it is clear that Spitzer expects the lack of a factual history to be balanced by the presence of a linguistic history. Even his early psychoanalytic analyses, such as that of Philippe, necessitated the mapping out of a particular linguistic form and its relation to other possible choices. Spitzer's easy reference to Philippe's "peculiar use of causal expressions . . . the unliterary, colloquial *à cause de*" ("Wortkunst und Sprachwissenschaft," 175), depends upon a very thorough knowledge of linguistic history. Any student of *Stilistik* or *Stilforschung* would be expected to have this knowledge, and it is a part of the foundation underlying Spitzer's recognition procedure.[11] The fact that many critics lack an equivalent training in historical linguistics often leads them to downplay such linguistic knowledge, while Spitzer's own description of his procedures— "Reading, close reading is as it were my only trick of the trade" (183)— unfortunately encourages them to do so by masking his underlying belief in the importance of the context to the analysis.

That misreading results more from Spitzer's vagueness in describing the components of the historical context than it does from any argument on his part that historical context is of little importance. In fact, Spitzer has been charged with analyzing content and not form precisely because he introduces the author's conceptual and cultural framework into the stylistic analysis.[12] His defense against that particular charge rests on his definition of style and on the difference he posits between *Stilforschung* and *Stilistik*. The preliminary goal of any stylistics, Spitzer claims, is to uncover various textual details and to assign them places in the work as a whole. But Spitzer's literary stylistic analysis only achieves validity with a simultaneous uncovering of the author's strategy behind the arrangement of those stylistic details.[13] Uncovering the author's motivation neither lowers the quality of the linguistic arguments, nor (to answer a related critical argument) does it fail to understand the basic nature of art and the artwork. Literary analysis has always tried to look into the author's workroom, Spitzer argues, and while excessively biographical studies have been hounded out of criticism by Croce and others, "the psychic biography," as far as it affects the production of a work of art, is both "worthy and in need of scientific" study. To describe style is to describe the relation of language to the author and the authorial context. No other claim will be granted, and although the nature of that relationship remains uncertainly defined, it continues to be a basic component of Spitzer's program for modern scientific stylistics. [14]

Ironically, Spitzer's linguistic call for the scientific treatment of style has led fellow literary critics to complain that he "neglect[s] the aesthetic evaluation of the work" (184). Spitzer counters the argument here by defining his primary goal as interpretation, not evaluation. "I, for my part," he declares, "would like to leave aesthetic judging to other authorities"; like Walzel and Curtius, he is aware of the dangers of evaluation and would prefer to stop the investigation when he has discovered "the center of a personality, the point (or inner stratum, circle) which explains all of [the writer's] utterances" (184–85). That goal admittedly introduces the possibility that Spitzer will read stylistic elements *into* a personality or a culture: "Perhaps I read *élan vital* in things which have no inner relation to Péguy's personality? Perhaps Péguy 'mechanically' adopted the punctuation habits of one of his teachers? Nevertheless, I deny that the adoption could have been altogether mechanical: there must already have been an inclination favorable to it" (180–81). [15] The arguments, in brief, remain those of his early work. In order to analyze style it is necessary to formulate the psychogram of the author; such a psychic portrait unites the various stylistic features into an integrated whole. This portrait also provides a secondary check or proof, since it and the elements which constitute its formation are interdependent.

These are the methodological beliefs that match the stylistic beliefs, and they are ultimately rooted in the authority of Spitzer as their claimant. Biographical facts or psychological models of human behavior are not to be used to support the primary analysis: "No," Spitzer states, "research concerned with what is individual and 'intuitional' in literature must itself remain individual and intuitional, must not degenerate into stereotype" (186). [16] Such claims emanate from Spitzer's determined effort to maintain a nonpositivistic component within his stylistics, a component that increasingly comes to depend upon Spitzer's growing sense of personal authority within Romance linguistics and upon the nature of his own methodology. For now, the critical arena is such that his arguments stand as much on the merits of the readings that they produce as on any agreement about their critical validity.

The strengths of those readings, as well as Spitzer's continuing desire to unite style, history, and author in his critical thinking from 1925 to 1935, are particularly evident in two applied works from this period. "Zum Stil Marcel Prousts" (1928) follows Spitzer's stricture concerning the study of contemporary or near-contemporary authors. The portrait of the psyche that is offered in this essay displays both his increasing distance from a closely applied psychoanalytic model and the continuing presence of his earliest stylistic goals. The second essay, "Zur Kunst Quevedos in seinem Buscón" (1927), ignores the previous historical restrictions for which Spitzer had called.[17] Yet even as this last essay demonstrates Spitzer's move into noncontemporary texts, it reveals the strain of holding author and text together, not in terms of the historical moment, but as a function of the general intellectual spirit of the age.

Spitzer opens his discussion of Proust, as he begins many of his essays, by presenting a figure sympathetic to his critical goals and relating that figure's methods to his own critical approach. In this essay that figure is E. R. Curtius. Curtius is a philologian without being a pedant, a scholar capable of the "microscopic examination of the macroscopic tableau" offered by the text, and a critic who expands the study of stylistic details into interpretations of wide-ranging issues and ideas. Most important of all, Spitzer declares that Curtius possesses a "keen sense of linguistic nuances and their aesthetic effect" (397), thus voicing the final significance claimed by Spitzer for his model of linguistic and literary creativity. The presence of these capabilities and qualities in the respected figure of Curtius argues for their general value, and they provide the authority that Spitzer needs in order to unite literary criticism and linguistics into the academic discipline of stylistics.

Curtius not only seconds Spitzer's goals, however; he also offers a set of procedures that Spitzer rightly identifies as closely resembling his own sharpening portrait of the philological circle:

> In order to uncover the soul of Proust in his works, Curtius uses the same method that Proust instinctively used (which matches that which I have been proposing for some years now); the critic reads, struck at first by an oddity of the style, pauses over the oddity (a phrase transparent in some way) letting the character of the artist appear, finds in pursuing his reading a second, then a third phrase of the same type, and ends by presenting a "law" whose application permits him to take up again "the psychic elements of an author's style" (Curtius, "The critic's task"). The issue is the search for the "motif

and the word," the psycholinguistic search—I again will maintain
that this method (which one could sum up thus: "read, read, and
read again!") applies not only to Proust, but to any author whose
language one truly wants to "understand." [397–98]

Spitzer clearly is using this portrait of Curtius to describe his own critical
reading in full detail, arguing for the general applicability of such an
approach and reaffirming his belief in the psycholinguistic roots of style.
The straightforward clarity of the presentation is intended to offset the
unmentioned absence of any external models of support (beyond the figure
of Curtius himself), while the quick reference to stylistic "law" echoes the
objectivity of neo-grammarian procedures.

In keeping with the move toward a broader view of the authorial *Seele*,
the Proustian psyche is defined as a blend of spirit and mind that lies
outside the supposedly more pedestrian range of the original psychoanalytic model—the psychohistory of the author will not be speculated upon,
whether there is any strong biographical material available or not. Spitzer
eliminates such supposed intrusions in terms resembling those he used
previously to argue against positivism. He declares, for example, that the
"naturalistic biological explication" of Pierre-Quint, "is without interest
in the study of the work of art" (468n). Personal creativity is subsumed
under the larger cultural value of art and aesthetics, while intellectual
control rivals, if it does not yet replace, emotional intensity as the hallmark
of the creative psyche.

This stressing of literary value does not lead to a corresponding absence
of linguistic detail. The lodestone of Proust's style—the sentence and its
various manipulations—provides a specific, if more sedate, stylistic center
than that provided by the neologisms and shifted forms of the Morgenstern
study. The basic forms that the language offers are not to be altered by
Proust but stylistically retuned. This view of controlled creativity as the
root of Proust's style reflects congenially on the portrait of the controlling
artist that Spitzer now seeks. Language and style unite under the aegis
of the aesthetic, the artistic, the intellectually controlled. Struggling at
times with the portrait that he is after, Spitzer begins to achieve his
purpose as he aligns his views on the unfolding sentence patterns of Proust
with the creative activity of the writer. In certain fictional passages, Spitzer
argues, the progression of the periodic sentence becomes a "direct consequence of the intellectual vision" of Proust, "an activity of the ordering
reason" (399). Elsewhere Spitzer relates Proust's awareness of the mallea-
bility of perceived events to his knowledge of the tenuous but powerful

relationship between language and the world. The split between the objective world and an internalized reality expressed via language "preoccupies Proust: he applies himself at one and the same time to the word as well as to reality, to the gap between the word and the reality that it pretends to express, and to the creation of a new reality existing for itself" (440). The theme of language versus reality that appears in the Morgenstern essay thus reappears in this study of Proust, but does so in a way that implies greater mastery than that granted to Morgenstern.[18] This new sense of the controlling psyche threatens to drift toward rhetorical views of choice rather than Romantic views of expression, however, and the direct link between psyche and writing needs to be reworked on some level. Spitzer finds the appropriate vehicle for his argument in the relationship that he posits between Proust and his characters.

On the surface, the characters and their expressions are safer repositories of a necessary link between style and language than the author, since they can embody linguistic creativity without involving their creator in a deterministic union of psyche and expression. Spitzer can claim that Proust treats the speech of his characters as "a biological manifestation of a whole personality" without implicating Proust himself in that biological union. Under the creative pen of Proust, "to speak is to reveal the personality" (436), while that creativity can be allowed to rest upon Proust's own active engagement in "the warmth, the fullness, the spontaneity of speech" (436). The biological/cultural union of language and style remains indissoluble, a part of an artistic and organic whole. Sociological ties, on the other hand, are not as binding as the biological: Proust "is not married to his characters, but well divorced from them" (454). The sundering of such social ties is seen as a necessity by Spitzer if he is to elevate style to the level of aesthetic knowledge.

In this new analysis of style, linguistic creativity, now displaced onto the intentionally formed speech of Proust's characters, still unites expression and psyche in the way in which Spitzer so clearly wants to believe. The full value of style to language (and thus to Romantic epistemology) continues to be demanded—paradoxically underwritten by the "spoken" language of the dialog. The controlling artist thus still presides over the creation, while linguistic expression reaches its highest form in the mouths of the characters. This separation grants to Spitzer both the Romantic and pre-Romantic or rhetorical models of style that he seeks. The characters provide the first; the control of Proust, creatively unfolding his style before the responsive reader, the second. Indeed, when discussing gradation within Proust's syntax, Spitzer goes so far as to describe the stylistic method as a "rhetorical process" (421). But his sense of the rhetorical process has a particularly Romantic feature—a belief that the controlled literary style still harbors the authorial psyche as well, hidden but not absent, a Romantic hero in rhetorical clothing. The description of Proust's aesthetic/intellectual control thus allows Spitzer to generalize the framework of psychic motivation, to lift it out of the biographically banal and into the universal realm of the artistic. In Proust's repetitions, new starts, and gradations of syntax "does one not sense," Spitzer asks, "something like the obscure need which all creators (and the artist Proust) have to create and to construct reality, something like an effort in the direction of being, the passionate, repeated seeking for the true life?" (423).

The expansive vision behind such a description displays Spitzer's determination to justify stylistics as a legitimate intellectual discipline with a right to exist between the academic mansions of linguistics and literary criticism. The original argument for the value of stylistics remains: language is at the heart of all intellectual activity and literary style is at the heart of all language use. Left behind are the psychological models that originally had been of use in supporting these beliefs. There is no clear reference to psychoanalysis and no clear definition of what constitutes the aesthetic intention or act, although the full weight of Spitzer's argument for a stylistics that unites language and psyche rests upon such intentional activity. Instead, Spitzer's argument continues to depend upon the assumed intellectual value of art and literature that is a part of the heritage of Romantic organicism.

Whatever problems that assumption may raise today, using that Romantic epistemology nevertheless offered a reasonable degree of support in 1928. Thus, Spitzer's move toward aesthetic justification still provides him with a defensible high ground for his ongoing forays against the growing positivism of linguistic science. Taking the offensive, Spitzer upbraids linguists for failing to see stylistics as the key to linguistic methodology. As an outside authority for this continuing argument, Spitzer points to Proust himself, who "pursues an interior research" into the motivations behind language—a pursuit whose value the neo-grammarian linguist still ignores, preferring to see in language change only a "particular case of natural evolution" (442).

In short, the article on Proust demonstrates the mediation of those issues that are central to Spitzer's thinking along the lines established by his growing sense that contemporary critical readings may not require (indeed, even discourage) the use of strong external models to support an interpretation. Positivist linguistics remains symptomatic of the ills of an overly mechanical approach to language, and all other approaches are judged in relation to it. But in the face of linguistic and critical interest in formal, nonhistorical properties of language and texts, Spitzer compromises with a cultural psyche. Intellectual history becomes the key descriptor for the creative act; the writer becomes the aesthetic avatar of the age.[19]

The reasons for that aestheticization of history are myriad, but the resulting implications for stylistics are displayed quite clearly in Spitzer's essay on Quevedo, published shortly before his essay on Proust. "Zur Kunst Quevedos in seinem Buscón" (1927) paints a stylistic portrait of an author from the pre-Romantic environment that Spitzer wishes to include within his broadening discussions of literary history. His analytic procedures are essentially the same; the shadow of the philological circle is present, if not sharply outlined, in the procedures described by Spitzer. And the argument opens, once again, not with a stated reaction to the work itself, but with a reaction to another author—here, Vossler and his discussion of the picaresque. In a 1926 paper on realism, Vossler outlined his view of the basic structure of the picaresque: it is a conflict between the temporal and the eternal that is mirrored in the ongoing conflict between the amoral or immoral activities of the picaro and the corrective values of the narrative voice: "the more easily the picaro loses his wits, and lets himself be seduced by the mirages of the world, the more the narrator returns resolutely to durable and real values."[20] For Vossler, the result of this break between narrator and character is a divided presentation that fluctuates between wordly cynicism and spiritual didacticism. Basic human conflicts are not internalized so much as they are presented through the separate terms of the picaro's activity and his subsequent moral correctives. Such is the nature of *El Buscón* in which Pablo, "with neither fear nor human respect," relates his actions and humiliations in a flat rendering of human and spiritual vacuity.

Spitzer dislikes this separation between narrator and character, and he feels drawn by the vitality in Pablo, the strong moralizing notwithstanding. The result is a reading in which Spitzer refuses to see the voices of the text as completely separate functions, and an interpretation in which the text's separate voices are subsets of the author's larger creative intention. The deep disillusion displayed in the *Buscón* is not an aspect merely of Pablo or of a disembodied narrative judgment; the central feature uniting all elements of the text, Spitzer declares, is the style of Quevedo. The tension between *Weltsucht* and *Weltflucht*, a tension produced by our sense of the separation between "the world and eternity, the life on earth and the life of the other side" (8), reaches full expression in the essential *desengaño* (disillusion) revealed in Quevedo's style. This internalization within Quevedo of Vossler's structural tension allows Spitzer to rework the conflicts of the narration into a unified aspect of the author's sensibility rather than a set of fragmented homilies spoken by the author's puppets. The argument thus follows the basic pattern of Spitzer's stylistic analyses from this period. The central explanatory feature of a work of art is found within a particular sensibility expressed in the work's style, a style anchored in the authorial figure responsible for it: Quevedo displays his art in his ability to reproduce and heighten the effect of a baroque *desengaño*, letting it be felt by the reader through the style and tone of the text. The next issue, then, is how Quevedo is to be described and how the style is to be attached to the portrait provided.

Here, as was true for the essay on Proust, the authorial sensibility is described partially on what might be seen as rhetorical grounds. The author's sensibility is allowed to shine through the style, but that style is to be under control, not directly expressive but rather productive of the author's vision, a spiritual and emotional, as well as a rational, construct. The style of the earlier studies was to be read as a biological necessity in full Romantic bloom. The aesthetic drive now put forth as the key link between style and psyche avoids such direct bio-psychological determinism. Indeed, Spitzer is very close to anticipating what Wayne Booth will later describe as the implied author,[21] a term that Booth arrives at after first considering style and technique. Significantly, both are rejected because they are too often relegated to simple mechanics or "the merely verbal" (*The Rhetoric of Fiction*, 74). According to Booth, "We can be satisfied only with a term that is as broad as the work itself but still capable of calling attention to that work as the product of a choosing, evaluating person rather than as a self-existing thing. The 'implied author' chooses, consciously or unconsciously, what we read; we infer him as an ideal created version of the real man; he is the sum of his own choices" (74–75). The closeness of this description to what Spitzer seeks for his author is obvious, but there is an important difference as well, one that reminds us of Spitzer's current importance to critical thinking. Booth leans toward defining this implied author in terms of a post-Romantic reading that arises from the "intuitive apprehension of a completed artistic whole" (73), a beginning point which clearly matches Spitzer's. But Spitzer will remain committed to defining his author's style as a function of history—a commitment that anticipates Mary Louise Pratt's revision of the implied author in 1981 as a function of the society and its ideology.[22]

Spitzer does not recognize the possibilities offered by such a new description of history and its relation to the individual personality. Yet faced with a desire to maintain the Romantic significance of style in a pre-Romantic author, Spitzer wisely shifts the motivation for the style from the personal and individual to the cultural. The individual style expresses more than the individual's personal history; Quevedo's style expresses the sensibility of sixteenth-century Spain. The spirit of baroque *desengaño* speaks to the readers of the *Buscón* through its style.

The linguistic foundation for these arguments rests on Spitzer's claim that the sense of *desengaño* is achieved not only through the content, but through the way the style displays Quevedo's mistrust of language and the world—and their relation to each other. In a statement reminiscent of his study of Morgenstern, Spitzer discusses wordplay in general and the particular service which it performs for Quevedo. "It is certain," Spitzer declares, "that these spiritual word-plays have the function of diverting the reader, and that they are born out of the verve of Quevedo, in an epoch strongly inclined to wielding concepts and, by consequence, to playing with the diverse meanings covered over by a single word. . . ." And with a rhetorical question, Spitzer provides the final link between author and culture: "Cannot one see a mirror of the *desengaño* of the Spanish baroque in the particular nature of Quevedo's wordplay?" (28–30)—a wordplay that, in Spitzer's interpretation, is put "to the service of the break-up of illusion." The style provides connections that "contradict all reality and all logic, creating, so-to-speak, an 'intralinguistic' reality limited to the sole domain of language (which is an unreality from the point of view of the world outside of language)." The wordplay is "perfectly suited" to producing false illusions and to the disabusing of them (28–30).

Spitzer finds particular examples of such wordplay on all linguistic levels: puns and double-entendres (47), plays on synonyms (36), plays on proper names (39), words and phrases in unexpected contexts (18), antithetical constructions in which "the second contradicts the first" (20ff.), the use of subordinate clauses to undermine the sense of the main clause (24), exaggerated and misplaced quantitative comparisons (58), replacement of qualities by quantities (63), inflated diction (66), and others. All of these elements are used by Spitzer (as they were in the Morgenstern and Proust studies) as evidence of Quevedo's profoundly pessimistic view of the relation between language and reality, self and universe. But the enumeration of particular features provides only a fragmented view of the style. A more substantial tie between the textual elements and Quevedo's cultural sensibility is needed to solidify the argument, just as a significant link between Morgenstern's wordplay and his creative psyche was needed to cement that study together.

As he did with Proust, Spitzer finds the tie he needs within the characterizations. The key analytic procedure in the study of Proust—the displacement of the direct relation between authorial psyche and style onto the speech of the characters— again grants the author a degree of control over the style while at the same time admitting an expressive function (in this case, that of unmasking the falsity of existence and conveying the essential spirit of *desengaño*). Spitzer finds in Quevedo the creative talent that turns language into "the conducting-wire of a psychic trait" (54). The uncovering of that talent ensures the Romantic flavor of Spitzer's analysis, while his portrait of the author escapes the danger of individual psychological determinism, but produces a separation between author and man that appears here even more strongly. The first-person narration of *El Buscón* is a "fiction," Spitzer declares, and it serves to hide Quevedo, whose experiences are a "private affair." He is "the sole master of his sentiments and his impulses and knows to maintain a distance between himself and his hero" (124).

Willed or controlled expression and its growth within the historical situation are the two keys to this particular view of style. Yet the strain of holding author and culture together, and yet apart, is extreme, and the separation between author and narrator disappears at certain times, especially during discussions of the text's various leitmotivs, which Spitzer describes as "translations of affective complexes" (55). These complexes, central to the style of the work, tend to shift rapidly from character to narrator to Quevedo—with various blendings of all occurring intermittently. Of whom is Spitzer speaking, for example, when he notes that these affective complexes, "once aroused, cannot be repressed" (55)? At least part of the complex belongs to Quevedo, since Spitzer immediately hastens to refute Castro's suggestion that such motifs are "obsessional." Not so, argues Spitzer, noting that the motifs are a part of the overall theme (thus implying that they are yet another feature of the controlling plan of the text). Yet Spitzer's own definition of these motifs places them within Quevedo's psychic makeup as well. The fact that Quevedo "crystallizes" wordplay around a concept such as *comer* (eating) may "signif[y] nothing more than a great sensual excitability on his part to the concept of nourishment" (55). Yet how does that explanation reduce the personal element? In haste Spitzer follows that admission with the declaration that such excitability is simply a part of the animal within all of us, thus weakening its psychological implications by reducing it to the level of instinct. Not finished, however, he later discusses how nourishment and other simple natural functions "have been, for Quevedo, poisoned by pessimistic images" (63).

These varying declarations reveal no clear division between authorial obsession and authorial control in this particular analysis, demonstrating instead a confirmed intermingling of both. Author and historical context remain at the heart of Spitzer's definition of style and language, but he has no adequate model of epistemology to support his theory. The available sociological or psychological descriptions of linguistic behavior cannot vie with those offered by an organicist aesthetics; consequently, they are left out of the portrait of Quevedo's sensibility. Spitzer continues to reject the available psychological frameworks because he sees them as eliminating the larger historical frame in favor of a deterministic individualism. One such framework is contained in Castro's suggestion that a "psychological biography" of Quevedo could account for the influence of Bosch's "misery" on Quevedo's representations (50). But Spitzer argues that Quevedo finds the physical deformities that he portrays interesting in themselves. They are an observed element of reality and not just personal fantasy. The subtext of Spitzer's argument is obvious: artistic intention involves a form of creativity beyond the descriptive capacities of most psychological models. Yet Spitzer refuses to sunder the text from its author.

The results of Spitzer's desire to keep individual and literary motivations related are clear in his discussion of Cabra. He notes that the strength of Quevedo's fictionalizing power is evident by the number of writers who have found Cabra's portrait a perfect example of realism. Spitzer, in contrast, places Cabra midway between the real and the ideal, the sensible and mere appearance. "[Cabra] remains, in fact, the incarnation of the difference between the ideal and the real," a palpable incarnation of *desengaño*. His body is at one and the same time, "presence and fiction, his soul is perhaps at the same time ideal and illusion" (49–50). Cabra, like Quevedo, can be at home neither in the real nor in the spiritual world, but only in the world of Quevedo's sensibility, Spitzer argues. He is, finally, "a caricature" (49), and Spitzer extends that point through a number of arguments to reveal the portrait as a linguistic tour de force.[23] The portrait of Cabra is thus revealed as minutely detailed; yet the supposedly objective representation produces not a realistic portrait but a linguistic sketch that blends the opposing movements of *desengaño* into a single stylistic statement. In place of an actual object realistically described we find "an intellectual exercise" (46) or portrait, a study in the relativity of our perceptions. The resulting caricature bears no relation to an objectively conceived realism; the sum of these traits only produces an "automaton" from which arises, "after the Bergsonian definition of the comic ('the mechanical placed over the living'), the comic effect" (45).

Much of Spitzer's analysis, including the reference to Cabra's portrait as caricature and his statements on the comic, are similar to those of Bergson, with perhaps none being more appropriate than Bergson's sense that "comic absurdity gives us from the outset the impression of playing with ideas" (*Laughter*, 186). This sense of play, carried from the word to the idea, evokes Spitzer's comments that intellectual play lies behind artistic creativity, as does Bergson's sense of comedy as a manipulation of the real, of "appearance seeking to triumph over reality" (96). Yet Spitzer's continuing emphasis on the intellectual control in this implied authorship leaves a nagging sense of incompleteness. Cabra, after all, represents the depths of hunger, a subject that Spitzer has attached to a "great sensual excitability" in Quevedo. Spitzer's analysis of Cabra repeats, but does not overcome, the tension established between these two representations of hunger—one encompassing an intellectual purpose of the author; the other, a visceral response. The tension between the ideal and the real exists not only within *El Buscón* or Quevedo; it also exists within Spitzer's desire to discuss the author's psyche and the lack of a satisfactory psychological model for doing so.

That unavailability stems, at least partially, of course, from Spitzer's own decision that a model of everyday pathology must somehow introduce positivistic values while lowering those of the aesthetic. The strain produced by that division is apparent in the way Spitzer's description of comedy and caricature differs from Ernst Kris and Erich Gombrich's discussion of the same material.[24] Their discussion also defines a historical context for caricature, and they supply a motive force for its production that is congenial to Spitzer's own concept of *desengaño*. Speaking of

pictorial caricature, Kris and Gombrich argue that the power attached to
caricature is "symptomatic of a complete change in the artist's role and
position in society which marks the sixteenth century, the century of the
Great Masters." The heart of that change lies in the artist's recognized
right to go beyond exact reproduction in pursuit of a deeper "reality of
his own" (198).

The reference by Kris and Gombrich to the artist's ready manipulation
of reality recalls Spitzer's definition of the core issue in Quevedo's style:
"Thus the language of the Buscón oscillates between *engaño* and *desengaño*. The author unmasks the falsity of his characters, their attempts to
make and display themselves as other than they are, whether in their
character or in their social status" (67). Spitzer's concept of *desengaño*
remains, however, on a plane above that of the "factually" historical or
the essentially human; the motive for Cabra's portrait rests in the general
sensibility of the age. Kris, on the other hand, suggests a second motive
behind this desire to undercut false appearances, a motive that adds a
sense of human behavior within the confines of a society's institutions:

> [According to one of the early definitions of pictorial caricature],
> which originated in the seventeenth century within the circle of the
> great Giovanni Lorenzo Bernini, caricature seeks to discover a like-
> ness in deformity; in this way, so runs the theory of the time, it
> comes nearer to truth than does reality. This settles the nature of its
> achievement; it serves the purpose of *unmasking* another person,
> familiar to us as a technique of degradation.[25]

Kris is arguing that the process of degradation, of unmasking appearance
in order to reveal the actual as well as undercut the seemingly real, engages
us in socially framed aggression. And this sense of the basic aggression
inherent in caricature allows Kris to continue on and freely explore the
actual historical motivations for certain specific caricatures—while still
implying that these are aesthetically significant forms of expression.

Spitzer himself does not hesitate to describe aggression and cruelty as
a formative motive behind the text: "With the cruelty of the artist—what
artist is not cruel?—[Quevedo] has made from his own life a work of art,
and he wants, full of curiosity about himself, to reproduce that life in his
work" (78). Yet Spitzer finally cannot make a detailed use of any particular
psychological motive for art, because it appears to lower the aesthetic
significance that he seeks for literature. As was true with the study of
Proust, Spitzer qualifies his statement even as he is making it, quickly
generalizing Quevedo's motives into those of all artists and substituting

the artwork for the artist. The factual must be avoided lest the study drop from the literary level of *Motiv und Wort* to the literal level of simple *Wörter und Sachen*. And just as the literary material must be defined as more than simply linguistic, so must the creative, authorial psyche be separated from the social motives of the writer.

Support for the reading thus comes not from models formed to describe the psychological workings of the individual mind, nor from the social purposes behind particular behavior, but from historical models created to describe the workings of a culture in its language—and the premier model remains that of philology. The ethos of *desengaño* is to be established not only in terms of *El Buscón*, but in terms of the cultural sensibility out of which it arises:

> It is certain that these plays with the words for the spiritual have the function of diverting the reader, and that they are born from the verve of Quevedo, . . . But is that not to say that the play of words is only conceivable, in the end, in an epoch that has lost its confidence in words, to which a naive and normal use of words has become strange, and which makes of them a mirror of its doubts? Can one not see in the particular nature of the wordplay in Quevedo's work the reflection of *desengaño* in baroque Spanish? [28–29].

This bridge between individual style, artistic sensibility, and the culture's sense of itself (as evidenced in its language) upholds the full intellectual significance that Spitzer insists upon for style and stylistics. But while such artists and their styles may rest safely within the high tower of culture, it is difficult to decide if they reside there as rulers or prisoners, writers or emblems. Is the distance between the author's style and the culture's aesthetics too vast to allow the writer to survive the trip? Is the move too quickly taken in order to consolidate style's rapid advance to these halls of power? Exactly how are the two related? What supports the bridge that has been thrown here between the two, a span that extends not only from the text to the psyche, but from the psyche to the entire culture's aesthetics?

To ask these questions is not necessarily to deny the validity of Spitzer's reading but to ask for greater support for his insights. Such readings can be found. In this essay Spitzer finds support by noting similarities between his work and that of Vossler, Castro, and Hatzfeld. Nor is a reading such as Spitzer's limited to the period in which it was written. Claudio Guillén offers a reasonably similar portrait of the picaro—thirty-four years after

Spitzer first made his arguments. The picaresque, Guillén argues, "stresses the insufficiency of man. It presents the world as vanity, delusion, theatrical performance. The *pícaro* acts immorally by virtue of the most exacting of ethics, and his realization that all men fail to be honest or truthful."[26] It is a sense of the ambiguity of behavior and morality that extends into the eighteenth century:

> The Spanish-type *pícaro* asked himself not "What shall one believe?" but "How will I act?" With the seventeenth century, the connection between faith and action had become problematical. Man, halfway to the assumption of his own destiny, yet undeviating in his allegiance to his creed, found it increasingly difficult to translate belief into individual behavior. These moral and social ambiguities remain operative through the eighteenth century, from Defoe to Le Sage and Smollett. [102].

The difference between these arguments and those made by Spitzer is that Guillén is describing a wide historical and generic thoroughfare that carries us from the general themes of picaresque novels to the cultural attitude that produces them. Spitzer has built a much narrower bridge between one author and the culture, and passage over it seems more dangerous as a result, requiring finer arguments and more specific proof. Such a reading might have been achieved by broadening the concept of intention and style to include psychological, sociological, or historical issues. These arguments would have allowed the passage from individual to culture to be made more smoothly. Yet the inclusion of those features would necessarily lower the value of Spitzer's arguments in a pre–World War II critical marketplace devoted to aesthetic truth. The only other possibility left to Spitzer is to provide a linguistic model that carries its own descriptive value and intellectual weight. Unfortunately, the growth of positivistic linguistics removes that option as well. Spitzer is caught in a double bind: the linguistic and critical environment requires a more scientific form of stylistic analysis, but the available models are so framed that they are damaging to the Romantic epistemology that lies beneath all of Spitzer's entire thinking on style.

In 1923 in *The Meaning of Meaning*, Richards and Ogden announced their own program for overcoming that separation of values. "It has been felt," they declare, "that the study of language as hitherto conducted by traditional methods has failed to face fundamental issues in spite of its central position as regards all human intercourse."[27] Meaning in language lies at the heart of humanistic study, yet "[p]hilosophers and philologists alike have failed in their attempts" to arrive at an understanding of this central issue (6). Faced with this situation, Richards intends, like Spitzer, to provide an intellectually sophisticated means of pursuing such study; unlike Spitzer, he is more willing to avoid the issues of author, history, and context in his critical model. Within the academic framework being constructed for Anglo-American criticism at the time, critical analysis is increasingly legitimized by nonhistorical methods and procedures.[28] But working within the Romance tradition that links text to history, Spitzer cannot see that option as valid.

Nor, it must be stated, does Spitzer necessarily sense a need to deepen and extend the historical support for his reading. In 1927 Spitzer's work is sufficiently validated by the critical environment of comparative Romance studies to justify avoiding further historical analysis. In addition, his work continues to carry the added cachet of intellectual daring as well as scholarly depth. Spitzer's study of Proust, Hatzfeld notes, belongs to "the very early stages" of Proust studies (the predecessors that Hatzfeld names are Curtius, Pierre-Quint, and Cremieux, all of whom are addressed by Spitzer in his own study [49]). Spitzer dares to construct his stylistic bridge because the atmosphere is right for it, because the growing call for scientific procedure has not yet drowned out historical declarations made in the name of philology, and because Spitzer by now has established sufficient authority to justify the attempt. Yet as the reach of Spitzer's stylistic span increases, the resulting strain also increases the need to provide stronger justification for the beliefs upon which the reading rests. "Zur sprachlichen Interpretation" represents the last procedural blueprint for his stylistics that Spitzer will offer from within the Continental academic arena.

"Zur Sprachlichen Interpretation von Wortkunstwerken" (1930)[29] appeared three years before the Nazis forced Spitzer to depart from Cologne and six years before his move to Johns Hopkins University in the United States. It occurs, then, at a high plateau in his Continental career, and it marks another stage in his shift toward a reading procedure based increasingly on his own authority and beliefs, and dependent upon the critical values assumed within Romance literary theory in 1930. Yet much, if not all, of what supposedly constitutes the focus of Spitzer's newer approach—compositional technique, characterization, worldview—characterizes the material of the old approach as well. At the same time, the belief in the relationship of language change and psychic activity is, as

Wellek notes, even "more sharply" formulated ("Leo Spitzer" 313). The essay thus continues to pursue the Spitzerian theme that the text is to be viewed as more than a mere "linguistic phenomenon" (314), a theme augmented by Spitzer's continuing unhappiness with the growing power and restrictiveness of general linguistic methods. In the midst of this shift in linguistics, an equivalent shift toward ahistoricism in Anglo-American criticism, and a political situation characterized by an "inward-looking nationalism" in Germany (Bellos, *Essays*, xvi), Spitzer responds by insisting upon addressing larger, cross-cultural issues in stylistics.

Spitzer opens the essay by stating that he will avoid theoretical arguments and display his techniques and methods through practical examples. He then includes a single paragraph excursion in which he outlines his approach in more specific terms than any previously attempted. The background elements are still present, specifically the reference to his method as originating "in a practical application of Vossler's thoughts" (4). The primary features of that application are Spitzer's own, however. The method is based on the premise "that any *psychic* or *spiritual* excitement which deviates from our normal mental habits finds its utterance in a corresponding verbal deviation from normal usage so that, inversely, we may infer an emotional center of the psyche from any deviation from the linguistic norm, and that a verbal peculiarity must mirror a psychic peculiarity" (4).

The definition, carried along by its language of objective detail and procedure, attempts to eliminate any supposed generalities made in earlier statements while maintaining the relation between psyche and language at full strength. Yet the language cannot by itself relieve the tensions gathered around that relation. Once again, the implied direct link between psychic change and linguistic change places a huge burden of explanation upon a psychic construct that is invoked not in terms of the writer as a particular psychological or historical figure, but as a cultural spokesperson whose writing enacts the sensibility of an age. The weight of that theoretical burden produces subtle creakings in the bridge between the style and the psyche, the psyche and the culture. The language of psychoanalysis, no longer drawn upon to shore up this portrait of the creative writer, is replaced here by the phrasing of a more positivistic psycholinguistics. Creativity is paradoxically yoked to the quantifying terms of norm, deviation, and habit. But this language exists mainly to hint at an objectivity in methodology without actually endorsing any external model of behavior, mental or otherwise.[30]

Having dropped the Freudian link between language and psyche, Spitzer elaborates on the relation between language and history in a way that clearly echoes the heritage of Humboldt and his belief in the reciprocal formation of language and intellect. The creative literary impulse "becomes itself more solid, anchored in something as relatively durable as an objective linguistic utterance." At the same time, the linguistic formation gains a new "spiritual dimension" from the infusion of this creativity. The process produces a "solidification of the psyche in the language and the growth of the language through the psyche" (4).

Spitzer thus maintains a view of language and the proper means of its study that remains colored by organicist values even as he undertakes to expand his stylistics backward in time.[31] The continuing presence of these beliefs and the tensions they produce are evident in the contrast between the objective language used in the essay's opening theoretical statements and the later applied interpretations. In discussing Léon Daudet's work, for example, Spitzer outlines the stylistic process in a decidedly open-ended description of creativity that bears no close resemblance to the language of norm and deviation. Spitzer's goal in this analysis is the "pulsing and fermenting sap of the soul" as displayed in the "verbal growths and buds" of Daudet's work (5). The sexual connotations are apparent, but the procedures used to justify the arguments remain those of the philological circle. "The surest method for finding a writer's or poet's center of sensitivity" is declared, once more, to be that of reading "until something in the language strikes you" (5). A cycle of verification is to take over after that insight is achieved, offering further interpretive justification for the reading that arises from out of the initial response: "Once you compare several linguistic observations it is nearly certain that you can find their common denominator, draw a line to the soul and even establish their correspondence with composition and structure as well as with the world view of the work" (5).

The features of the philological circle are all present in this description: the reference to the psychic portrait of the author; the role of this portrait as both an image to be drawn and a backdrop against which the material is judged, the focus on thorough reading as the only means of ensuring an initial recognition of important features. The reference to literary biography made in "Wortkunst und Sprachwissenschaft" is now gone, and the concentration on the work as a whole leads, at least in the primary stages of the analysis, to an interest in the work alone. But the seemingly Practical or New Critical overtones of this process remain undeveloped.

The freestanding, historically independent text has no place within Spitzer's work. The issue is never how to get rid of the historical elements of the text, but how to describe them and their particular influence on the text's production in a way that entails epistemological significance.

Historical linguistics remains as one possible framework, and describing textual analysis as dependent upon a link between *Wort und Werk* allows Spitzer to bring in overtones of the *Wörter und Sachen* procedures of Schuchardt: "We have seen that our method so far can be summarized by the motto: *word and work*. The observations we made on the level of the word could be applied to the whole work. Hence there must be in the writer's mind something like a pre-established harmony between the verbal form and the intention of the work. My whole analysis is based on this axiom" (10). But the nature of that controlling authorial psyche continues to be devoid of avoid any detail smacking of a possibly excessive historicism. At one point Spitzer even strips away the authority provided by his linguistic training, making an argument for "simply reading on and noting what speaks to us, not just as philologists and experts, but as human beings, as simple readers who know just enough French . . ." (10).

The intention behind this abrogation of critical authority is clear enough. Spitzer is trying to balance the skills required by the philological method with a generally available aesthetic effect or response. But behind the "simple" reader is the experienced reader, and a reader who knows just enough French to attempt a reading can hardly read the text under study—Villon's sixteenth-century "Dames du temps jadis"—in the same way as a Romance scholar. Spitzer's suggestion only anticipates the difficulty presently faced by arguments for open readings, and he quickly eliminates that approach. His subsequent argument for contextualizing the ballad presents the historical vision that lies behind his work. "We must above all," Spitzer tells us, "allow the poem its exact place, save it from the nowhere-land of anthologies" (10). That call undercuts the innocence of "just reading," and it is followed by a sketch of two contextual areas that extend beyond the borders of the poem itself. Spitzer first places the ballad into the body of Villon's work, then uses the theme of *Ubi Sunt* to provide a second, literary context. Finally, the catalog of names from classical and medieval literature and the names of various French personages provides a weak historical context as well.

In the surroundings created by these physical and literary contexts, rather than in those merely found within the simple language of the text, Spitzer proceeds to an analysis of the central motif of the ballad—the refrain of each strophe: "Mais ou sont les neiges d'antan?" The movement from the harshness of the preceding "Testament" into the lyric beauty of the ballad is mirrored in the development of the *Ubi Sunt* theme within the poem's refrain: "The function of the ballad . . . in Villon's "Grant Testament" and the function of the refrain within the ballad becomes a symbol for us, a symbol for a new faith in man's natural fate which overcame the waning-of-the-Middle-Ages mood" (16).

What gradually becomes apparent is that too little of the Spitzerian concern with stylistics can be discerned in this brief study. There are glimmerings of a linguistic interpretation of the poem in the concern with the words "mais" and "antan," a discussion that adds weight to the reading by at least broaching the topic of historical usage: "The word *antan*, slightly archaic even in Villon's time, in its position at the end of the line indicates a past which has been erased, as it were, become poetic, as if covered by ivy. *L'année passée* would simply fix the point in time, *antan* is yesteryear beyond recall . . ." (13). But neither of these references is very substantially developed, and the entire discussion touches only lightly on the particulars of the poem. Indeed, Spitzer has a growing conviction, he now surprisingly states, that stylistics—or any other isolating study of linguistic detail alone—"must be abolished, must dissolve in an analysis of the work as a whole" (29).

This statement has been noted by Wellek, who argues that it indicates a substantial shift in Spitzer's thinking about stylistics. "In this article," Wellek claims, "Spitzer abandons the ideal of a 'stylistics' with which he has been wrongly identified. He disapproves—as early as 1930—of the attempt to make stylistics a special 'science' and he even vows to work toward its disappearance in literary scholarship" ("Leo Spitzer," 314). But only two years later Wellek notes in his introduction to Spitzer's posthumous *Classical and Christian Ideas of World Harmony* that Spitzer is "of course, best known for his extensive work in stylistics."[32] And the declaration by Spitzer is not all that exceptional when considered in relation to the body of his work. It is a critical attitude already visible in the tendency of Spitzer, as Bellos notes, to insist upon defining his own work as *Stilforschung*, as stylistic research rather than as the more traditional German *Stilistik* or Bally's *stylistique*, both of which devote themselves to a more empirical study than Spitzer cares to undertake.[33] The statement thus expresses Spitzer's continuing rejection of positivist linguistics and of any stylistic procedure that mimics such a nonmentalistic approach to language, rather than a denial of any of his essential beliefs about style. He is attempting to move away from the fragmentation and atomization that he sees as attached to current historical comparativism and to move toward a unified reading.

But the unification of history and aesthetics that Spitzer seeks is not easily achieved, and he admits to an uncertainty over his reading. "I do not know," he declares, "how far my interpretation of linguistic points has been convincing. Perhaps the reader will even find that I have done too little of it" (29), Spitzer admits, and in a renewed search for a larger historical framework for style that would encompass those factual features that he mistrusts, Spitzer now offers a historical frame more congenial to his linguistic training: the linguistic norm.[34]

For Spitzer, the concept of norm is always defined in terms of a historical norm, and there are two specific problems tied to it. The first arises from Spitzer's Humboldtian emphasis on creativity. Since creativity is a major factor in Spitzer's language theory, and since writers of literature are defined as highly creative users of language, the idea of norm threatens to force Spitzer into a singular pursuit of literary language alone. In practice, Spitzer extends his work into nonliterary areas as well, and his culture-based etymological studies or "word-histories" as he refers to them, counter the possibility that linguistic creativity exists only as a function of literature.[35] Yet the hierarchical implications of creative progression and development are always there, as they are in every attempt to establish a norm, literary or otherwise, and they remain a part of the model of organicist development that lurks throughout Spitzer's literary value system. The second problem arises, paradoxically enough, from Spitzer's nonhierarchical (and erroneous) blending of spoken and written language. Speaking as a historical linguist, Spitzer discusses the importance to linguistic study of finding new formations. "These cases are precisely the most interesting for the student of linguistic formation," he argues, "because they allow us to catch *in flagrante* the neologism's passage from individual language into common language (from *parole* into *langue*, to use Saussure's terms)" (6). It does not seem strange, given Spitzer's background, that the *parole* of which he speaks is a literary text.

Because of these contradictions and loose definitions, Spitzer finds it no easier to actually define the norm than the structuralists of the 1960s and 1970s. Spitzer's refusal to provide any specific definition of the norm is a sin of commission, however, rather than omission. The verification of a stylistic feature in literature is intended to be no less (and no more) certain than the verification of a particular etymology. Texts can be investigated, dates confirmed, and a general picture of language use provided, as long as the analysis does not descend into historical determinism. The methodology for pursuing that analysis is contained in the procedures put forth as the philological circle. Those procedures are designed specifically to provide as much room as possible for a critical reading that depends upon interpretation for its verification, not upon mechanically repeatable scientific procedures.

The sense of objectivity found in the opening language of "Zur Sprachlichen Interpretation" thus resides in the language itself and in the historical linguistics of Spitzer's training, rather than in any significant shifts in thinking or specifics of method. At the same time, Spitzer continues to move beyond his early linguistic training in order to establish not a closely regulated analytical procedure but a coherent set of beliefs as well as the authority to express them. "In my youth," Spitzer recalls, "language was taken as a possession handed down by our forefathers and treated, in historical grammar, *without feeling* as the end product of a growth, as an instrument of communication which had grown, developed according to its own laws. Rightly so! But we are just as right to take language as something created, as the expression of feelings and therefore accessible to feelings" (30).

The full sense of authority that rings in Spitzer's words comes from his belief in the goals of European Romance scholarship. But the claim made in the academic environment of the time is being shaken by the looming breakup of Europe, and Spitzer will shortly be moving into an Anglo-American critical arena with different views of literary and linguistic priorities and procedures. Spitzer's beliefs in the juncture between literature and history will remain intact, but they also will become progressively less acceptable in these changing critical and linguistic environments. The authority on which Spitzer could depend when writing on the Continent will, at least temporarily, be lost amid the changes taking place as he flees from Nazi Germany and is eventually appointed to the faculty of Johns Hopkins University. By 1936 Spitzer will be surrounded by the Anglo-American critical arguments that have been developing beyond his immediate critical milieu. The resulting critical issues will center no longer around Spitzer's method alone, but around the reasons why he simply could not pursue the adaptations demanded by others, and what the implications would be for stylistic method as a whole.

NOTES

1. Leo Spitzer, "Wortkunst und Sprachwissenschaft," (1925), "Zur sprachlichen Interpretation von Wortkunstwerken," (1930). Bellos provides a quick overview of the history of these essays. See *Essays*, xiv–xviii.

2. "Linguistics and Literary History," *Linguistics and Literary History: Essays in Stylistics* (Princeton, N.J.: Princeton University Press, 1948), 1–39. This later essay remains the primary source of Spitzer's critical thinking for most English-speaking critics. An edited and reduced version, for example, appears in Donald Freeman's *Linguistics and Literary Style* (Holt, Rinehart and Winston, 1970) as "one of the classic studies in what might be called philological stylistics" (21). Much of the discussion is, however, a recapitulation of earlier statements.

3. Karl Vossler, *The Spirit of Language in Civilization*, trans. Oscar Oeser (London: Kegan Paul, Trench, Trubner & Co. Ltd., 1932), 21.

4. Examples of Vossler's rapid movement from the level of psychology to that of theology are not hard to find: "If, then, we wish to fathom the hidden, psychic meaning of the speech of man, we need the inquisatorial spirit, which has been developed to a higher degree in the confessional than in the lecture rooms of psychology" (*The Spirit of Language*, 47), or, while discussing Racine: "Spiritual connections that can be proved by psychology and social history are of course to be found among contemporaries and compatriots. And we ourselves have spun ingenious yarns of this kind between the hermits' cells of Port-Royal and the boards of the Racinian theatre. But Racine's work as such really has nothing to do with all this," (Vossler, *Racine*, trans. Isabel and Florence McHugh (New York: Frederick Ungar Pub. Co., l972), 134.

5. Jean Starobinski, "Leo Spitzer et la lecture stylistique," in Leo Spitzer, *Études de Style* (Paris: Gallimard, 1970), 17–18.

6. I. A. Richards, *Practical Criticism* (London: Kegan Paul, Trench, Trubner & Co. Ltd., 1929), 10.

7. I. A. Richards, from *Science and Poetry* (1926), in *Modern Literary Criticism*, Lawrence A. Lipking and A. Walton Litz, eds. (New York: Atheneum, 1972), 150.

8. Spitzer believes that his claim for complexity of description is sufficient argument. The degree to which those values will shift, disappear, and reappear is clear in Riffaterre's use of the same argument forty years later for different purposes. Riffaterre is passing judgment on "Les Chats de Charles Baudelaire" by Jakobson and Lévi-Strauss (*L'Homme*, 2 [1962], 5–21). The argument is that any such approach will never be objective, since it lacks a framework for predefinition, which would serve to limit

the possible elements for investigation. (Riffaterre, "Describing Poetic Structures," in *Structuralism*, Jacques Ehrmann, ed. [New York: Doubleday & Co., 1970], 188–230.)

9. Helmut Hatzfeld, "Stylistic Criticism as Art-Minded Philology," *Yale French Studies*, 2 (1949), 66, 62–70.

10. David Lodge, *Language of Fiction: Essays in Criticism and Verbal Analysis of the English Novel* (New York: Columbia University Press, 1966), 54.

11. Spitzer spends little time discussing the role of the reader in his theory of style. His discussion is not directly concerned with reader response, but with the trained literary critic's ability to discuss the material under investigation. The only analytical problem he recognizes is that stylistic studies have not progressed to the point where the critic can adopt the sensibility that is correct for the text. Spitzer attempts to deal with this question later, but the solution always remains that of bringing the past alive.

He does recommend beginning the stylistic program with analyses of authors who write "in one's native tongue and preferably with contemporaries because, in more distant verbal climes we do not have a live feeling for the language to help us." Spitzer obviously sees the situation as temporary and preparatory, a focus on the "*hic et nunc* as preparation for the *olim et tunc*" (183). Presumably, the continued study of style would make inroads into earlier works, making both the style and the language of their respective periods accessible to the critic.

12. This is essentially the central point of Bennison Gray's discussion in "The Lesson of Leo Spitzer," *Modern Language Review*, 61 (1966), 547–55. Gray claims that by discussing the meaning of textual elements, form is subsumed under content, and the discussion is not of style at all. In addition, Gray argues that the text reveals itself completely through itself, and that the introduction of the author is an unnecessary complication.

13. Spitzer always enjoys presenting the stylistic analysis as a parallel unfolding of the stylistic presentation. The analogy becomes especially important in several studies, especially that of John Donne in Spitzer's "Three Poems on Ecstasy." The essay is discussed in chapter 5.

14. Precision of description, the hallmark of the sciences, continues to be a part of Spitzer's goals. He argues that demonstrating the frequency of a trait "allows the inference of a psychic constant," and makes possible "the precision we are used to in linguistics and which we want to apply to stylistics." The use of statistical data is even a possibility, since they provide the most reliable form of quantification (although Spitzer finds them "too boring" for his own use, [184]). The reliability of such data

is, of course, only as sound as the interpretation placed upon them.

15. Spitzer's statement will be important later, when he comes to deny the possibility of discovering an authorial psyche in writers prior to the eighteenth century and its concern with personal expression. In fact, critics can and will argue against Spitzer that all writers, even those writing in periods which value the ability to manipulate given models and forms more than individual expression, are legitimate subjects for an investigation of style in terms of historical and ideological determinants. As Spitzer himself notes here, even partially "mechanical" adoptions reveal an inclination, and there will exist in all writers those constructions which are products of their particular stylistic sensibilities.

16. Spitzer will have to reject the overtones contained in intuition, however, when he agrees with Cherniss's attacks on the Stefan George school of criticism. See chapter 5.

17. Leo Spitzer, "Zum Stil Marcel Prousts," *Stilstudien* (Munich: 1928), 2nd Printing (Munich: Max Hueber, 1961), trans. Alain Coulon, "Le style de Marcel Proust," in *Études de style*, Jean Starobinski, ed. (Paris: Gallimard, 1970), 397–473, and "Zur Kunst Quevedos in seinem Buscón," *Archivum Romanicum*, 11 (1927), 511–80, trans. B. Dauer and C. Dauer, "L'Art de Quevedo dans le *Buscón*" (Paris: Ediciones Hispano-Americanas, 1972). All page references are to the French translations.

18. The shift from poetry to prose also lessens the interest in expressivity somewhat and allows for the shifted focus on control. But the real difference in the readings remains dependent upon the sense of the psyche that Spitzer is about to put forth.

19. Final authority for the readings of that writer's historical framework resides primarily within Spitzer's own personal status and critical ability. Reactions to that authority over the last sixty years reflect the fluctuating values of the literary marketplace. Helmut Hatzfeld remembers finding the essay "fascinating" in 1928, but is disturbed in 1981 by its "rather lofty criticism, which the casual or non-preoccupied reader would not be able to derive from the examples cited." Today's reading requires external justifications that the essay does not need in 1928. (Helmut Hatzfeld, "Leo Spitzer's and Stephen Ullmann's Stylistic Criticism," in *Language, Meaning, and Style: Essays in Memory of Stephen Ullman*, ed. T. E. Hope [Leeds: University of Leeds Press, 1981], 49).

20. Karl Vossler, "Realism in Spanish Literature of the Golden Age" (quoted in Spitzer, "Zur Kunst Quevedos," 2). See his *Introduction to Spanish Literature of the Golden Age* (Buenos Aires: España, 1945).

21. Wayne Booth, *The Rhetoric of Fiction* (Chicago: University of Chicago Press, 1961).

22. See chapter 7 for the full implications of Pratt's argument on the resolution of Spitzer's desire to link author, style, language, and history.

23. Perhaps the most straightforward clue is Quevedo's bald-faced claim that he exaggerates nothing in his obviously hyperbolic description, although there are also a number of less forthright but equally revealing features: (1) the use of portmanteau words to exaggerate the description and elevate Cabra to the level of an exemplar (e.g., *archipobre y protomiseria*), (2) the use of metaphors and similes that compare body parts to things with which they have nothing in common, (3) comparisons introduced by "as if," and (4) the larger structure of the description itself, which faithfully follows the "requirements of a scholarly treatise" (44–46). For Bergson's discussion see esp. *Laughter*, in *Comedy*, ed. Wylie Sypher (New York: Doubleday Anchor, 1956).

24. Ernst Kris and E. H. Gombrich, "The Principles of Caricature," in *Psychoanalytic Explorations in Art* (New York: Schocken Books, 1952), 189–203.

25. Ernst Kris, "The Psychology of Caricature," in *Psychoanalytic Explorations in Art*, 173.

26. Claudio Guillén, *Literature as System: Essays Toward the Theory of Literary History* (Princeton, N.J.: Princeton University Press, 1971), 98.

27. C. K. Ogden and I. A. Richards, *The Meaning of Meaning* (New York: Harcourt Brace Jovanovich, 1923), vi.

28. See Richards's *Poetries and Sciences* (New York: Norton, 1970) for a fuller discussion of his attitudes.

29. Leo Spitzer, "Zur Sprachlichen Interpretation von Wortkunstwerken," *Neue Jahrbücher für Wissenschaft und Jugendbildung*, 6 (1930), rpt. *Romanische Stil- und Literaturstudien*, Marburg: Elwert, 1931), 4–53. Page references are to the reprinted edition.

30. Later in the essay, Spitzer will multiply the possible relations on both sides of the equation, allowing for a variety of psychic impulses behind a particular stylistic effect, or offering the possibility of one impulse producing a variety of effects. The discussion of mind and language as functioning according to a cause-and-effect formula does not appear outside of the definition. Spitzer's larger vision of the psyche rests in quiet opposition to any such movement toward the clinical or behavioristic.

31. In the posthumous "Les Études de style et les différent pays" (*Langue et littérature. Actes du VIIe Congrès de la fédération internationale des langues et littératures modernes*. [Paris: « Les Belles Lettres, » 1961], 23–38), Spitzer offers two reasons for the uncertainty and struggle that surround his attempts to define this psyche. The first reason given

is that his early work was limited primarily to authors of the modern period, since authors prior to the eighteenth century were not writing so "personally." In the centuries prior to the eighteenth, it is "the *topos* which predominates . . . not the complex individual" (29). As his second reason, Spitzer declares that the early studies were influenced by a variation on the biographical fallacy.

Both claims stress the shift toward describing the artwork as a controlled aesthetic statement (as opposed to a psychologically determined expression) that occurred in the later stages of Spitzer's career. Spitzer is willing to argue in 1960 that only after the eighteenth century would authors allow their personal expressions to enter as a major constructive principle in the writing. Prior to this period, he argues, writers worked within preset *topoi*, using such formulas as were provided by established sources such as the Bible or classical writers.

This latter claim runs counter to Spitzer's early sense of the interplay between linguistic constraint and literary creativity. As was noted above, Spitzer declares in his 1925 analysis of Péguy that any stylistic choice could be seen to bear the mark of the individual, whether external constraints upon the choice existed or not. By 1960, however, the impetus for the creative manipulation has shifted from the sensibility of the author to that of the age. The particular *topoi* still are not defined simply as available literary material (that would be similar to embracing a taxonomy of figures), but are seen as linguistic exemplars of the culture. To go further into the motivations for an individual's particular choices amongst these materials remains problematic for Spitzer.

32. Leo Spitzer, *Classical and Christian Ideas of World Harmony* (Baltimore, Md.: Johns Hopkins University Press, 1963), v.

33. Bellos, *Essays*, xxi. Yakov Malkiel also has no difficulty in describing Spitzer's work in general as the pursuit of stylistics: "Another characteristic of Spitzer's focus is his steady concern with stylistics, as a compromise, so to speak, between his literary and linguistic leanings. This proclivity is traceable to his doctoral dissertation . . ." (Malkiel, "Comparative Romance Linguistics," 906n).

34. In "Les Études," Spitzer will note some similarities of thinking between his work and that of the Russian Formalists in order to explain his reasons for moving away from linguistic positivism, as he defines it. Spitzer's reference is to the early structuralism of Shklovsky, whose "Art as Device" (1917), appeared at the same time as Spitzer's essay on Morgenstern. Spitzer states that he first encountered the work in 1956.

35. Studies of this nature can be found in Spitzer's *Essays in Historical Semantics* (1948; rpt. New York: Russell & Russell, 1968).

4 Transplanting the Arguments
The Debates over Bloomfield's Linguistics and Lovejoy's History

In 1945, while Spitzer was still feeling unconnected with his American critical audience, an article entitled "German Words, German Personality and Protestantism" appeared in *Psychiatry*. It stands as a signal example of the misapplication of Spitzer's methods and beliefs.[1] The article begins well enough, sounding the notes of cultural and linguistic development that have become familiar: "It should be possible," Thorner notes, "to follow the development of a society's sociological and psychological structure by tracing the formation of new words and the changes in meanings of old ones." The emphasis on sociology and psychology leaves the question of compatability between Spitzer and Thorner open, but Thorner's concluding, war-inspired declaration ensures a necessary separation between his goals and those of Spitzer. "In the interest of manageability," he declares, "the scope of this essay will be restricted to . . . the stress on the coercive in human relations, as it is displayed in Germany and, by contrast, in the English-speaking countries" (403). What follows is an ideological leap from language to judgment, an interpretation that begins with a few selected linguistic formations and then moves on to portray the differences between coercive and affective control in German and American personalities—a set of differences that are to be rooted, finally, in the family structures of both groups.

Spitzer and Arno Schirokauer wrote a reply in 1949 after Thorner, in a decidedly misguided sense of collegiality, "had been kind enough to send an offprint" (185n).[2] They did not attempt to "endorse or refute" (185) Thorner's psychological assumptions and conclusions, choosing instead simply to deny each of the etymologies upon which the essay rested its argument. The remainder of the study was left to float rather aimlessly upon the air of its ideological assumptions. The exchange remains a minor note in Spitzer's career, but it demonstrates with graphic irony the academic roles that Schirokauer and Spitzer were forced to play because of this convoluted combination of their scholarly methods with a wartime ideology. Both men were trained philologists; both left Germany before the war (Schirokauer had left in 1930); both had become members of the faculty of Johns Hopkins University. Now both were put in the position of critiquing an overly eager misapplication of a basic philological assumption—that language reveals culture—as it was presented by a writer only too willing to attack the German mentality and to praise in opposition the more "civilized" English-speaking countries. Spitzer and Schirokauer must have winced over the misreading that had been committed in the name of philology.

The most problematic aspect of Thorner's article, however, is not its biased presentation but the implications that such misreadings have for philology and its historical interpretations. Schirokauer and Spitzer correct the erroneous etymologies that Thorner provides and, having done so, they feel no need to address the philological link between language change and cultural shift—it is a given of the correctly applied philological analysis. Others, who had less invested in historical and philological methods, would not be so generous. The interpretive discussions encouraged by the assumptions of comparative and historical philology—and, in particular, by the idealism that had been so strongly nurtured within Romance philology—were not only being scrutinized by other linguists in 1940, they were being noisily attacked by proponents of neo-grammarian and American structural linguistics.[3]

Neo-grammarian ideals had been championed in the United States by Leonard Bloomfield (a former student of Meyer-Lübke's), and they were firmly rooted when Spitzer arrived in 1936. The linguistic study of the period was dominated by attempts to formulate a science of language founded upon empirically verifiable methods of analysis. An approach such as Spitzer's, which depended greatly upon the critical interpretation of meaning, occupied the opposite end of the linguistic spectrum. The Meyer-Lübke/Schuchardt split that occupied Spitzer's early career thus transferred in full force to the United States, with time and distance only increasing the acrimonious quality of the arguments and adding some further differences along the way. The most basic of these changes was that Spitzer's authority simply carried less weight outside the supporting framework of Continental Romance linguistics. World War I had already lowered the influence of philology within Anglo-American study; the interest in general linguistics had done the rest.

At the same time, the ideals of the New and Practical Criticisms displayed a similarity with the goals of Bloomfield's neo-grammarian work, although the complex values attached to literary criticism were not necessarily in keeping with the importance that linguistics attached to the value of descriptive power and efficiency. The New Critical tradition can hardly be accused of lowering the importance of the aesthetic readings that it insisted upon attaching to the linguistic forms of a text. But both New Critical and neo-grammarian approaches shared a determined avoidance of the social or the historical in favor of the formal. New Criticism's determined mugging of author and reader, undertaken to protect the text from outside fallacies, matched nicely with the contemporaneous antipathy in linguistics toward including external features of use and behavior in linguistic description. The fortress built upon these shared concerns left little room for a stylistics such as that envisioned by Continental comparativists like Spitzer, even if the historical comparisons were primarily textual at base.

The resulting diminution of Spitzer's (and much of comparative linguistics') historical approach during the next thirty years coincided with a series of attacks and counterattacks from 1940 to 1950 that defined the rest of Spitzer's career, as well as the basic format of stylistics. Among the more notable linguistics clashes were those involving Spitzer, Leonard Bloomfield, and Robert Hall. To these arguments over the place of history in linguistics must be added Spitzer's further arguments over the interpretation of history itself. Spitzer's concentration on the historical in language erupted into a published exchange with A. O. Lovejoy over the nature of literary expression, the place of sociological and psychological issues in historical description, and the basic nature of the proper historical analysis.

In 1957 Spitzer would look back on this period and see it as one of two "periods of rebellion against stale patterns of academic scholarship . . . ; the German rebellion of the twenties against 'positivism' and, in America . . . the protestation in the 40es [*sic*] against the 'historical school.' "[4] The battles were not over stale scholarship alone, however, but against a relativizing of linguistic and literary value. The enemies were not simply the tools of science or history but the intellectual and academic banality of their goals, their supposedly senseless pursuit of a reductive vision of realism. In the discipline of philology, "as in the sciences," Spitzer declared, "the ultimate goal, however more arduous its attainment or approximation, must be Truth. . ." ("*Celestina,*" 24). But in 1943 the primary, if not sole, support for that high plateau of scholarly truth was a form of historical and comparative linguistic analysis that itself was being shunted rapidly into the background of linguistic methodology. In fighting to keep his philology in the foregound of linguistics, Spitzer was battling against the major ideological trends of the day.

Within linguistics, Bloomfield stood at the head of a movement traveling directly away from a diachronic linguistics heavily weighted in favor of meaning and toward a synchronic linguistics intent upon avoiding issues of meaning wherever possible. Scientific objectivity, efficiency, and predictability were the watchwords of a wartime era, and the resulting postwar ambience helps to explain why Spitzer was about to receive only passing attention within linguistic circles.[5] In addition, Spitzer's sense of the proper use of history in critical intepretation was affected by the plethora of articles appearing at this time, many determinedly political, that explained Germany in terms of its sociological and psychological leanings and past history. In essence, Spitzer faced severe pressure in both of the areas for which he produced his interpretions—the linguistic and the literary critical.

When Spitzer compares this period to his early rebellious years, it is thus both enlightening and ironic, for while both periods define a Spitzer in rebellion against the institutional and academic powers that be, the intervening years have transformed Spitzer's arguments about the role of history in critical interpretation into declarations that sound inherently conservative. The heart of that conservatism rests, once again, on Spitzer's uncertainty over the correct way to introduce specific historical issues into the larger epistemological frame that he demands for language and literature. When Spitzer links the German linguistic positivism of the twenties to the American historical analysis of the forties, he underscores his sense, right or wrong, that these approaches lack the desire to describe history and language in terms of a larger epistemology rather than just in terms of factual data.

At the same time, Spitzer provides us with a sense of his own personal need to uncover a meaning deeper than that provided by linguistic and historical fact. As Green has noted, it was during those same rebellious twenties that Spitzer's inheritance, sufficient to make him a millionaire, disappeared in the German and Austrian inflation of the time (*Literary Criticism*, 103). Green ascribes Spitzer's ability to cope with that severe change in economic status to a trust in Providence. However it is described, Spitzer's subsequent need to find some compensatory sense of stability is undeniable. We can add to Spitzer's wariness over relying too heavily on social institutions his mistrust of certain forms of historical analysis that Bellos describes as "one of the least savoury aspects of German academic life in the Weimar Republic" (*Essays*, xxiii). Bellos's purpose is to explain Spitzer's refusal to engage in the self-serving historical analyses of the Nazis. Yet even in the midst of such severe personal and political pressures, Spitzer refuses to ignore completely the place that historical context plays in critical analysis. As Bellos also notes, Spitzer defends both Germany and the historical study in his exchange with Lovejoy, much as he does when he rejects Thorner's attack. History and language remain at the heart of Spitzer's critical readings; the most adequate way of interpreting that history remains unanswered.

As we look at the rest of Spitzer's career, then, we should balance his search for larger Truths against his continued need to keep historical analysis as a part of linguistic and critical study, and against our own awareness that his critical difficulties will be at least partially resolved in the seventies and eighties, when both the New History and the analysis of ideology will lead to the investigation of the epistemological link between language, literature, and history. In this later movement we can find the union that ties together Spitzer's critical needs—needs which are asserted strongly in his critical battles from 1940 to 1960, even if the assertion itself was the most successful aspect of the struggle.

The first shot in the battle for linguistic validity was fired in Spitzer's essay "Why Does Language Change?," an address delivered in December, 1941, to the Philological Association of the Johns Hopkins faculty.[6] When the address was published in 1943, Spitzer added the notes, including in them the long final note that outlines his position in relation to the "mechanists" and to Bloomfield in particular. The closing note almost has the tone of an afterthought, shifting as it does from philological interpretation to an attack on positivism in linguistic theory. But the motivating forces behind it are part and parcel of Spitzer's approach to language. They appear in the paper's arguments for creative intention as the hallmark of linguistic change, and in Spitzer's distaste for the inadequacy of phonetic investigations engendered by the "positivism of the neo-grammarians" (415), a distaste readily apparent in his concern with the separation between phonology and phonetics: "Whereas the latter studies the possible acoustic phenomena which may be produced in all times and all places by human throats and mouths, the former treats of the actual conceptions of sounds as these have materialized in particular communities" (416).

Given Spitzer's regular linking of language and style to the individual or cultural psyche, it is not surprising that his differences with Bloomfield should be reinforced through a strong emphasis on the "actual conceptions" that are a part of language as defined by Spitzer. Sound production and interpretation are linked to the perceptual framework of the users, and any description of a change in that sound system must be accompanied by reference to the corresponding mental shift in the community: "Prior to the emergence of any sound shift, there must have been a change in the mental pattern of the sound . . ." (416).

Spitzer thus ties the study of sound change to the study of the changing culture, and his offhand reference to the phoneme as "the 'Platonic Idea' as it were" of individual sounds (416) is typical of his prevailing desire to relate all linguistic activity to epistemological activity. It demonstrates his refusal to grant any split between mind and brain, interpretation and response—an attitude that results in a ranked scale whose gradations consist of social and cultural factors in change. At zero position on this scale lies the purely descriptive study that postulates no cause but only writes a rule stating what occurred. Equally useless to Spitzer are biological and environmental explanations that relate language use to race and climate. More interesting to him are those descriptions that rely upon language mixing; they present a Schuchardtian picture of a people and a language in progress.

Language mixing is described by Spitzer in the traditional categories: external shifting occurs between regional and national groups, and internal change is brought about by differences among social groups. The first category—language mixing across the boundaries of different languages or dialects—is seen as an active factor in all language shifting. But Spitzer does not deal very long with this motive for change. Language mixing that involves the transfer of technical or mercantile terms—or of other specialized forms from one group to another—exemplifies the approach taken by Schuchardt's *Wörter und Sachen* methods rather than Spitzer's own *Motiv und Wort*. This does not mean that Spitzer rejects the validity of this category; he obviously cannot deny such a clear factor in language change (and he willingly devotes a large section of a later version of this article to discussing such commercial formations).[7] But his deep-seated

desire to situate language and language change within some larger epistemological frame leads him even further. He devotes most of his essay
to the second form of language mixing—that which occurs amongst the
repertoires of various distinct social groups using a single common language. The investigation of such mixings allows for the study of smaller,
more distinct groups and for the introduction of those psychological motives that Spitzer seeks.

Yet even when a particular description parallels a linguistic change with
subtle social or political changes, it may not portray the sense of motivation
that Spitzer is after: "Those theories which treat of [*sic*] linguistic change
as a result of social mixture, speak only of innovation, and innovation
undertaken for the purpose of improving one's social standing." The portrait that emerges from these motives, like the stylistic analysis that delves
too deeply into social history, is one that Spitzer has "never liked," a
vision of the "psychology of man as a social climber who, for worldly
success and out of pure vanity alone, is an innovator in his speech" (420).
Such a portrait is too caught up in the issues of the moment, and Spitzer
now suggests adding another interpretation in which traditional values
substitute for current social trends: "Perhaps, I thought, man creates
because he wants to preserve, because he wants to be a good, undistin-
guished member of the linguistic community to which he belongs. In this
case the real problem would be to find out why this original conservative
intention went wrong" (420).

Spitzer's arguments hint of nostalgia for a different time and place. Yet
they are also a determined championing of the multiplicity of human
motivations, and with them Spitzer can fly in the face of language theories
interested in efficient models of explanation. Spitzer's own disinterest in
following that trend is obvious, and he stresses his lack of interest by
deciding not to support his discussion with contemporary arguments, and
instead looking back to Menendez Pidal's 1926 *Origenes del español*.
Spitzer's choice is based on more than the specifics of the argument. The
appearance of Pidal's text in 1926 had served to signal a shift away from
Meyer-Lübke's neo-grammarian comparatism, and Spitzer undoubtedly
enjoys using the argument now in his own rejection of American neo-
grammarian work. But even Pidal's discussion does not go far enough for
Spitzer, since it only mentions "the need for expressivity, the desire to
pronounce more correctly, orthodoxly—but *impressively*" as a balance for
the commonly accepted motive of innovation.[8] Pidal "does not elaborate
on this paradoxical psychological attitude" (421); he does not question or

discuss the desire to be so correct as to be incorrect. The investigation fails "to explain the *primordial* phenomenon involved" (421).

The problem with Pidal's theory, in Spitzer's view, is that it merely adds another feature to an already generalized model of the speaking subject, one which symmetry naturally demands: if language change occurs due to a desire to innovate, then change should also occur through a desire to conserve. Having made this point, Pidal then reverts to physiological discussions. He fails to move into a discussion of motivation itself, preferring instead to simply label the phenomenon—and this is not sufficient for Spitzer. "Why, in fact," he asks, "was one sound split into two (this is no necessary consequence of expressivity in itself); how was it that this one sound seemed to present two aspects, so that the speaker was led to tackle it in two installments—his split attention resulting in a split vowel?" (422). Spitzer's answer rests upon the interpretation of the culture's psychological attitude, and it resembles the declaration he made in the study of Morgenstern and repeated in the essays on Proust and Quevedo. The " 'split attention,' " Spitzer declares, "undoubtedly reflects the awkward waverings of a people who had lost an instinctively sure linguistic taste: a state brought about, to some extent by racial mixture, but mainly by conditions of unrest" (422). This last step provides Spitzer with the bridge from language to psyche that he is after and moves the analysis up and out of the realm of historical linguistics and onto the plane of stylistics.[9]

The reach of the statement does justice to the scope of the change, and it places the cause of the change back among the users of the language. But is the explanation really rooted in human motivation? In anticipation of that question, Spitzer provides two more arguments that produce contemporary "data" in order to argue that cultural unrest and uncertainty, when combined with a desire for naturalness of expression, paradoxically lead to "unnatural" sound production and change. The first example explains Hitler's personal sound shift of *o* to *a* as the result of cultural uncertainty. The second discusses an *a* to *e* shift among newsboys in Istanbul as the affectation of a Parisian accent. In all cases, the affectation is due to "the impingement of cultural unrest" (423). This secondary proof established, Spitzer moves beyond the level of social explanation, and he roots the changes in a basic "striving toward an ideal," a striving "which is basic and permanent in man, [and] is different from any tendency toward social climbing" (423–24).

Spitzer's later hesitation over this kind of psychological interpretation only serves to highlight the importance that he attaches to it. "[I]n our present state of knowledge," he notes, "we are not able to isolate the psychological influence on phonological laws with the same assurance that is possible in the case of semantics, syntax, and morphology" (427). Yet that inability speaks not to the unimportance of sociocultural explanation in linguistics but to the lesser importance of a positivistic phonology. Spitzer's explanation, having taken mental behavior as the only sensible foundation for linguistic description, allows him to turn the scientific framework of neo-grammarian linguistics on its head. Phonology is much less easily related to psychological behavior than semantics is, and since the only really objective study in Spitzer's mind is that which deals with human motivation, the least objectifiable aspect of language is contained in its phonological function. Non-mentalistic descriptions of sound cannot even begin to describe what lies at the heart of language. In support of this reversal Spitzer notes that in phonetic development "there is an attempt to preserve the 'perfect' sound," but semantic innovation "seeks to preserve, or to restore the original intensity of the *idea*—at the sacrifice of the verbal material" (425). This sacrificing of the verbal material completes Spitzer's drive toward a linguistics based upon the intellectual and the aesthetic and his rejection of the pseudo-objectivity of phonology. The "anti-mentalist would reduce the aesthetic factor in linguistics to a matter of 'unofficial' private taste" (430n), but the aesthetic factor is the only valid goal within Spitzer's approach. True science encompasses more than empirical science.

To these qualitative arguments Spitzer adds the methodological weight of his own philological circle, here attaching it to the work of Schleir-macher, Dilthey, and Diez and specifically noting its reliance upon organicist models of language and thought. "There is the same circularity here as in the reasoning of Diez: both speculations are based on the 'idea' of the organicity of development (the 'organism' of Vulgar Latin, 'the organism of the psyche of an individual writer'—both of which unfold)" (431).[10] But this discussion of method rightly remains in a note; Spitzer's main arguments address linguistic values and not procedures. All language investigation is seen as the investigation of style, and the heart of any analysis lies in uncovering the consciousness of the language community. Such a goal finds its final realization in Spitzer's outline for an ideal grammar: "I would advocate, theoretically, the following order [for the grammar]: first, an all-embracing stylistics (all historic change in language rests upon the urge to self-expression); next, syntax (which is stylistics grammaticised); then semantics and morphology. Only in the last volume would come phonology" (428). If language shifts emphasize psychic shifts, the most fruitful areas of investigation will naturally be those in which meaning is a primary feature of the shift.

This reversal of phonology's normal opening position in pre-Chomsky grammars is an obvious attack on Meyer-Lübke and all those neo-grammarians who would insist upon objective phonological phenomena as the primary basis of linguistic study. When he added the footnotes prior to publication, Spitzer carried that attack one step further, using them to issue a dual challenge to the antimentalists and to Bloomfield. The first set of arguments addresses individual aspects of specific linguistic methods; the second set is concerned with human nature. For Spitzer, the two questions are, of course, inseparable. The method chosen betrays one's beliefs about human nature; the rubric of descriptive efficiency remains a false commandment, a concentrating of one's efforts upon linguistic systems rather than upon language itself.[11]

Method, then, provides the opening spark for Spitzer's attack on Bloomfield, but linguistic relevance is the real fuel that fires his arguments. Under Spitzer's gaze the non-evaluative, fact-based approach of modern descriptive analysis has become a reversed Cartesian doubting; it is a movement that pursues not the ultimate activity of thought, but only the pure descriptive procedure. Never given to moderate statements about the place of linguistics in academia, Spitzer declares the pursuit of such procedures to be the first step on the road to perdition:

> First one says: "let us not speak of the human mind because this would 'obscure our notions' "; later one behaves as though this human mind did not exist at all; this would be an anti-scientific, sophistical attitude; this is the attitude of this school of linguists who would prefer any mechanical and matter-of-fact explanation to a spiritual one. And to admit of a schism between the scholar-as-human-being, and the "official scholar," as Bloch proposes, is to betray a lack of ambition toward the goal of a unification of human nature; it is a surrender to modern mental disintegration. [430]

The apocalyptic tone of Spitzer's statement reveals the conservatism that is feeding off of his desire to preserve some aspect of his past in the face of academic and political uncertainty. Yet he does put his finger on a problem lying at the heart of much descriptive procedure. The desire for scientific factuality regularly produces a set of observational procedures that ensures that only measurable "facts" are found, possibly to the exclusion of other relevant material. The collection and removal of data from their contexts do not necessarily yield final truths; such procedures yield data available within the limits established by the procedures. The real difficulty in evaluating a method does not lie simply in asking whether or not the data are sufficiently objective, but whether the method is adequate to the larger values attached to its analytical purpose. Spitzer's arguments stress that the analysis must discuss the epistemological, perhaps the "moral," value of the information sought and found. His harshness derives from a belief that linguistics is being refashioned into an exercise in objectivity, an exercise that justifies itself simply through the fact of its own internal consistency. Indeed, that internal self-justification is as conservative as Spitzer's longing for the past. But although Spitzer is right to attack the supposition that scientific objectivity operates in a value-free, nonideological framework, he misgauges the strong appeal of that supposed objectivity in 1943. On the other hand, Bloomfield makes full use of the appeal of objectivity in his "Secondary and Tertiary Responses to Language," which contains a sarcastic attack on Spitzer's article that offers some evidence to justify Spitzer's combativeness. But Bloomfield's self-portrayal as the frustrated scientist battling the forces of nonscientific interpretation will carry the day during the war and postwar periods to 1950.

The title of Bloomfield's article provides its own combined statement of method and ideology. Discussions of language are seen as producing responses that can be classified (according to Bloomfield's taxonomy) as secondary or tertiary. A primary response to language is presumably either the use of the language or an associated activity—replies in conversation or the activities dictated by that conversation. Secondary responses consist of metalinguistic utterances about language, and while all discussions of language fall under this category, all are not equal. The most important are those made in "the systematic study of language—the utterances, above all, which . . . embody the past results of linguistic science" and which display "the general characteristics of scientific utterance" (45). Other secondary responses consist of nonscientific, culture-based assumptions and pronouncements; included here are the general social concepts of good and bad grammar, responses to dialects, and social and cultural evaluations of general language use. In short, this category of secondary response consists of the average speaker's recognition and judgment of any significant deviation from cultural linguistic norms; social pronouncements are allowed to take precedence over scientific fact. Such interpretive behavior is the dark side of the secondary response. To stimulate an equally misguided tertiary response one need only attempt to correct the bias. Such an attempt, Bloomfield tells us, will cause immediate offense and probably a trenchant moral retort—in essence, a tertiary response.

Bloomfield equates such general tertiary responses with the reactions of mentalist linguists to his own mechanistic approach, and he offers Spitzer's final note from "Why Does Language Change?" as an "illustration perfect in every detail" (53) of the typical tertiary response. He then closes his satire by offering a more viable approach to language—a scientific approach that is based upon his own social desires: "We have acquired understanding and the power of prediction and control and have reaped vast benefit in the domains where we have developed non-animistic and non-teleological science. We remain ignorant and helpless in the domains where we have failed to develop that kind of science, namely, in human affairs, such as the correlation of incentive with the distribution of economic goods, or the disposal of conflicting national interests" (55). Bloomfield may argue in favor of a context-free linguistics, but this argument makes free stylistic use of the social situation in which it is made. In 1944 the possibility of being able to predict, and even control, the social, economic, and political situation would have been powerfully attractive— as would the opportunity to gain "power" over new "domains." The general chaos caused by the war, to which Bloomfield's "national interests" quietly alludes, would have been only too apparent to his audience. In that atmosphere the implication that scientific method has the ability to correctly reproduce cause-and-effect behavior—or, at least, to describe elemental dependencies and the results of disturbing them—would be hard to ignore.

Yet it is easier to call for a bridge between scientific description and human behavior than to provide one—a fact that has been apparent since Spitzer first declared his pursuit of a scientific stylistics. Bloomfield is certainly not unaware of the difficulties. His whole essay, after all, is a behavioristic correlation of certain forms of behavior with certain linguistic situations and beliefs, and he willingly describes himself as "one of a number of workers who believe that animistic and teleological terminology (*mind, consciousness, concept,* and so on) does no good and much harm in linguistics, or, for that matter, in any branch of science" (51). He also knows that his rejection of mentalistic terms will lead to accusations that he ignores whole segments of human behavior. But while Bloomfield's stated goals of predictability and objective analysis may severely limit his theory, he can easily find support in the contemporary value attached to science and its presumed ability to eliminate all secondary or nonessential elements in its description of human behavior.

That descriptive efficiency, so attractive in the midst of global upheaval, makes Bloomfield's theory completely untenable for Spitzer. Behaviorist schemes describe the individual users of language, but they quickly disenfranchise their conceptions and interpretations. For a linguist committed to the description of individual creativity in language, Bloomfield's model will never be adequate to the question of style, and the belief that style should be central to linguistics is no more in doubt for Spitzer now than it was thirty-five years earlier. Stylistics, Spitzer states at the outset of his "Answer to Mr. Bloomfield," is part of "the complete field of linguistics," even though the editors of *Language* would not care to see it as such (245). That point made, Spitzer goes on to argue the inherent incompleteness of any mechanist approach to language. After all, antimentalists, by definition, cannot hold to the framework of their system and also write on stylistics. Spitzer's direct reply to Bloomfield thus continues to follow his argument, as outlined in "Why Does Language Change?," that stylistics contains the broadest and most adequate approach to linguistic study. As to the issue of whether a behaviorist model of discourse can adequately describe the complexity of language use, Spitzer's answer is an unqualified "No."

Arguments in support of this belief are not especially difficult to find. There is no question that language can be analyzed in terms of its identifiable segments, but such segmentation fails to address the synthetic power of language, a fact made clear by the inadequacy of most structural descriptions of syntax. Nor is the vision of mind provided by behaviorist psychology capable of addressing complex and subtle relations between history and language, context and use. Spitzer makes these points, and he declares his authority to make them: "Since I have been linguistically trained (in my juvenile days) by the neo-grammarians Meyer-Lübke and Brugmann (although I later developed away from them toward their adversaries Schuchardt, Gilliéron, Meillet, Vossler), it will not do for Mr. Bloomfield, instead of answering my questions, to put my objections against him on one level with the 'tertiary responses' of the layman who talked nonsense about Chippewa—and to deal with me 'diagnostically' " (248). Yet the model that Spitzer later offers as a substitute for Bloomfield's is not without its own problems, for Spitzer's usual arguments now soar beyond the aesthetic and enter into the theological, with great developments in science being equated with religious belief. Spitzer grants the mechanists their desire to avoid "such vague terms as 'soul' until they have redefined them in terms of biology and sociology," but he does so only to sarcastically contrast such thinking with that of the poets, who "belong to that odd majority who do not wait upon such a redefinition but count with the influence of language on the responsive souls of their fellowmen—i.e., with the influence of style" (246).

Spitzer's rejection of sociobiological arguments repeats the negative judgments he put forth in the study of Quevedo. His purpose is clear—to leave no doubt that he refers to a general human nature beyond that available to mechanists and other such theorists who intentionally limit the sphere of their study. It is a limitation with which Bloomfield chooses to live. He admits that one could "easily avoid" the difficulties incurred in discussing subjective topics such as meaning by adopting "the popular (*mentalistic*) view and say[ing] that speech forms reflect unobservable, non-physical events in the *minds* of speakers and hearers: for every speech form that is uttered, one need only claim the occurrence of a corresponding *mental* event" (102). The preferable route, however, is to admit that "the linguist cannot define meanings, but must appeal for this to students of other sciences or to common knowledge" (*Language*, 145). Grammar deals with form and with function, but meaning belongs to a grammatical tradition that has been left behind in the pursuit of scientific linguistics:

> It follows from this that in all study of language we must start from forms and not from meanings. For instance, our school grammars give such definitions as these: "A noun is the name of a person, place, or thing. . . ." The interpretation or application of statements like these would lead to disputes even in a college of metaphysicians. . . . If we said [instead], for instance, that a noun is any word which can be preceded by the word *the* to form a unit phrase, we should have a usable criteria which would offer only slight difficulty in the case of names (*the Tom I know*).[12]

Bloomfield's definition of form is undoubtedly useful, but it achieves the very effect that originally drove Spitzer away from Meyer-Lübke's linguistics and toward stylistics. The clash between Spitzer and Bloomfield over meaning is a clash over the goals and purposes of linguistic, scientific, and humanistic study. And while those goals and purposes appear to be limited to methodological and academic arguments, they cannot be separated from the larger overtones that language, science, and humanism carry for both men. For Spitzer, who is writing just ten years after fleeing the Nazis, any theory which even temporarily refuses to deal with the totality of human experience is guilty of moral blindness. "We mentalists," he declares, "though equally ignorant of the bio-sociological factors of anger, have no scruples in positing an entity 'anger' and in observing its activity. But we could not expect a scholar with the scruples of Mr. Bloomfield to study the influence of 'anger' on speech—which is a reality: just consider the style, even the phonetic style, of Hitler!" (246).

The full ideological range of their clash is visible in this comment. The direct reference to the political situation is not unusual, as the exchange with Thorner displayed so well. But it is also a mark of Spitzer's defensiveness, which arises from his growing sense that he is swimming against the tide of positivism. That he is not wrong is strongly displayed in another exchange with Robert A. Hall.[13] The conflict between Hall and Spitzer is not surprising in itself—Hall regularly identifies himself as a follower of Bloomfield, and Spitzer grants him that status, identifying Hall as "a certain member of the group of anti-mentalists [who] failed to RECOGNIZE the stylistic nature of a problem he was treating" ("Reply to Mr. Bloomfield," 246). Hall then enlarges the exchange by rejecting Spitzer's approach, and, in another exchange, by attacking Bonfante and the Italian neo-linguists on the formal grounds already established by Bloomfield: meaning does not provide the same objective basis for linguistics as the study of form and function does; language seen as individual expression cannot provide the scientific verifiability available when language is seen as a general communicative device. Given Hall's thinking, the conflict is inevitable; what makes it especially important is the fact that Hall is a Romance scholar and not only a general linguist.

The smaller battleground of Romance linguistics helps to explain the particular intensity of Spitzer's exchanges with Hall: the arguments take place on home ground, and they are fierce. Malkiel goes so far as to characterize Hall's belated volley, *Idealism in Romance Linguistics* (1963), as approachable only by the "immunized expert" ("Comparative Romance Linguistics," in *Current Trends in Linguistics*, vol. 9, 922n). His further comment that the text produced only "boredom and disappointment on both sides of the Atlantic" (923n) implies a gradual easing of tensions by 1965 and a desire to reunite Romance and general linguistics. But in 1944 Spitzer could only equate the differences between his views and those of Hall with a "Crisis in Modern Linguistics," as the title of Spitzer's essay describes it.

That essay, directed against a brief etymological note by Hall, produces the arguments for historical semantics that have become familiar by now. All of Hall's " 'material etymologies' . . . will be wrong," Spitzer claims, because of his atomistic approach. In an organicist version of semantic field theory Spitzer argues that Hall's etymological work must fail, "so long as the 'spiritual etymon' of the whole series has not been grasped: the over-all Etymon which gives meaning, which 'informs' all the 'material etymologies' " ("Crai," 156). Hall's Bloomfieldian approach, lacking a search for those higher motives, can provide no real analysis or interpretation of language change. The basic charges are similar to those made against Bloomfield, yet these arguments are rooted much more deeply in Spitzer's literary concerns, and they demonstrate even more clearly the degree to which he insists upon uniting all aspects of his linguistic and critical thinking.[14] "All word-formations obey stylistics" (160), he declares, and he demands that there be "no linguistics without philology; no philology without linguistics" (169n). The resulting blend of literary criticism, linguistics, and stylistics serves as a declaration of method and as a gauntlet thrown down before Hall. The particular weapons that Spitzer chooses comprise a set of familiar beliefs: historically motivated creativity is the basis of all linguistic behavior, and the aesthetic is a part of all scientific description.

In defining those beliefs Spitzer relies once more on a blend of psychology and aesthetics. The union of the two is intentionally hazy and exists primarily to provide a framework for a discussion of creativity in certain discourse situations:

> Here is involved a kind of phonetic symbolism which requires a crescendo in intensity . . . and the crescendo in intensity, in turn, represents an instinctive device of the speaker who would (unconsciously) counterbalance the diminishing attention of his interlocutor, which he anticipates while he is speaking. In fact, all stylistics is a more or less conscious psychological calculation based on the experience with language which any speaking man has had (again, a thorn in the flesh of the anti-mentalists!) All word-formations obey stylistics. [160]

Spitzer's rapid movement among these instinctual, unconscious, and conscious intentions can be explained, once again, by his desire to provide a mentalistic explanation, while he does not possess a particular model of mind with which to do so. In this particular case Spitzer's shifting description allows him to vent his negative reactions against behaviorist models that define language change in terms of habit. Spitzer's opposing concern with nonhabitual change leads naturally enough to his claim that language shifts are rooted in historically defined, conscious (i.e., nonhabitual), creative behavior. The seeming contradiction between such "conscious psychological calculation" and an "instinctive device" (or unconscious behavior) is produced by the same tension we have seen in Spitzer's discussions of narrative strategies and style. Here, as in the discussions of Quevedo and Proust, Spitzer is trying to walk a tightrope between creative expression and controlled statement without the support that a fully defined psychological or historical model would provide.[15]

That he has no specific model does not mean that Spitzer will qualify his argument, however. In fact, Spitzer conflates both of his arguments against Hall's formalism, explaining a stylistic value in terms of an "aesthetic or psychological tendency" toward verbal lengthening. Why or how that conjunction operates is not discussed by Spitzer. Behavioral models would obviously be too reductionistic, and psychoanalytic models are mistakenly judged by him as being too deterministic. The validity of a psychological/aesthetic conjunction is assumed, and his presentation must rest lightly on that assumption. Within the full safety of a Romance philological tradition such assumptions could be made, but the cracks now appearing in the Romance edifice make Spitzer's failure to provide some explanatory framework dangerous, at best. The dangers of idealism become even more evident as Spitzer proposes his second argument—that Hall willingly separates aesthetic and positivistic description. Spitzer rightly believes that linguistic description, be it a description of the "linguistic creation of poets" or of "the naturally poetic popular language" (168), must address certain fundamental givens or needs of behavior. The most important of these needs is captured within the concept of the etymon, "the driving force behind human speech" (168). Unfortunately, that drive is considered by Spitzer to be aesthetic at base. "Poetry is a linguistic phenomenon," Spitzer suggests, "and language is unthinkable without poetry" (168). That allusion to aesthetic values must suffice, since no social, psychological, or historical frame appears viable to Spitzer at the moment. But the absence of such an explanatory frame invites attack.

By 1946 Spitzer's philological methods were so clearly overshadowed by structural linguistics that all Hall needed to do in rejecting Spitzer's views was to offer up his own opposing views on the strengths of formalist description. "Linguistics," Hall declares, "is simply the scientific study of language" ("The State of Linguistics," 30), and in making that statement he rejects outright any arguments on aesthetic or mentalistic grounds. In the academic climate of 1946 the call for scientific methodology is self-validating. Two sentences later Hall addresses the psychological issue by agreeing that language forms "an essential part of human behavior" (30). The related and more basic issue of the model used to describe that behavior is hardly addressed, but the mantle of linguistic science covers over in Hall what conversely appears as a glaring lack in Spitzer. Indeed, Spitzer's own description does not force the issue. In an academic environment filled with psychological models, neither Hall's behaviorism nor Spitzer's Romantic aestheticism are very well defined. The difference lies in the status already granted to each model.

Whatever their weaknesses and strengths, the arguments have taken on a life of their own by this time and are continued by various other principals without producing any sense of progress or resolution. Bonfante, for example, enters the argument by providing a burgeoning list of fifty-one differences between neo-linguists and neo-grammarians.[16] But the essential issues cannot really be resolved. Acceptability is primarily a function of the linguistic and academic climate; neither side ever relinquishes its separate claims. Spitzer's work may display a more useful attitude toward the complexities of mind and behavior, but he offers no specific model that could be of use in pursuing his assertions. And while Hall may continually attack the Crocean philosophy that supposedly underlies Spitzer's model of language, he spends more time alluding to such a tie than Spitzer does in establishing one. Spitzer affirms that fact, noting once again that his early work relied not at all upon Croce, instead being "primarily influenced by that great Viennese seeker into the meaning of human behavior, Sigmund Freud" (501n). The reference, while pointing to a possible model, will not be sustained.[17]

The resolution of the other point of opposition—scientific versus aesthetic description—also is not achieved by these arguments, but is achieved instead through the influence and power of general linguistics and the diminution of the influence of Continental Romance philology. Hall even uses the Continental sources of Spitzer's ideas to support his attack, characterizing the intellectual atmosphere of Europe as "influenced by the aristocratic, theological background of mediaeval and Renaissance intellectualism."[18] In opposition to that supposed elitism, Hall offers "American work on language, [where] the burning question at present is whether this same anti-scientific attitude is to be allowed to block the further development of linguistics and its contribution to our understanding of human affairs, especially in our teaching" (34). By 1946 the battle over the status of Europe had not yet ended, although the growing global influence of the United States would help to guarantee the fading of Continental philology.[19]

To counter that influence the strongest arguments available to Spitzer remain those of depth and complexity. The descriptive power of structural linguistics can only be achieved through a corresponding loss of historical and contextual depth, a fact that Spitzer uses to advantage by concentrating in "Why Does Language Change?" on semantics—the Achilles' heel of general linguistics. In similar fashion, Spitzer's nonliterary etymological studies, such as the *Essays in Historical Semantics* (1948) and the post-humous *Classical and Christian Ideas of World Harmony* (1960), are a part of his battle to keep meaning and etymology at the center of linguistic description and to promote a linguistics that describes language as a form of creative activity. Language, Spitzer continues to hammer home in these studies, is not simply behavior; it is historically significant and meaningful behavior. It is discourse activity and not linguistic material that Spitzer wants to describe, and he stresses the drama of language by opening the *Essays* with an extended analogy between words and writers, comparing this book to its literary "foil," *Linguistics and Literary History*:

> While, in the latter, the protagonists are individual writers, whose literary personalities are studied in their written words, in their own particular style, here, in this volume, the protagonists will be words themselves, as used by writers of various periods. . . . Given the variety and extent of the literary material on which the word-histories have been based, it is evident that these have had to be conceived supra-personally, and that the personalities which have left their imprint on the words can only be those of civilizations although these, in turn, have naturally been formed and colored by the personalities of individuals (who, however, were only giving expression to the general feelings of their civilization). This treatment of the particular meanings assumed by certain words under the impact of the "style" of certain civilizations is what I mean by . . . historical semantics. [1]

Spitzer's description of language in terms of personality, whether indi-vidual or cultural, is intended to be more than metaphorical. Studying the words of a writer or a historical period only has validity for Spitzer if the analysis results in a further or more thorough awareness of the actual users of the language. The primary goal of all language study is the

unearthing of style, of the particular manner of expression which embodies, at the same time that it depends upon, the personality of an author
or a culture.

The central need facing this stylistic model remains that of adequately
defining the supposedly individual aspects of the style while also tying
that creativity to the larger historical and cultural situation. What constitutes the correct blend of individual creativity and historical determinism? The answer to that question continues to elude Spitzer and is further
complicated by his growing insistence on a larger organicist aesthetics
that escapes history via its expressive power. Once more Spitzer faces
the need to justify the epistemological nature of stylistics, and once more
the only model close at hand is that of Romantic organicism, here shifted
even more closely to the models originally offered by Humboldt. History,
like the literature and language which embody it, must be seen as an
organic development, with aesthetic expression conceived as the spiritual
essence that vivifies the organism.

These essays on historical semantics are thus the visible embodiment
of Spitzer's theoretical rejection of neo-grammarian positivism and set
forth his proposal for diachronic study as the core of linguistics. Sound
description is to be countered with the analysis of meaning; phonological
etymology is to be blocked by cultural philology. At the same time, Spitzer
denies that this stance removes him from the mainstream of linguistic
trends. He is no more willing to capitulate to the neo-grammarian arguments of Bloomfield and Hall than to those of Meyer-Lübke. Instead,
he impudently offers the belief that meaning provides "the most *concrete*
aspect of a word" (2), but the argument is clearly a form of bravado. "[I]t
is highly characteristic of the absence of critical feeling for values in our
times," Spitzer admits, "that the abstract results of mechanical comparativism, phonetic or morphological, seem in general more attractive to
the professional linguist than do the concrete finds of semantic comparison . . ." (2).

Faced with that attraction, Spitzer opposes the empiricist vision of
science by presenting his procedures as objective in their own right and
by arguing that the results of "mechanical comparativism" are more abstract than those of semantic study—precisely because the goal of the
former is a general law, not a discussion of linguistic particularities. Semantics is to be seen as the only truly concrete aspect of language because
it deals with the individual complexities of language in its context of use.
Other approaches merely study the framework or shell of language, poking

about a skeletal framework that lacks the vital flesh of human use. Linguists, Spitzer urges, must escape from this archaeology of the fragments and bones of language by forming a science that studies linguistic behavior rather than linguistic material.

Spitzer defines the procedures for such etymological analysis along the lines set forth in his early literary studies: a revision of Schuchardt's *Wörter und Sachen* procedures. The word or concept (either may be taken as a starting point) is to be investigated through the related words and concepts with which it comes in contact or whose usage it affects. The basic idea is essentially that of semantic field theory with Spitzerian overtones added.[20] Schuchardt's fallacy was to limit himself to the "utilitarian" level of language and then to attempt to define intellectual concepts by reference to it. Spitzer's semantic histories will circumvent this "naturalism" by focusing on words of "an intellectual calibre" and on "the language of cultured circles" (*Essays*, 3). Such a focus allows Spitzer's word-histories to address the same goals as those defined for the literary studies of Proust and Quevedo. Ideas rather than things are the historical and cultural detritus uncovered in this linguistic history, although the purely rational concept is not what Spitzer seeks. He does not pursue the thoughts of a particular period (which can be equated with the words of the dictionary); he seeks a culture's intellectual activity, "the style of thinking" displayed by the history of the language (14n).

The justification that Spitzer offers for constructing this stylistic bridge between conceptual terms and the intellectual/aesthetic attitude of an age is a blend of Humboldt and Sperber. A word or concept is not an empty unit; it is an act motivated by aesthetic and emotional interest, and the particular interest or appeal constitutes what Sperber has called a "fixing factor." Rephrased by Spitzer, a period "for which architecture is an ideal, will use architectural metaphors, . . . at the expense of other possible metaphors—in all of which the 'fixing (cultural) factor' will have been the architectural obsession" (*Essays*, 5).[21] In place of the assumed value of efficient and powerful methods of description, Spitzer offers a description of language as a multidimensional activity and, beyond that vision, as an embodiment of the beliefs and attitudes of western culture. He repeats the argument that Sperber's "semantic tendencies" are equivalent to the "so-called phonetic laws" of the general linguists (*Essays*, 5), but admits that the real value of the volume "stands or falls" on its expansion of etymology beyond *Bedeutungswandel* into *Kulturwandel* (13n). Like the words and concepts they consider, these essays gain their full intellectual significance from their synthetic treatment of the concepts they attract into their orbit. The ultimate "fixing factor" for western culture—a vision of world harmony—becomes the ultimate argument for their value. Spitzer's etymological study, while initially historical, thus attempts to transcend naked historical fact in order to reach the higher realms of epistemology. Caught between a stable but ahistorical positivism in his scholarly field and the social chaos of his now-lost academic world, Spitzer (not surprisingly) wishes to root his historically informed philology in a supposedly more significant panhistorical human sensibility.

The best example of the implications (and contradictions) of this approach grows out of Spitzer's unhappiness with the work of A. O. Lovejoy, his colleague in both ideas and institutions. Some crossover would seem to be natural: both scholars are concerned with the same particular issue—the status of ideas within an historical framework; both decry the compartmentalization and specialization of the academic environment.[22] These similarities fade upon closer study of their work, however, and the inevitable public exchange to which it led. Over the long run their arguments center on what qualifies as an adequate description of history, and the political situation again adds its own fuel to the supposedly bias-free scholarly debate. What begins as a discussion of the nature of ideas within history closes as an argument over the place of Romanticism in the German consciousness.

Spitzer's general argument is that Lovejoy seeks to characterize "idea" as an unemotional and rational construct, an argument that is clearly heavy-handed.[23] In 1940 Lovejoy's lead essay in the opening volume of the *Journal of the History of Ideas* (and the beginning of this exchange) does argue that "the intellectual historiographer will still do well to entertain the hypothesis that logic is one of the important operative factors in the history of thought," but he immediately qualifies that statement by noting that "he cannot accept this assumption in the extreme form in which it was once widely held" ("Reflections," 20). He cannot, as he explains, because there has been a general, widespread shift in thinking about the role played by the unconscious in the workings of the mind. The influence of Freud has been felt by Lovejoy as well as Spitzer, and the merely rational has no real place within his theorizing, even though its assumption would be helpful in the production of efficient analytical methods.

Spitzer's real difficulty with Lovejoy arises less from the excessive rationality of Lovejoy's definitions and more from his work's implication that aesthetic values—specifically, those defined by organicist views of literary expression—may not provide the best criteria on which to base a literary history. In Spitzer's view this lowering of the aesthetic in favor of historical and psychological "fact" threatens to taint Lovejoy's studies with positivism, a threat that is only increased in 1941 when Lovejoy presents the ideal analytical procedures for the historian of ideas, a set of procedures that he illustrates by defining Romanticism:[24]

1. The historian locates key recurring terms in the texts and attempts to determine "what and how many distinct ideas appear to be expressed by, or associated with, each of these terms" (262).

2. Having uncovered, clarified, and listed each of the key ideas of the period, the historian looks for the relations between the ideas. Such relations are of three kinds: logical, psychological, and historical (264).

3. The ongoing growth of the separate ideas within these complexes must be followed as each one reasserts itself and enters into subsequent combinations (268).

As outlined, the procedure appears valid, manageable, and—important at this time—objective. In fact, the method's seeming ability to function in an orderly and progressive fashion provides a good part of its appeal. It is an attraction that Spitzer does not fail to notice: "the very appeal of [Lovejoy's] article rests precisely upon the bold *implications* of his study, upon the scientific attitude *underlying* all his propositions."[25] That appeal does not apply to Spitzer, however, who sees in it the sacrificing of intellectual complexity for scientific efficiency, the creation of a "scientific program" (194) deep within the history of ideas—and of Romanticism.[26]

Spitzer responds to Lovejoy's vision of Romanticism (and its willing analysis of the German consciousness as well) by proposing a synthetic approach to the history of ideas (*Geistesgeschichte* versus history of ideas) that mirrors the one he proposed for his history of words. Spitzer "put his finger on the differences between Lovejoy's and his own method," Wellek agrees, "when he emphasized totality, unity, climate of an age, emotional atmosphere, the links and transitions between words rather than the distinctions between unit-ideas and a rationalistic criticism of their implied 'metaphysical pathos' which were Lovejoy's peculiar *forte*" (introduction to Spitzer's *Classical and Christian Ideas of World Harmony*, vii). This qualitative argument against reducing the complexity of the issues is bolstered further with a claim that Lovejoy cannot fully deliver on the scientific procedures to which he appeals. Yet each of these declarations is qualified by the fact that Lovejoy's arguments are quite close to Spitzer's own stylistic program, as the similarity of Lovejoy's historical

analysis to Spitzer's etymological studies makes very clear. In fact, Spitzer
actually adopts the essential features of Lovejoy's method in his attack,
and Lovejoy responds by noting that Spitzer's discussion produces its own
list of unit ideas, even while ostensibly denying their validity.[27]

The ensuing arguments quickly boil down the issues devoted to the
merits of the respective methods to a question of interpretive quality:
whose presentation of the relationship between Romanticism and Germanic consciousness is more adequate? Spitzer suggests (in a slap at
Lovejoy's appeal to science) that Lovejoy's chemical formula for Romanticism lacks a full listing of essential elements (197). Lovejoy's three-part
compound of organicism, dynamism, and diversity fails both to address
the full complexity of the situation and to maintain the scientific rigor to
which it appeals. Nor will a simple multiplication of the number of unit
ideas add objectivity to the description. In fact, such random addition
only demonstrates the very subjectivity that Spitzer uses to deny the
objective validity of Lovejoy's appeal. The sheer number of essential ideas
does not serve to validate the interpretation; it is the degree to which
these abstract ideas can be shifted from the plane of the abstract and onto
the historical that serves to underpin each man's argument. That fact
becomes most clear in Spitzer's rejection of the wartime sentiments of
Lovejoy, whose attempt to shift from describing Romanticism to analyzing
prewar and wartime Germany rings with the familiar echoes of ideological
interpretation. Lovejoy does not actually claim that his features describe
the only influential aspects of twentieth-century German ideas. Yet the
step from history of ideas to social interpretation has been made, and it
leaves behind a lingering sense of excessive haste.

Lovejoy has made the interpretive jump from idea to society that Spitzer
himself has been accused of taking too quickly and too often. Ironically,
then, Spitzer proceeds to demonstrate the clarity that banal historical
materials can add to the definition of intellectual history by using them
to deny the general portrait of the Germanic tradition that Lovejoy offers.
In the essay that marks the beginning of this exchange, Lovejoy argued
for the inclusion of specific, even biographical, events within the aesthetic,
the intellectual, the ideational description—and was chastised by Spitzer
for doing so. Now Spitzer uses those same devices to produce one more
corrective to a wartime misreading, as he asks so succinctly, "Why not
first look at the actual picture?" (194), and then proceeds to do so, drawing
a quick sketch of the educational offerings within Germany's secondary
schools and universities and weaving a web of factuality around the inter-

pretation that reminds us of Spitzer's rejection of Thorner. The resulting sketch, colored by historical facts (or at least by Spitzer's remembrance of them), provides a social setting in which the argument takes on life and depth. The sketch remains a construction, a critical intepretation, but it is given an implied accuracy through the addition of particular social and historical details. In essence, Spitzer has countered the scientific tone and appeal of Lovejoy's argument with that of historical realism.

Unfortunately, Spitzer's belief in the necessity of these historical specifics depends upon an increasingly hermetic organicism for validation rather than upon a revised vision of history and epistemology. By 1941 Spitzer had already opposed the reading of poetry to the pursuit of a history of ideas in the newly formed *Southern Review*,[28] and it would be only a short step from those arguments to the methodological statements of *A Method of Interpreting Literature* (1948). These declarations would affirm Spitzer's choice of a Romantic epistemology to support his historical vision, a choice that would be further solidified by his overly quick dismissal of Kenneth Burke, who was himself struggling to oppose the ahistorical formalism of New Criticism. In these arguments, as we will see in the next chapter, lie both the reasons for Spitzer's continuing desire to unite history, style, and language, and his continuing dissatisfaction with the available critical and linguistic models of the day.

NOTES

1. Isidor Thorner, "German Words, German Personality and Protestantism," *Psychiatry: Journal of the Biology and the Pathology of Interpersonal Relations*, 8, no. 4 (1945), 403–17.

2. Arno Schirokauer and Leo Spitzer, "German Words, German Personality and Protestantism Again," *Psychiatry: Journal of the Biology and the Pathology of Interpersonal Relations*, 12, no. 2 (1949), 185–87.

3. American structural linguistics and the later structuralist literary criticism are not the same discipline. The former grew out of the work in general linguistics begun by Bloomfield and reached its height in work done by Fries, Hockett, and others during the mid–1950s.

4. Leo Spitzer, "A New Book on the Art of *The Celestina*," review of *The Art of "La Celestina*," by Stephen Gilman, *Hispanic Review*, 25 (January, 1957), 23.

5. As late as 1973 Chatman and Levin found the situation little changed, admitting that American linguists and literary critics "have not shown

much interest in the great European stylistic tradition . . ." (Seymour Chatman and Samuel Levin, "Linguistics and Literature," in *Current Trends in Linguistics*, ed. Thomas A. Sebeok, vol. 10 [The Hague: Mouton, 1973], 274). It is a separation that currently shows signs of adjustment, as the difficulties attached to objective analysis in both literary theory and linguistics become more apparent. But the answers sought in critical analysis do not necessarily match those pursued by linguistic science, and the salvos fired by Spitzer and Bloomfield in 1943 and 1944 are still echoing today.

6. Leo Spitzer, "Why Does Language Change?," *Modern Language Quarterly*, 4 (1943), 413–31. Bloomfield's response to this essay is contained in his "Secondary and Tertiary Responses to the Language," *Language*, 20 (1944), 45–55. The last comments in the exchange are in Spitzer's "Answer to Mr. Bloomfield," *Language*, 20 (1944), 245–51.

7. See his "The Individual Factor in Linguistic Change," *Cultura Neolatina*, 16 (1956), 71–89.

8. Don Ramon Menendez Pidal, *Origenes del español* (Madrid: Espasa-Calpe, S.A., 1926), 421. See Malkiel ("Comparative Romance Linguistics," *Current Trends in Linguistics*, vol. 9 [The Hague: Mouton, 1972]), 835–925 for a quick discussion of the impact of Pidal's text.

9. Robert Hall denies the validity of every aspect of this explanation, but he does so with no less cultural speculation than that provided by Spitzer: "Spitzer ascribes this presumed anarchy and restlessness of the Romance-speaking peoples before A.D. 1000 to an urge for conformity . . . but the validity of this conception is becoming increasingly open to doubt, and even if it were tenable, it is quite doubtful whether the mass of speakers of the then-nascent Romance languages had the 'ideals' which Spitzer ascribed to them" (*Idealism in Romance Linguistics* [Ithaca, N.Y.: Cornell University Press, 1963], 73–74). Arguments based on doubt are still interpretations, however.

10. Spitzer's long final note is an extended argument for the validity of the circle as seen in other approaches to language: "thus it was that Diez started with the observation . . . that no one Romance language is reducible to another, and then proceeded to construct his 'Urpflanze,' the 'unknown quantity' Proto-Romance = Vulgar Latin, finally concluding with the reverse procedure by which he verified his assumption that 'Vulgar Latin' as conceived by him, could explain all the Romance languages. Nothing is more orthodox than such 'circular reasoning.' Similarly, when I have observed what I call a 'stylistic fact' . . . in the language of a writer, I tentatively suggest a possible psychological root, in the writer, of this particular usage—later to test whether the assumed psychological root is

able to explain other stylistic observations which may be made concerning his individual language . . ." (430–31n).

11. The clearest statement of that dislike may appear in his 1955 review of R. A. Sayce, in which he tries to put his American audience "on its guard" against the false illusions produced by the term "method." In America, Spitzer believes, a method is too readily thought of as "a kind of magic key that, once discovered, lets anyone who has it enter straight away into a new world." But that statement only echoes attitudes found throughout the work, such as the early disparaging comment made in "Wortkunst und Sprachwissenschaft" that Spitzer does not want his method to become a "sausage-grinder" for literary studies. Leo Spitzer, "Stylistique et critique littéraire," *Critique*, 11 (1955), 597.

12. Leonard Bloomfield, "Meaning," in *A Leonard Bloomfield Anthology*, ed Charles Hockett (Bloomington: Indiana University Press, 1970), 103.

13. The exchange covers four articles and a book: Hall, "IT. MER. *poskráy, poskrílle* ECC.," *Italica*, 20, no. 4 (1943), 198–200; Spitzer, "Crai e Poscrai o Poscrilla e Posquacchera Again, or the Crisis in Modern Linguistics," *Italica*, 21, no. 4 (1944), 154–69; Hall, "The State of Linguistics: Crisis or Reaction?," *Italica*, 23, no. 1 (1946), 30–34; Spitzer, "Correspondence on Robert Hall, The State of Linguistics: Crisis or Reaction?," *Modern Language Notes*, 61 (1946), 497–502; Hall, *Idealism in Romance Linguistics* (Ithaca, N.Y.: Cornell University Press, 1963).

14. Spitzer decorously characterizes Bloomfield, in yet another broadside from this series of exchanges, as coloring his arguments with "the tempering quality of a smile" befitting "this intelligent and learned scholar" (*MLN*, 500). The reason for the change seems to be that of contrasting such a portrait of Bloomfield with the figure of Hall available from these exchanges.

15. The same issues, as found in the Quevedo essay, clearly are in Spitzer's thoughts. See his reference to Quevedo on 162.

16. G. Bonfante, "The neo-linguistic position," *Language*, 23 (1947), 344–75.

17. Spitzer might fit best into a model based on Husserl's phenomenology. But there is really no more philosphical argumentation in Spitzer than there is psychological, and actually a good deal less. In fact, Spitzer brings all three approaches together in a note to "*Explication de Texte* Applied to Three Great Middle English Poems," in *Essays on English and American Literature*, ed. Anna Hatcher (Princeton, N.J.: Princeton University Press, 1962), 193–247. (See chapter 5). Auerbach has mentioned both Croce and Husserl as influences on *explication*. Among the

"many other currents" flowing through *explication*, Spitzer "personally would list Freud's analysis of the psychological laws governing the expression of the subconscious" (194n).

18. Hall also draws the portrait of the scientist (and especially the American scientist) as capable of divorcing all personal prejudice in the pursuit of some higher (albeit scientific) truth. "[I]n American scholarship," he declares, "it is considered the utmost bad taste to inject one's personal religious beliefs into scientific discourse" (32n). The charge is off the mark, to say the least, and exists more as an ideological comment on scientific truth than as a useful description of Spitzer's admittedly spiritualized readings.

19. The war and postwar atmosphere that colors many of the more unpleasant references may explain the nastiness of these exchanges. Whatever their source, the personal attacks by both men are incremental, and it is difficult to establish who strikes the first low blow. Spitzer's comments on Hall are decidedly aggressive, but then, so is Hall's unfortunate characterization of European thought as containing "an essentially reactionary hostility to objective science" and as being influenced by the inheritance of an "aristocratic, theological background of medieval and Renaissance intellectualism" (33–34). Spitzer's personal experiences with the Third Reich may have led to his counter characterization of Hall's views as "Marxoid" and "jingoistic," but that hardly condones the statement. The lowest point, however, occurs with Hall's speculations on Spitzer's mental health and sexuality (*Idealism*, 76–77), an attack that occurred two years after Spitzer's death, thus precluding any possibility of reply.

20. Spitzer makes the comparison himself in *Classical and Christian Ideas of World Harmony: Prolegomena to an Interpretation of the Word 'Stimmung'*, ed. Anna Hatcher (Baltimore, Md.: Johns Hopkins Press, 1963), 1. A quick introduction to the theory as it relates to stylistic issues can be found in Stephen Ullmann's work, specifically in *Meaning and Style* (New York: Harper and Row, 1973). Field theory is discussed on pages 23–33.

21. The reference to "architectural obsession" is reminiscent of remarks made about Morgenstern, Proust, and Quevedo, and it renews Spitzer's attempt to validate his reading through reference to psychological issues, if not through the application of specific psychological models. Mentioning Sperber and pathology provides Spitzer with the external psychological model that he recognizes as important, while never really serving as a procedural step within these studies themselves. The echo of Schuchardt's "overly-naturalistic" approach sounds its warning here, and Spitzer only approaches the psychological—he does not embrace it.

22. See Lovejoy's comments in "Reflections on the History of Ideas," *Journal of the History of Ideas*, 1 (1940), 4–5.

23. Wellek comes to the same conclusion in his introduction to *Classical and Christian Ideas of World Harmony*, viii.

24. A. O. Lovejoy, "The Meaning of Romanticism for the Historian of Ideas," *Journal of the History of Ideas*, 2 (1941), 257–78.

25. Leo Spitzer, "Geistesgeschichte vs. History of Ideas Applied to Hitlerism," *Journal of the History of Ideas*, 5 (1944), 191–203. The comment is from page 197. See Green, *Erich Auerbach and Leo Spitzer* (109–14), for a further discussion of the spiritual overtones in Spitzer's arguments with Lovejoy.

26. Spitzer would continue to argue that Lovejoy's work was essentially positivistic, referring to him in 1952 as a "logical positivist" lacking the ability to read the general "artistic self-irony or humor" in the work of historical essayists. More interesting than these intentional misreadings is the hint of where Spitzer's motives lie, a hint that appears in his flat comment on the verifiability of aesthetic readings. "Any aesthetic evaluation," he declares, "must, of course, always be subjective" ("The 'Ideal Typology' in Dante's 'De Vulgari eloquentia,' " *Italica*, 32 [1955], 75–94).

27. A. O. Lovejoy, "Reply to Mr. Spitzer," *Journal of the History of Ideas*, 5, no. 2 (1944), 204–19. The statement appears on page 205.

28. Leo Spitzer, "History of Ideas versus Reading of Poetry," *Southern Review*, 6 (1941), 584–609.

5 Historical versus Organicist Criticism
Spitzer, Burke, and the Context of Style

The exchanges between Bloomfield, Hall, Lovejoy, and Spitzer highlight the struggle that Spitzer faced in establishing his stylistic theories within an Anglo-American academic tradition. Spitzer's arguments make it clear that his own procedures rested upon two pillars of support that were being (or had been) seriously eroded by the current streams of thought. The importance of historical interpretations of language or literature had faded, and the status of Romance philology as the academically preeminent discipline in linguistics was gone.[1] As 1950 neared, the pursuit of general linguistic methodologies brought with it an established interest in synchronic rather than diachronic studies, while approaches geared toward describing or enhancing particularities and differences in individual languages or linguistic behavior were replaced by those devoted to general linguistic features. The situation demanded of Spitzer what had been demanded so often of those pursuing the study of style—stylistics would be granted academic credibility only if it successfully achieved two goals: (1) the creation of a stylistic method that displayed the same procedural consistency as that demonstrated by general linguistic methods, and (2) the presentation of arguments demonstrating the superiority of a contextual and historical description of language to the one pursued by general linguistics. The move to a more complex description of language could not simply be asserted, however, nor could a method be created in a vacuum. Achieving both goals required the formation of alliances with other academic disciplines and the acquisition of methods of analysis that would offer support and validation for this wider view.

Such were the needs. They are not difficult to recognize, since they have faced Spitzer at all points in his career. Nor does he fail to respond to them. *Linguistics and Literary History* (1948), along with *A Method of Interpreting Literature* (1949),[2] once more provide the outline of the Spitzerian philological circle, together with clarifications and explanations added to strengthen its objectivity. At the same time, Spitzer refers to external approaches and similar work done by other critics. But the postwar environment would prove to be more hostile than ever. Structural linguistics was not the only dominant acontextual approach to language at this time. New Critical interest in ahistorical criticism still maintained its hold on American critical thought, and while its grip was beginning to weaken, its influence would continue for the rest of Spitzer's career. On top of these difficulties, Spitzer will face one additional complication of his own making: the exchange with Lovejoy has made it clear that Spitzer will continue to justify his interpretive framework in terms of a large set of cultural and aesthetic values resting only upon his assumption of (rather than his definition and elaboration of) certain set views of history and aesthetic response.

This placement of historical and aesthetic interpretation in opposition to methodological positivism will seriously affect Spitzer's description of the user and the context of use. Over the previous forty years Spitzer has come to believe that this incipient positivism has watered down the epistemological basis of every scholarly field that he has embraced. Linguistics, literary criticism, stylistics, and psychoanalysis have all demonstrated a propensity for such reductionism and, faced by it, Spitzer chooses to defend his method in isolation, limiting the arena of discussion to "ideas couched in linguistic and literary form." With that characterization Spitzer intends to grant stylistics a safe middle ground as a historical study rooted in aesthetics: ideas apart from their context will be left to the history of philosophy; ideas as "informing action," studied by the fields of history and social science (*Linguistics and Literary History*, 32n). Yet that careful separation hints at territorial partitioning, and with it Spitzer will be very close to acquiescing to a split between the epistemological visions of science and those of the humanistic disciplines, a separation that he himself attacks in *Linguistics and Literary History* (36n) as granting positivism an unnecessary predominance in linguistic study.

During the late forties and fifties this methodological uncertainty colors the work not only of Spitzer and Lovejoy but also that of fellow critic Kenneth Burke. Experiencing the same distaste as Spitzer for the rising values of scientific mechanism, Burke embraces a functional attitude toward art, resorting to arguments resting on a rhetorical view of the activity of style and history. Spitzer, in search of values more lasting than those he has experienced personally in society, instead relies upon the historicization of aesthetics. There are also good critical reasons for this stance—reasons that outstrip even his own personal desire for stability. New Critical arguments, while never fully endorsed by Spitzer, nonetheless offer some support for his arguments against an excessive focus on the Romantic individual. The most important support that the literary/critical ambience offers, however, is its defense of the aesthetically defined text. Although Spitzer holds back from coloring his critical portraits with specific historical details, that tactic is still endorsed by a critical milieu that fervently downplays the importance of context in interpretation. Linguistic and critical movements thus apply their own varying pressures to those particular points of stress in the bridge that Spitzer constructs between language and history. Spitzer's presentation of the link between writing and historical context remains vague in the climate fostered by the New Critical interest in the freestanding text. But his continuing belief in the necessary presence of that historical link places him outside both the dominant critical and linguistic frameworks, while the pressure to drop that link amounts to a linguistic and critical fiat that Spitzer feels no obligation to obey. The critical methods that he puts forth at this time, described at separate times as the "philological circle" and "*explication de texte*," continue to stress his refusal to join the movement toward an ahistorical analysis of literature or language.

The opening pages of *Linguistics and Literary History* repeat the arguments for stylistic study that Spitzer put forth on the Continent. He reviews his early career, including the dissatisfaction with Meyer-Lübke's linguistics and Becker's criticism, and points to the possible merging of both areas in stylistics. As he moves toward defining his approach to language and literature, Spitzer demonstrates his own beliefs by providing an etymological analysis, thus mirroring the opening to his *Essays in Historical Semantics* and its discussion of personal etymologies and neologisms. The ensuing emphasis on the psychological and cultural motivation for change parallels the emphasis of the *Essays*, as does the belief in linguistic personalities underlying the discussion. The derivation of "conundrum" and "quandary" serves Spitzer as the platform from which he can denounce the positivists' limited description of language. Creative wordplay and word development are declared to be "psychologically and culturally motivated: language is not, as the behavioristic, anti-mentalistic, mechanistic or materialistic school of linguists, rampant in some universities, would have it: a meaningless agglomeration of corpses: dead word-material, automatic 'speech habits' unleased [*sic*] by a trigger motion" (*Linguistics and Literary History*, 8).

These beliefs are recognizable by now—the problems remain. To display the complexities of language is not the same as providing a definitive argument against or replacement for efficiency of description. With that in mind Spitzer presents the philological circle to his English-speaking readers:

> [The critic] must work from the surface to the "inward life-center" of the work of art: first observing details about the superficial appearance of the particular work (and the "ideas" expressed by the poet are, also, only one of the superficial traits in a work of art); then, grouping these details and seeking to integrate them into a creative principle which may have been present in the soul of the artist; and, finally, making the return trip to all the other groups of observations in order to find whether the "inward life form" one has tentatively constructed gives an account of the whole. [19]

The most obvious procedural question to be argued in 1948 is whether the process is vitiated by the possibility that any such reading may rest upon an initial subjective insight. As a partial counter to that argument, Spitzer finds support in similar procedures undertaken by Dilthey, Schleirmacher, Plato, and Heidegger, among others. But his real argument comes not from other practitioners but from the authority provided by an achieved analysis and the subsequent placing of this achieved critical portrait within the historical pantheon of writers related to it. It never enters Spitzer's mind that the critical reading of a text might be an untutored gestalt or a readerly response. The critical pursuit rests upon the critic's ability to reveal the internal and historical complexity of the text.

Countering earlier studies in which he left the historical placement of a style to others,[3] Spitzer now repeats the issues of his argument with Lovejoy. Within one page of the description of the philological circle, Spitzer outlines the full range of his anticipated stylistic reading. To complete the stylistic study, here exemplified by a quick sketch of Rabelais, "we must place [Rabelais], as the literary historians would say, within the framework of the history of ideas, or *Geistesgeschichte*" (20).[4] Spitzer's method thus bears the stamp of an admitted hierarchy of readers, at the top of which stands the linguistically trained critic. The philological circle defines a critical response that rests its initial insight—and its subsequent verification procedures—upon the critic's ability to recreate the context surrounding the work's production. How that initial insight and its verification are to be achieved defines the authority of, and remains the province of, the critic. It also remains the source of the charges of subjectivity that will dog Spitzer throughout the close of his career.

The charges clearly rankle Spitzer (especially in an era judging critical worth on the basis of objectivity), and he is quick to provide a series of defenses for the validity of his insights and his authority to make them. The arguments range from invoking the spiritual correctness of his method to denying the importance of method entirely. The first appeal for justification will naturally be that of philology. Language and its intellectual context are inseparable. To see one is to see the other: "what repeats itself in all word-histories is the possibility of recognizing the signs of a people at work, culturally and psychologically. To speak in the language of the homeland of philology: *Wortwandel ist Kulturwandel und Seelenwandel . . .*" (9). The etymological study thus reveals both the linguistic history of various forms and the psychological and cultural framework of the civilization enacted by them. The particular connection between the language and its users goes beyond history, however, suggesting "a web of interrelations between language and the soul of the speaker" (10).

The presence of this creative soul is important enough to be repeated again later. Language change may be unconscious (general language change) or conscious (literary creativity), but both types of change are united by the encompassing "soul of the speaker(s)" (31n). This personal and cultural *"Geistesgeschichte"* is familiar from the argument with Lovejoy, but it easily extends back to the thinking of Vossler, Grimm, and Humboldt. Spitzer does not choose to justify this blend of the historical and the spiritual by referring to nineteenth-century linguistic and literary tradition, however, but by suggesting a relationship between the humanist and the theologian. "[I]t is not by chance," Spitzer declares, "that the 'philological circle' was discovered by a theologian [Pascal], who was wont to harmonize the discordant, to retrace the beauty of God in this world" (24). This sense of harmony, which will motivate the work of *Classical and Christian Ideas of Harmony*, is seen by Spitzer as the underlying basis of all synthetic analysis, which proceeds "not only by the gradual progression from one detail to another detail, but by the anticipation or divination of the whole" (19).

The recourse to spiritual insight and argument is not new, but these interpretive heights are ethereal, and Spitzer's subsequent descent and movement back into the general discussion of method is welcome, indeed. Recalling his 1925 claim that literary methods are not sausage grinders for literary texts, Spitzer here acknowledges that the philological circle is not "the systematic step-by-step procedure which my own description of it may have seemed to promise" (25). Moreover, he notes, the word "method" may itself be problematic, since he admits to using it in a manner apart from the word's normal connotations. Method is not to be seen as a series of preordained operations but as (quoting Laland's *Vocabulaire de la philosophie* s.v. *méthode I*) " 'a habitual procedure of the mind,' " an *Erlebnis* or attitude, as it were (38n). It is a definition of method calculated to set Spitzer's interpretive procedures apart from supposedly objective, generally applicable methods of analysis, and he openly declares that his own talent for reading may affect the recognition of the stylistic detail and its place in the stylistic framework: "This gift, or vice (for it has its dangers), of seeing part and whole together, at any moment, and which, to some degree, is basic to the operation of the philosophical mind, is perhaps, in my own case, developed to a particular degree . . ." (25–26).

The recognition of a stylistic feature is thus (as Spitzer has always argued and continues to argue) a result of reading and re-reading in order to judge the specific work of the individual artist. As it is phrased by Spitzer, the "click"—the recognition of the importance of a feature—is achievable only if the reader becomes "soaked through and through with the atmosphere of a work" (27). While this focus on reading harbors a belief in levels of reading ability, Spitzer does allow for the acquisition of this talent: "the click will come oftener and more quickly after several experiences of 'clicks' have been realized by the critic" (28). Yet the essential procedural issue remains—the method requires insight rather than technique, and its proofs gather around a series of critical arguments rather than a set of data.

Spitzer has provided these methodological descriptions before, but now he appears to find them insufficient in countering the objectivist trends he finds himself fighting. Unable to find any other acceptable procedures close at hand, and lacking a middle term for his stylistic equation that unites language and psyche, Spitzer increases the spiritual aura of his arguments in order to provide, if not an acceptable substitute for positivism, at least a polar opposition to it. The resulting argument for the intellectual importance of his method goes well beyond the bounds of methodological necessity. An element of spirituality in the learning process has always been an aspect of Spitzer's approach, and especially of his rebuttal of whatever he sees as positivistic reductionism. But at this point he unfortunately includes the critic's moral stance as a component of the critical reading. Artist, artistic organism, and critic are united in their feeling for the stylistic expression of the text, a feeling that is most readily available to select acolytes:

> [T]he capacity for this feeling is, again, deeply rooted in the previous life and education of the critic, and not only in his scholarly education: in order to keep his soul ready for his scholarly task he must have already made choices, in ordering his life, of what I would call a moral nature; he must have chosen to cleanse his mind of everyday small details—to keep it open to the synthetic apprehension of the "wholes" of life, to the symbolism in nature and art and language. [29]

This replacement of the aesthetic with the near-ascetic marks a watershed in Spitzer's call for the authoritative reading. It is a Romanticist call to the elevating powers of creativity, to the apotheosis of the individual in a stable world of art.

As the daily events of history vanish from Spitzer's critical reading, it is best to see this description as the only role that Spitzer can envision for a scholar displaced from his academic and personal setting in prewar Europe. The political chaos marking the last fifty years has laid bare the rather worldly nature of the academic and intellectual power structure, and Spitzer responds with a series of moral and political arguments that counter these upheavals with a set of higher immutable values.[5] Not surprisingly, Spitzer's view of the ideal academic environment often defines a prewar European scholarly world, such as that offered in his "The Formation of the American Humanist."[6] This 1950 MLA address repeats the call for a scholarly morality equivalent to that found in *Linguistics and Literary History,* and Spitzer continues to stumble over his spiritual aestheticism in his search for some order in the midst of the ongoing upheaval in his personal, social, and academic environment. What would appear to be large oscillations between discussions of the high spirituality of literature and analyses of the commonplace (such as an analysis of a Sunkist juice advertisement)[7] are really Arnoldian—not Barthesian—attempts to justify the relevance of scholarship to the culture at large.

In the midst of the struggle for the revitalization of academic life as he sees it, Spitzer chooses to restate and reform his methodological attitudes from within the terminological framework of a more Continental criticism. The critical procedures outlined in *A Method of Interpeting Literature* (a set of lectures offered at Smith College one year earlier in 1948) are less specific than the title implies, but they admittedly center on the use of *explication de texte*, and the presentation hearkens back to the source, both intellectual and geographical, of Spitzer's early work. According to Erich Auerbach, whom Spitzer cites in a later note, explication has three essential modes. Classical *explication* "provid[es] the factual data (historical, linguistic, cultural, exegetic) necessary for the correct and complete understanding of the text." Pedagogical *explication* serves to help French students approach a text. The third form (used "among the scholars in Romance especially by L. Spitzer") seeks "not to rediscover in the texts things already known, but to reach 'new first-hand observations' " which then must be integrated to the known and may lead to reevaluation of the particular author or work.[8]

In the lead essay of *A Method of Interpreting Literature*, Spitzer blends the first and the third forms, stating that *explication* is the primary mode of analysis to be followed and that, negative reactions from the texts' authors notwithstanding, he intends to follow the critic's need "to draw on his historical knowledge" in order to interpret that blend of rational and spiritual expression that constitutes poetic language (2–3).[9] The procedure is, according to comments made later, that of "*ex ungue leonem,* the technique, characteristic of the *explication de texte*, of seeking, in the linguistic details of the smallest artistic organism, the spirit and nature of a great writer" (64). That procedure is clarified by the opening discussion of John Donne's "Exstasie." The poet's particular rhetorical stance in "Exstasie" is described as that of "a believer" who, having a conception of ecstasy "firmly established in his mind . . . wishes to convince his audience" of its validity (11). The stylistic technique is one of quantification and accumulation of evidence (12) and of hyperbole (13), both enlivened by the "rhythm of a simple spoken speech" (14). At its midpoint the analysis remains on this formal, almost New Critical plane and is stylistic only in the simplest definition of that concept. It might more accurately be called "structural" in its close investigation of the specific features of the text. For it to be stylistic, in the Spitzerian framework, this structural description must be related to the author's perceptual framework, and the interpretation must move into the realm of literary and linguistic history.

This final step begins with Spitzer's brief midpoint summary. The poem is the concretization of "an intuitive state of mind," Spitzer argues. He then follows this claim by describing creativity in much the same manner as he did in Proust. Searching for a compromise between history and cross-cultural aesthetics, Spitzer declares that Donne has created the timeless representation of "an experience which must have developed in time" (15). In this way, the specific historical experience is lifted out of history so that Spitzer can allow Donne to direct the experience without being determined by it. "Donne does not re-enact what is within him, but points us to something above him" (14), Spitzer declares, thus ensuring that the aesthetic project transcends the individual experience.

But this construction of an implied author only provides a fulcrum for the analysis of the second half of the poem, which Spitzer finds "poetically less successful that the rest" (15). With a not very subtle pun, Spitzer speculates on the composition of the poem's closing lines. "Any reader must feel here a poetic anti-climax," he notes wryly, and then suggests in a trailing aside that the reader "may even suspect composition of that last part at a different time" (15). The speculation is offered as a way of addressing Spitzer's belief that the poem drops from the higher ecstatic and aesthetic level to a weaker, more mundane plane: "Donne . . . wished to make the ecstatic vision tributary to the daily life which must follow," but he has failed. And in that failure, Spitzer indicates, we see not just the abstract poet, but Donne as he falls, Icarus-like, from the heights of the sublime. We are led to feel somehow "that Donne, himself, . . . was more intimately convinced of the reality and beauty of the spiritual union than of the necessity of the body for that union. It may well be that the basically Protestant mind of Donne is responsible for this self-contradictory attitude" (16).

The tension that Spitzer finds in Donne's theme serves to underline a familiar tension in Spitzer's own thinking. Just as the poem struggles to close the gap between the sublime and the mundane, so the analysis struggles to accomodate both an aesthetic encomium and a specific historical description. Once more, the tension between a Romantically based, synthetic aestheticism and a particularizing formal analysis makes itself felt, and now Spitzer points directly to that unsolved interpretive equation by noting the similarity between Donne's intellectual struggles and those of the present, most particularly those of Spitzer the critic. The tension of Donne's writing "has made [him] so dear to our age," Spitzer declares, because this is "an age sore perplexed, mistrusting intellectual emotion— preferring, perhaps, clarity of analysis to syntheses which it can no longer whole-heartedly ratify" (18). Spitzer's reading of the poem thus reenacts his basic critical problem: How is the post-Romantic literary-critical desire for cross-historical significance to be satisfied by an analysis of the pedestrian materials of linguistic form and individual authorial experience? What justifies a bridge thrown between author and style, writer and text, history and universal expression?

Spitzer's answer in 1950 is indirect, resting mainly in whatever personal arguments Spitzer can provide, since both linguistics and literary criticism have decided that there can be no justification. The introduction of Donne's experience ensures the contextual coloration that Spitzer's stylistic theory requires—the presence of a particular intentional construct within a historical framework. But that requirement only exists as a part of Spitzer's individual definition of style and stylistics. The necessity of moving from text to author rests almost solely on Spitzer's authority: agree to his definition of style and you agree to the necessity for reading as he does. To argue that speculating on Donne's authorial intentions and compositional difficulties is both unnecessary and invalid is to deny Spitzer's epistemological arguments about style, a denial that has been made regularly, of course, but one which Spitzer simply (and rightly) ignores. If we grant Spitzer his definition (and there is no pressing reason not to), the only valid complaints are those that address the quality of the reading and the degree of speculation upon which it depends. Simply put, the most pertinent question is whether the interpretation that grows out of "the smallest artistic organism" can provide sufficient support for a full stylistic analysis, given the need to postulate a context and an authorial psyche that defines the individual work.

The answer must be no—an answer with which Spitzer would agree— and one that drives the wedge of history between his stylistics and the acontextual arguments of the New Criticism. While Spitzer shares the critical interest in organicism, the historical drive of his reading places him more surely within the Continental criticism from which he again has begun to draw his strength. When Spitzer interprets the work of Voltaire in the next essay, an assumed familiarity with the corpus of Voltaire appears throughout the study and is joined by historical as well as literary materials. Far from being the analysis of an isolated piece, this essay is a close study of a work that first is placed within the milieu of all of Voltaire's writing and then is encompassed by the context of French letters. The actual process of interpreting the literature thus does not differ drastically from the philological circle as it was outlined three years earlier in his essay "Linguistics and Literary History." Both studies, limited on the surface to brief individual works (but united through the reading skills of Spitzer) proceed through the formal details of a work (broadened to include general themes as well as linguistic details), find significant points of usage, and finish with the formation of a stylistic portrait based upon, as Spitzer says of Voltaire, a glimpse at "the inner geology of psychical strata" (97). The analytical changes seem to be in name rather than procedure, and that particular change serves primarily as a means of declaring critical empathy with French methods.

The view of what constitutes acceptable historical detail certainly remains that of the philological circle. Spitzer's opening to *Linguistics and Literary History* satirizes the "sensitive plant" who would avoid analyzing the aesthetic phenomenon (30n). Yet the analysis of history outlined there displays some of his own phobias about entering the forbidden territory of historical reality, of which Meyer-Lübke supposedly taught more than did Becker. "[I]t was unquestionable," Spitzer tells us, "that Latin *a* had evolved to French *e;* it was untrue that Molière's experience with the possibly faithless Madelaine Béjart had evolved to the work of art *École des femmes*" (4). The separation is clear: Spitzer's literary history deals with literary sensibilities, not with particular historical issues. The artistic soul remains the best unifying factor that Spitzer can find; the aesthetic response, the best bulwark against the positivistic reductionism Spitzer fears.

The equation having been found, it still is not easy for Spitzer to identify the components of this spiritual and cultural psyche that unifies history and expression in an organicist aesthetics. Part of the justification for this framework consists of Spitzer's proposal in *A Method of Interpreting Literature* for a type of "symbolizing thinking" (132n), a proposal that he ties to the philological circle of *Linguistics and Literary History*. What is needed, he declares, is "to see the relationship between an everyday detail which is, all too often, simply taken for granted, and a spiritual entity in itself not unknown, but only vaguely and separately conceived— this is, I believe, to take a step toward the understanding of the well-motivated, coherent, and consistent organism which our civilization is" (132n). This declaration occurs in the essay on advertising, an essay that also repeats Spitzer's desire to make his analyses more immediately relevant. The argument that advertising offers "a fulfillment of the *aesthetic* desires of modern humanity" (132) provides Spitzer with a blend of the aesthetic and the cultural. At the same time, the reference back to *Lin-*

guistics and Literary History echoes Spitzer's attempt to introduce "ideo-logical patterns" as a way of uniting history and literary expression.

Both definitions lack specificity, but they add two more bricks to the pile that Spitzer has been collecting in order to construct his bridge from text to context. The foundations for that bridge were laid with Spitzer's early use of Freud, his rejection of Vossler and Croce, and his insistence on a stylistics rooted in linguistic history. Spitzer's old arguments are now repeating themselves in his rejection of an overly sensitive aestheticism and his use of some historical and biographical data to provide a fuller *explication de texte*. This flurry of study and cross-reference leaves Spitzer on the edge of producing a justification for his stylistics based not on a general literary foundation, but on a unified foundation of the historical, social, and psychological issues holding together the real bridge linking cognition and style.

Yet a Romantic concept of literary relevance jars with this vision. Spitzer makes his study of the Sunkist advertisement relevant by declaring that it is "popular art," if not high art. But hidden behind this democratization of artistic expression lies Spitzer's desire for a hierarchy in which art and the artist, as the uppermost level of intellectual consciousness, provide Spitzer's stylistic arguments with the relevance required for Spitzer to battle the academic setting of 1950 and its attachment to positivism. By making literary history the ultimate arbiter of cultural sensibility, Spitzer collapses social history into literary history. And while he will not disavow the Freudian influence on his early work, it becomes clear that Spitzer's desire to avoid "the all-too-human 'complexes' which, in Freud's opinion, are supposed to color the writing of the great figures of literature" provides an impetus for looking at the history of ideas and ideational issues. It does not, despite Spitzer's use of the phrase, display a deep interest in "ideo-logical patterns" (32n).

In presenting these arguments Spitzer implies that his shift away from Freud rests upon a necessary separation between individual human com-plexes and cultural ideological patterns, a belief underscored by his ref-erence to the "all-too-human" quality of the Freudian complexes. But the separation that Spitzer posits remains a function of his incorrect sense that psychoanalytic interpretation separates personal formation from cul-tural description, and his opposition is at least partially justified by those psychoanalytic readings that Trilling graciously terms "sensational but unfortunate."[10] In 1918 Spitzer had dared to walk through the door that Freud had opened between language and the mind. By 1949 it would have been difficult to overcome the general antipathy created by early psychoanaltyic readings that Claudia Morrison, less reticent than Trilling, has characterized as "offensively dogmatic, over-simplified, and woefully lacking in appreciation of aesthetic expression." These early attempts at practical psychoanalytic interpretation "represent the worst kind of formula-writing," and such reductionism makes them anethema to Spitzer.[11]

Spitzer confirms his beliefs about Freud and ideology in response to Kenneth Burke's work.[12] It is a key response, for it occurs at a moment when Spitzer has the chance to extend the purview of historical context by embracing the work of a scholar who, like Spitzer and Lovejoy, is struggling to refine the historical reading. At the same time, in Burke's own struggles we find a repetition of the same difficulties dogging both Spitzer and Lovejoy's attempts to find the correct framework for an adequate historical reading. In all their work, then, we can recognize a similar mapping of the pressures that the aesthetic interpretation places upon the historical reading.

The particular similarities between Spitzer and Burke run the gamut from a concern with method (rooted in a distrust of mechanistic science and excessively rigid methodologies) to an interest in Freud as a validating figure for literary criticism (and a rejection of fixed psychoanalytic interpretations). All their similarities display a deep undercurrent of belief in the centrality of style within literary description. Like Spitzer, Burke also refuses to equate all of science with positivist approaches, although the call for objectivity is not rejected outright but met with a claim for equal objectivity in poetic description. Spitzer's often-repeated goal of a "more rigorously scientific definition of . . . style" is echoed in Burke's own belief that his psychology of poetry comes "as near to the use of objective, empirical evidence as even the physical sciences" (21). What Burke seeks in his criticism is not simply a given set of procedures equal to those followed by the physical sciences, but a set of coordinates that would allow for the integration of the social sciences and literary criticism into a kindred human science. He thus pursues a humanistic literary criticism that will serve as "the logical alternative to the treatment of human acts and relations in terms of the mechanistic metaphor (stimulus, response, and the conditioned reflex)" (105–6).

Burke's goals demonstrate a concern for the complexities of literature and a healthy mistrust of positivistic descriptive procedures that match well with Spitzer's concerns. At the same time, his general critical procedure of reading, analyzing, and re-reading fits nicely alongside Spitzer's philological circle.[13] Nor does Burke sense that this mistrust of overly specific procedures relieves him of the need to define a critical methodology. Like Spitzer, he may contrast the complexity of the creative process with the procedures of analytic methodology, but the pressure to offer a critical method remains. To fail to do so in the unfolding academic environment is to be faced with charges of subjectivity and critical weakness. Burke, who is well aware of that pressure, announces that he feels "prodded" to describe his methods "because my procedures have been characterized as 'intuitive' and 'idiosyncratic,' epithets that make me squirm" (68). But there is more than discomfort at work here: "It is 'poetic' to develop method; it is 'scientific' to develop methodology . . . [and] the ideal of literary criticism is a 'scientific' ideal" (130). Proposing a particular methodology qualifies the literary critic for work. Once qualified, the critic's real task begins: to define the quality of that work both intrinsically and extrinsically.

Burke's own procedural definition includes the use of Freud in an attempt to describe literature and style in terms of certain " 'associational clusters' " (20). Spitzer agrees that this clustering approach is "very close to the Freudian (and to my own, as far as it was influenced by Freud),"[14] although he finds Burke's particular application troubling. Like Spitzer, Burke recognizes the problems that dominate much psychoanalytic criticism of the period and, again like Spitzer, Burke finds that much Freudian analysis of art is "handicapped by the aesthetic of the period—an aesthetic that placed the emphasis wholly upon the function of self-expression" (280). Unlike Spitzer, Burke decides to qualify rather than reject the place of the individual in this expressive frame. His argument for the applicability of psychoanalysis broadens the importance of historical fact rather than assuming that such analysis will lead to historical and biographical determinism:

> Only if we eliminate biography entirely as a relevant fact about poetic organization can we eliminate the importance of the psychoanalyst's search for universal patterns of biography (as revealed in the search for basic myths which recur in new guises as a theme with variations); and we can eliminate biography as a relevant fact about poetic organization only if we consider the work of art as if it were written neither by people nor for people, involving neither inducements nor resistances. Such can be done, but the cost is tremendous in so far as the critic considers it his task to disclose the poem's eventfulness. [285–86]

Burke's description uses biography as a link between the particular and the general, the historical and the universal. Critical and imaginative works are not simply universal expressions, they are also "answers to questions posed by the situation in which they arose"; even more importantly, the works are not merely answers, "they are *strategic* answers, *stylized* answers" (1). As such, they are a definable part of general literary and psychological processes and not the personal "phobias and idiosyncrasies" (*Linguistics and Literary History*, 32n) that Spitzer sees as the structural fault of the psychoanalytic study.

Burke thus replaces Spitzer's general aesthetics of style by arguing for a stylistics that is validated by general patterns of motivation and behavior, and then he uses that argument to deny the historical determinism of his model. All situations have "public content," he notes, "and in so far as situations overlap from individual to individual, or from one historical period to another, the strategies possess universal relevance" (1). In place of the spiritual universals of Spitzer, Burke offers a universality of common behavior—a rhetorically universal act as opposed to an aesthetically universal sensibility. While this whole call for universalism remains problematic, Burke's vision is clearly more rooted in daily behavior than Spitzer's.

Spitzer and Burke thus begin with shared views and struggle equally with the tension between a universalizing aestheticism and a deterministic historicism. Yet their attempts to resolve that tension go in opposing directions. "The main ideal of criticism," as Burke conceives of it, "is to use all that there is to use" (23), and because he defines style as a particular strategy for a particular situation, all material—including that from disciplines such as history, anthropology, sociology, and psychology—can be used to develop the description of that scene and the validity of his reading of it. Burke's encapsulation of the situation-strategy design justifies that inclusivity. "The poet is not poetizing in the middle of nowhere," he argues; "though his poem may be viewed purely within itself ('in terms of' its internal consistency), it is also the act of an agent in a non-literary scene" (viii). At the same time, Burke provides a ready answer to the charge that such an approach limits criticism to those authors who are biographically available: "Please get me straight: I am *not* saying that we need know of Coleridge's marital troubles and sufferings from drug addiction in order to appreciate 'The Ancient Mariner' and other poems wherein the same themes figure. I am saying that, in trying to understand the psychology of the poetic act, we may introduce such knowledge, where it is available, to give us material necessary for discussing the full nature of this act" (73).

But we cannot simply assume that Burke, faced with the same desires and the same restricting critical ambience, succeeds in producing the intepretive model that keeps eluding Spitzer. The desire to provide a particular contextual framework for every study can and does lead Burke into some unbridled speculation, most particularly, linguistic specula-tion.[15] It is worth noting that Burke has difficulty precisely in that area in which Spitzer is most expert. More important, however, is the degree to which Burke's focus on the drama and rhetoric of the historical moment is refracted by the aestheticism of his own critical period. Burke's insis-tence on the historical structure of ideology (as opposed to Spitzer's con-stellation of ideas) underscores the Romantic coloration of Spitzer's vision of literature. But the power of the critical moment also makes an equivalent victim of Burke. Both Fredric Jameson and Frank Lentricchia have pointed out that Burke does not fully resolve the tension present in his link between the historical particular and the universal. Jameson "regret[s] that Burke finally did not want to teach us history, even though he wanted to teach us how to grapple with it."[16] Lentricchia is even more specific: "Contra-dictory as such a suggestion will sound, I think it necessary to characterize one level of his theory as a *rhetoric of nature*, with his emphasis on rhetoric moving us deeply into the affairs of the world that we make, even as his emphasis on unchanging, culturally and historically unmodifiable capacities of response would seem to move us beyond."[17]

Spitzer's rejection of Burke on the same grounds as his rejection of Freud and his "all-too-human complexes" mirrors Lentricchia's descrip-tion of Burke's divided attempt to resolve the tension between the his-torical and the universal. And while Spitzer's own method fails to offer a satisfactory substitute, his continuing hope that psychological methods offer some kind of answer surfaces in his subsequent inclusion of Freud on the list of *explication*'s formative influences. Along with Auerbach's enumeration of Croce's aesthetics, Husserl's phenomenology, Wölfflinn's analyses, and many other currents running through the background of *explication*, Spitzer "personally would list Freud's analysis of the psycho-logical laws governing the expression of the subconscious" (Spitzer, *Essays in British and American Literature*, 194n). Having introduced Freudian theory as part of the philosophical background of *explication de texte*, Spitzer takes time to expand upon the general influence of Freudian thought on his work and its misinterpretation by Wellek and Warren in their *Theory of Literature*. Unlike Auerbach, who fails to mention the influence of Freud, Spitzer feels that Wellek and Warren do little else: "the authors have only taken into consideration my earlier Freudian beginnings in which mental deviation from the normal in modern, mostly pathologically warped writers was shown to explain linguistic deviation or innovation, not my maturer work in *explication de texte* which deals with writers of all periods and attempts to explain particular stylistic traits by their historical or cultural background" (194n).[18]

By broadening his vision of the psychoanalytic reading, Spitzer implies that a psychological stylistics need not apply "only to the study of 'pathological' writers," and argues that the philological circle, as undertaken within *explication de texte*, moves from the detail to "an inference as to the (at this state still hypothetic) psyche of the author or the period" (194n). Spitzer is willing, moreover, to uncover this psyche in any historical period. But while psychology may be used to justify this descriptive plan, there is little development of the particular way in which a Freudian or other model of mind will be integrated into the Spitzerian analytical model. The movement from the psychological discussion to the presentation of the psyche remains, as Wellek later notes, an invocation of "the standard of historical representativeness" ("Leo Spitzer," 328). Like Burke, Spitzer is caught between his desire to define style via a historical psyche and the critical requirement of more universal aesthetic values.

An explicit model of the individual psyche and its creativity could provide a more specific historical context—a context that could in turn provide further validation for the stylistic analysis—but Spitzer does not try to counter the methodological superiority of positivism with a similar refinement in procedures. Instead, he offers a vision of organic synthesis to oppose the temporal, cultural, and social fragmentation ascribed to positivistic methods. Spitzer's concept of literary production remains rooted in the Romantic definition of individual creativity, as his own statements indicate. Even as he rejects Burke's " 'individual' associations," he characteristically refuses to reject the idea of "great literary 'individuals' " (32n). Style remains the individual manipulation of the language within an historical context, while Spitzer's Romantic belief in the creative power of the individual leads to a paradoxical overwhelming of the specifics of context: "Whoever has thought strongly or felt strongly has innovated in his language; mental creativity immediately inscribes itself into the language, where it becomes linguistic creativity; the trite and petrified in language is never sufficient for the needs of expression felt by a strong personality." The "strong personality" of the artist overshadows the paradoxical union/rupture between the individual and the historical that results from this organicism. The artist's expressive strength allows the individual, as cultural hero, to escape from specific historical events, even while embodying the culture's wider historical desires and beliefs.[19]

The difficulty created by Spitzer's Romantic solution of the historical/ universal tension is clear. He has moved, in his words, from the " 'all-too-human' complexes" of Freud to "ideological patterns" (*Linguistics and Literary History*, 32n). But he also has limited ideology and psychology to the realm of the ideational and the aesthetic rather than allowing for a broadening of the ideological frame to include the situational commonplaces of history and behavior—those explanations that Burke declares to have been "*unnecessarily*" exiled to the social sciences by the "rise of aesthetics" within literary criticism (x). And if Burke's insistence upon defining ideas and ideology in terms of the particulars of history fails to provide an ultimate resolution of the tension between the historical and the aesthetic interpretation, neither does Spitzer's attempt to provide a different vision of literary history save him from the contradictions between his desire for historical interpretation and the dominant value attached to literature by the Romantic epistemology of New Criticism.

As late as 1960 Spitzer would echo the rubrics of New Criticism by declaring that the biographical fallacy partially explains his movement away from psychological stylistics. But the full degree of New Critical opposition to historical issues qualifies Spitzer's allegiance, and he consigns himself to partial isolation by his insistence on this historical reading. The resulting division in Spitzer's theoretical goals is readily displayed in his divided response to Harold Cherniss's attack on "The Biographical Fashion in Literary Criticism."[20] Much of Cherniss's presentation depends upon an argued difference between the historian and the philologian. He does not wish to enter into "the old and rancorous debate concerning the relationship of philology and history" (280). But even as Cherniss announces that intention—declaring that the true study of literature is the study of literature for its own sake—he readmits the tension surrounding the debate by acknowledging that contextual features seem to be a useful accompaniment for any reading. "If a work of literature is the significant expression of thought," he asks, how is understanding possible "without intimate knowledge of the physical and spiritual environment, of the political, economic, and social conditions in which the thought was formulated and to which its expression responded?" (281). It is the question of a classical philologian, and the rest of Cherniss's article consists of a determined effort to limit the damage done by his honest admission that historical and biographical material inform the philological analysis.

Cherniss's article is thus an attempt to regulate, since it cannot seem to eliminate, the presence of the historical context in literary criticism. By and large he does so by offering extreme versions of historical interpetations, thus rendering the process absurd. It is in this vein of argumentation that he mentions the practical impossibility of fully re-creating any work's historical context (according to Cherniss, the "necessary conclusion" (282) of the call for historical contextualization). While he willingly subscribes to "the doctrine that no detail of knowledge is useless," Cherniss questions whether the total reconstruction of a historical context will "not justify despair in the strongest and most ambitious spirits" (284). Since full historical reconstruction lies beyond the critic's capacity and can be dismissed, only biography remains as a final means of contextual interpretation. There are easy negative arguments here as well, however, and Cherniss seizes on the complaint that interpretation is impossible in those cases where no biography does or can exist.

But as Cherniss moves to embrace this straw man, he inadvertently stumbles over the paradox of his argument. The role of the critical reading, as Cherniss sees it, is to lift the text out of the merely historical in order to ensure its position as high art. In order to ensure that end he downplays the value of biographical material: "the external incidents of the author's life have meaning only so far as they are assimilated to his personality, and literary significance only so far as they have been transmuted by that personality into artistic form" (287). Cherniss's argument for this aesthetic transubstantiation declares that the historical substance of the text is not what it appears to be. When offered up as art, the historical material of the author's life and personality mysteriously becomes something else, and in so doing becomes unimportant as history. Yet this statement, like the others, does not really argue against the value of biographical or historical materials in a critical reading; it only substitutes an aesthetic value for the supposedly weak value of the historical.

Like Cherniss, Spitzer believes that the aesthetic concerns of criticism and philology are the primary means of ensuring the intellectual value of the critical reading. Unlike Cherniss, however, Spitzer remains committed to his stylistic goal of portraying authorial sensibility. Any such intention lies beyond the pale for Cherniss, who parts company with Spitzer over both goal and method in a specific attack on the intuitional reading of the Stefan George school. Spitzer admits that a reliance upon intuition, "with its deliberate implications of extraordinary mystic qualities on the part of the critic," vitiates the reasoning of the Stefan George school (34n). Spitzer wishes to put "intelligent reading" in its place, and with a quick combination of ideas, he links Cherniss's later use of the phrase with a discussion of the philological circle: "the procedure from details to the inner core and back again is not at all vicious; in fact the 'intelligent reading' which Professor Cherniss advocates without defining (though he is forced to grant rather uncomfortably that it is 'a certain native insight, call it direct intelligence or intuition as you please') is based precisely on that very philogical circle" (34n). In rejecting Cherniss's arguments on this point, Spitzer also is rejecting the analysis that proceeds in a contextual vacuum, and his reasons for doing so are apparent in the difficulties that Cherniss faces as he carries his theory to its logical conclusion.

Having eliminated all but the text itself from his reading, Cherniss is left to validate his approach via the reader, and he faces the same difficulties there as those generated by today's reader-centered arguments. The immediate possibility of supposedly incorrect readings must be dealt with, and Cherniss does so with a quick call for the universal significance of literature and its foundation in "a set of ideas, emotions, and values which thus far in the history of the civilized world at least have always been recognized as having validity beyond the arbitrary taste of any individual or the customs of any locality" (290). The Romanticism of this vague portrait is readily apparent, and Cherniss's earlier comment that such values are available to "all men as men" further undercuts the universality of his vision with an ideological bias all its own. That bias is deepened further by Cherniss's move to thin the ranks of those men and to control their behavior, hastily making sure that any unwanted interlopers are stopped at the door. He does not mean to imply that "anyone, by reason of his humanity alone, can understand any literary work that is set before him" (290). There is a hierarchy of readers and readings to be acknowledged here, and with that one fell swoop of elitist interpretation, Cherniss undercuts his argument for a universal reading. The only means of accomplishing true appreciation, he admits, is through the "intelligent reading" (290)—a reading accomplished through the help of those "other studies" that reappear here at the end of the article.

Cherniss's essay thus produces two unexpected critical insights at its close: it provides an unintended but devastating reversal of the innocent reading, and in doing so it reestablishes the importance of external ma-

terials for criticism. It also reaffirms, yet again, the value of the historical
issues that Spitzer refuses to abandon. Faced with Cherniss's call for the
self-contained and self-absorbed text, Spitzer asserts the value of providing
a portrait of the author and the context of production. Spitzer's thinking
on style thus has the merit of rejecting the New Critical pseudodemoc-
ratizing of the text. But that rejection does not guarantee the subsequent
appearance of an acceptable interpretive model, and Spitzer needs that
model for two reasons: to resolve the historical/creative tension in his
stylistic portrait and to provide the methodological clout needed to combat
the nonhistorical criticism of the period. Simply recognizing the importance of an historically oriented interpretive model is not equivalent to
escaping from the pressures of the aesthetic reading—as Burke's own
difficulties so amply display. Spitzer's rejection of the ahistorical reading
is destined to become a Pyrrhic victory of sorts. With the now-burgeoning
field of general linguistics in control of most linguistically oriented criticism
by 1955, stylistics is about to embark upon twenty years of formalist
description, try as Spitzer will to demonstrate its limitations. His long
clash with the young Michael Riffaterre, which is discussed in the next
chapter, perfectly displays the tenor of those years.

NOTES

1. See Yakov Malkiel's comments in "Comparative Romance Linguistics," *Current Trends in Linguistics*, ed. Thomas A. Sebeok, vol. 9 (The
Hague: Mouton, 1972), 835–925. Among the discipline's other needs,
Malkiel notes the importance of reestablishing "a much-needed rapport
with general linguistics, which has somehow been lost in the last few
decades" (835–36).

2. Leo Spitzer, *Linguistics and Literary History: Essays in Stylistics*
(Princeton, N.J.: Princeton University Press, 1948; rpt. Russell & Russell,
1962) and *A Method of Interpreting Literature* (Northampton, Mass.:
Smith College, 1949; rpt. New York: Russell & Russell, 1967).

3. See, for example, his comments in his study of Racine: "As is my
custom in style studies, I shall take Racine as a star in himself, as an
entire, internally stable cosmos. I leave to other scholars the task of
presenting these attenuations, taken here as it were absolutely, in terms
of their relationships to pre-existing models, that is to say historically"
("Die klassische Dämpfung in Racines Stil," *Archivum Romanicum*, 12

[1928] 361–472; "Racine's Classical *piano*," in *Leo Spitzer: Essays on Seventeenth-Century French Literature*, ed. and trans. David Bellos [Cambridge: Cambridge University Press, 1983], 4).

4. The argument also relates Rabelais to Pulci and recalls, not only the argument with Lovejoy, but that with Hall, since Pulci arises in that discussion. Very little is wasted by Spitzer; very little is unrelated to other ideas or arguments.

5. In 1945 (the same year that the preface to *Linguistics and Literary History* was completed), Spitzer published "Das Eigene und das Fremde." The article, as described by Bellos, provided a "blueprint" for the revitalization of the study of the German languages: "It was the fundamental text for Hans-Robert Jauss and his generation, the text which made sense of their position and of the project of studying a foreign literature" (Bellos, *Essays*, xxiv). (Leo Spitzer, "Das Eigene und das Fremde. Über Philologie und Nationalismus," *Die Wandlung*, 1 [1945–46], 566–94.)

6. Leo Spitzer, "The Formation of the American Humanist," *PMLA*, 66 (1951), 39–48. The life of scholarship that Spitzer portrays is attractive enough in its scholarly dedication, but it smacks of the priestly. Rather than being free to enjoy "the sober sweetness of a life entirely devoted to scholarship," the young American scholar finds "his" time fragmented by the demands of the classroom and of early publication. True enough. But the rest of Spitzer's argument does "make things worse," to turn his words back on himself. "And to make things worse," he hesitates to tell us, "our students marry too early and thus are forced to give preeminence in their decisions to financial questions." Still there are some saving graces in an early marriage; students "avoid the soiling effect on mind and body of prostitution and debauchery; they will lead a pure life, enabled as they are to search for its meaning together with a companion worthy of them" (41). The attitudes are at best annoying, at worst misogynistic.

7. Leo Spitzer, "American Advertising Explained as Popular Art," *A Method of Interpreting Literature* (Northampton, Mass.: 1949; rpt. New York: Russell & Russell, 1967), 102–49.

8. Spitzer, "*Explication de Texte* Applied to Three Great Middle English Poems," *Archivum Linguisticum*, 3 (1951), 1–22, 157–65; rpt. in *Essays on English and American Literature*, ed. Anna G. Hatcher (Princeton, N.J.: Princeton University Press, 1962, 193–247; rpt. New York: Gordian Press, 1984), 193–94n.

9. Spitzer argues that the literary critic "who is able to draw on his historical knowledge, may discount the periodically recurring revolt of poets against critics who would explain their poetry" (1–2), and he does so by explaining some lines by Shapiro in terms of his wartime experiences.

10. Lionel Trilling, *The Liberal Imagination* (New York: Viking Press, 1950), 36.

11. Claudia Morrison, *Freud and the Critic* (Chapel Hill: University of North Carolina, 1968), 99.

12. Spitzer, *Linguistics and Literary History*, 32n. Spitzer is referring to Burke's *The Philosophy of Literary Form* (1941; rpt. Berkeley: University of California Press, 1973).

13. In *The Philosophy of Literary Form* Burke offers a number of quick vignettes that point to the read, analyze, check, and read again process of Spitzer: "To know what 'shoe, or house, or bridge' means, you don't begin with a 'symbolist dictionary' already written in advance. You must, by inductive inspection of a given work, discover the particular contexts in which the shoe, house, or bridge occurs. You cannot, in advance, know in what equational structure it will have membership.

"By inspection of the work, you propose your description of this equational structure. Your propositions are open to discussion, as you offer your evidence for them and show how much of the plot's development your description would account for. 'Closer approximations' are possible, accounting for more. The method, in brief, can be built upon, in contrast with essentializing stategies of motivation that all begin anew" (89).

And again, Burke states later: "The critic should adopt a variant of the free-association method. One obviously cannot invite an author, especially a dead author, to oblige him by telling what the author thinks of when the critic isolates some detail or other for improvisation. But what he can do is to note the context of imagery and ideas in which an image takes its place. He can also note, by such analysis, the kinds of evaluations surrounding the image of a crossing; for instance, is it an escape from or a return to an evil or a good, etc.? Until, finally, by noting the ways in which this crossing behaves, what subsidiary imagery accompanies it, what kind of event it grows out of, what kind of event grows out of it, what altered rhythmic and tonal effects characterize it, etc., one grasps its significance as motivation. And there is no essential motive offered here. The motive of the work is equated with the structure of interrelationships within the work itself" (267).

14. Leo Spitzer, *Linguistics and Literary History* (Princeton, N.J.: Princeton University Press, 1948; rpt. Russell & Russell, 1962), 32n. Although he doesn't say so, it would seem likely that Spitzer's concept of "symbolic thinking" may also have been influenced by Burke. See the previous discussion of *A Method of Interpreting Literature*.

15. See, for example, his discussion of the origin of language (*The Philosophy*, 12–16).

16. Fredric Jameson, "The Symbolic Inference; or, Kenneth Burke and Ideological Analysis," in *Selected Papers of the English Institute,* ed. Hayden White and Margaret Brose (Baltimore, Md.: Johns Hopkins University Press, 1982), 90.

17. Frank Lentricchia, *Criticism and Social Change* (Chicago: University of Chicago, 1983), 92.

18. Spitzer equates Wellek and Warren's refusal to accept his methodology with the positivism that he regularly opposes. He declares that Wellek and Warren argue, "in the manner that has become traditional with the school of unregenerate positivists from which these critics are usually miles away . . ." (194n), that his procedures lack objectivity. Whether Wellek felt that his 1960 eulogy of Spitzer was a response to Spitzer's challenge is not clear. But he continues to reject the philological circle, no matter what the starting point: "However ingenious Spitzer's observations and interpretations may be, it seems to me impossible to prove that the *etymon,* the *radix,* or simply the *Weltanschauung* of the writer was inferred purely on the basis of linguistic observation. It would be impossible to show that the stylistic traits were all deduced from a knowledge of the author's temperment or world view" ("Leo Spitzer," *Comparative Literature,* 12 [1960], 317). Wellek's implication that Spitzer claims to begin with a *tabula rasa* is not completely accurate.

19. Leo Spitzer, *Linguistics and Literary History,* 15. This statement occurs in a section of the essay arguing that not just modern writers, but writers such as Dante, Quevedo, and Rabelais reveal an "inward form" expressed through the "outward crystallization" of language (18). The argument concludes with Spitzer's note on Freud and Burke.

20. Harold Cherniss, "The Biographical Fashion in Literary Criticism," *University of California Publications in Classical Philology,* 12, no. 15 (1943), 279–92. Wellek and Warren also argue for a negative equivalency between the cultural sensibility and the biographical that Spitzer is trying to define: "Indeed, however ingenious some of its suggestions may be, psychological stylistics seems open to two objections. Many relationships professing to be thus established are not based on conclusions really drawn from the linguistic material but rather start with a psychological and ideological analysis and seek for confirmation in language. This would be unexceptionable if in practice the linguistic confirmation did not itself seem frequently strained or based on very slight evidence. Work of this type often assumes that true, or great, art must be based on experience, *Erlebnis,* a term which invokes a slightly revised version of the biographical fallacy." (*Theory of Literature* [New York: Harcourt, Brace and Company, 1942], 187–88).

This argument actually conflates a complaint about the verifiability of the reading with a rejection of Romantic expressionism. There are some valid arguments to be made about both questions, but they need to be more clearly separated before any answers are reached.

6 The Ascendancy of the New Linguistic Stylistics
Context-Free Style and the Desire for Method

Anglo-American literary stylistics underwent a period of rapid growth from 1955 to 1970, a growth fostered by trends in both literary criticism and linguistic theory. In criticism, the high aesthetics of Leavis and Richards in Britain and of the New Criticism in the United States had peaked, and any stylistics attached to them was facing a period of decline. At the same time, Saussurian, American structural, and trans-formational-generative linguistics finalized the departure of historical studies from the forefront of linguistic study.[1] In 1953 Charles Bruneau provided a succinct verdict on the future of stylistic study: the *stylistique* of Bally was to be the precursor of pure stylistics, by which Bruneau meant scientific and linguistic stylistics.[2] Spitzer's literary stylistic studies were "excellent," Bruneau admitted, but they were also less pure, more applied and, most problematic of all, nonscientific. Such studies were to be exiled to the realm of "another order" (11), thus repeating the separation established in 1910 between *stylistique* and *Stilforschung*, but one which now (thanks to the immense value attached to scientific procedures) left literary stylistics scrambling for validity. The choices facing the study of style were obvious: stylistics could adapt to the linguistic goals of scientific efficiency, or it could accept a reduction in intellectual and academic status. Method, increasingly, was the word of the day.

The ensuing struggle to blend scientific method with literary analysis is exemplified in the early work of Michael Riffaterre, whose *Le Style des Pléiades de Gobineau: essai d'application d'une méthode stylistique*, "Criteria for Style Analysis," (1959), and "Stylistic Context," (1960) were a bold attempt to unite Spitzer's Romance tradition with that of Bloomfield's linguistics.[3] It was an attempt befitting Spitzer's own early struggles, but Riffaterre's work was troubled from the outset by an excessive commitment to the linguistic formalism of the day, a commitment that entailed a necessary lowering of interest in the historical and social forces that shaped a style. Eventually Riffaterre himself would feel that constraint and move on to the larger environs offered by semiotics. But stylistics would continue to follow the formal and ahistorical course established by linguistic theory, keeping pace until 1973, when the isolated text was finally shattered through a growing interest in the role of the reader in critical interpretation.[4] Interest in a contextually defined stylistics would be reawakened, but only after twenty years of sleep.

During this twenty-year hiatus there were, of course, other approaches to style that did follow Spitzer's lead, as the title of Helmut Hatzfeld's "Stylistics as Art-Minded Philology" (1949) indicated.[5] Spitzer occupied a central role in Hatzfeld's definition of the "new stylistics" as Hatzfeld saw it from within the confines of Romance philology. But the seeds of future difficulties already were planted within Hatzfeld's emphasis on art, rather than history or linguistics, for his philological stylistics. Just as Spitzer had collapsed history into literary history, Hatzfeld leaned away from the labors of contextualizing style and toward a more loosely defined "Art-mindedness" (65). The resulting "crucial question" for Hatzfeld was a familiar one: How were "the decisive stylistic traits of a text" (66) to be formally defined while still linking them to the artist?

In 1949, Hatzfeld was willing to believe that the answer might lie in Spitzer's philological circle, a procedure that "would establish the new stylistics as an exact, controllable method" with "immense" consequences for criticism (66). The actual control over the circle through verification and external justification was to remain problematic, however. Thirty-two years later Hatzfeld would characterize Spitzer as "never satisfied with the merely aesthetic evaluation," and as searching "desperately for a way out or beyond this limitation" ("Leo Spitzer and Stephen Ullmann's Stylistic Criticism," 53), but in 1950 the exit offered by a wider view of history would not have appeared as a feasible part of that "exact, controllable method" for either Hatzfeld or Spitzer. Instead, Spitzer would continue to argue for the interpretive strength of the philological circle and its variant, *explication de texte*, on grounds more aesthetic than specifically historical.

This continued avoidance of objective procedures increased the distance between Spitzer's philology and general linguistic theory and exacerbated the already chafed relations between the linguistic mainstream and his Romance linguistics—even among critics less zealous than Hall. Discussions of Spitzer's readings during the fifties tend to divide themselves along roughly the same lines as those established by Spitzer himself: innumerable articles open with a positive reference to the talent and authority of Spitzer's interpretive powers, only to follow that praise with a less positive qualification of his methods and procedures. The qualification might address the basic analytic procedures of the method, or some portion of the method, such as the psychological features that it described, or the linguistic beliefs that lay beneath both. Whatever the point of qualification, the situation was clear. In this particular critical climate the value of method over interpretive talent was assured. Achieved interpretations were lauded, but general theoretical procedures were required.

Raphael Levy's 1949 review of *Essays in Historical Semantics* and *Linguistics and Literary History* offers a quiet preview of critical response to Spitzer that would characterize this period.[6] Much of Levy's review is dedicated to the refinement of various etymologies that appear in the *Essays*. When he takes up the more literary *Linguistics and Literary History*, Levy provides only a rather muted argument for openmindedness toward methods of stylistic inquiry. There is more than a hint that Levy wants to put some distance between linguistic history and literary criticism, and his transition from one book to the next sounds a somewhat uncertain note. "The procedure which jibes in one investigation is not necessarily the one which will jibe in another" (327–28), he remarks. These are uncharted waters, Levy clearly implies. "The reader," he warns, "will be disappointed if he expects to find what he is accustomed to call Linguistics and Literary History, but he will be amply rewarded if he wishes to learn more about Stylistics and Literary Criticism" (332). In 1950 Jean Hytier was more direct. His "La Méthode de M. Leo Spitzer"[7] opens with a lavish description of Spitzer's knowledge and authority as a reader and closes with a specific rejection of the Spitzerian method. Hytier endorses the "vigorous and brilliant" efforts of Spitzer's career (42); he notes Spitzer's far-ranging use of materials from literature, history, theology, philosophy, and psychoanalysis (43); and he describes Spitzer's keen understanding of artistic originality and literary tradition (43). Yet all of this praise only postpones Hytier's task of analyzing Spitzer's method—and finding it lacking.

Hytier approaches Spitzer's procedures from two directions: the or-

ganicist beliefs that lie beneath Spitzer's work and the actual procedures
that Spitzer follows. Addressing the issue of Spitzer's Romantic organicism, Hytier notes that Spitzer's historical sense is qualified by his desire
for a unifying spiritual essence within literature. Hytier is willing to grant
that some works have such an internal dynamism—"a fundamental inspiration" that unites subject, structure, and style (53)—but not all texts
are formed through such a unifying principle. In place of a belief in organic
structure Hytier offers a belief in constructed edifice; to the root aesthetic
drive behind a poem he opposes the poet's intentional struggle for unity
of expression. For Hytier, the literary text does not have the unique
simplicity that it holds for Spitzer, and the Romantic organicism that
allows Spitzer to envision art in this fashion has given way in Hytier to
a much more mundane linguistic activity. Significantly, Hytier does not
believe that Spitzer's own readings depend upon such unity. Spitzer's
critical interpretations are seen as resting on something other than the
organic nature of the text, his declared procedures, or a mysterious stylistic
essence. "Between the rhythmic scheme and the determination of the
essence diderotique," Hytier declares of Spitzer's essay on Diderot, "lies
all the talent of Spitzer" (55).

This talented interpretion does not need to be seen as subjective,
however. For Hytier, the simplest solution to that problem is to see the
procedure not as a method of discovery but as a method of exposition and
argument. If it pleases Spitzer to link the stylistic features of a text to an
initial intuition, "let's not quibble," Hytier decides (55). That white lie
accepted, the real heart of the argument can be shifted to issues of argument rather than of discovery.[8] And while Hytier's complaints about
those arguments stress the importance of including external contextual
and historical elements that would clarify and justify the stylistic portrait
that Spitzer puts forth, Hytier believes Spitzer recognizes, indeed announces, these elements even as he lays claim to an innocence in reading.

Hytier's basic qualifications are clearest in his discussion of the baroque,
where he refuses to entertain the definition of history and poetic creation
that Spitzer offers for that concept.[9] Instead, Hytier insists upon a definition of historical statement that is rooted in specific events and intentions. "It would be vain," Hytier supposes, to suggest to Spitzer that
Racine's supposed *Weltanschauung* lacks a close congruence with the
actual realities of Racine's life and beliefs. Hytier sees Racine as "a Christian for whom mythology is a source of poetry. . .and not a metaphysical
reservoir" (51–52). To Spitzer's larger cultural vision, Hytier simply adds

the vision of a historical individual formed by his situation, thus following the line of argument taken by Lovejoy and Burke. The view from this position may be less breathtaking, but it has the advantage of providing greater specificity and substance. The cultural portrait is fleshed out in an array of tones provided by events and ideas from the period, supplementing the more aesthetic vision provided by spiritual attitudes alone.

This need for a retreat from the aestheticization of literary history is not felt by Hytier or Lovejoy or Burke alone. Ten years later Wellek returns to endorse Spitzer's description of the baroque. But he is forced to qualify his endorsement, noting that while Spitzer is "quite aware of the dangers of reckless speculations about the nature of specific historical periods . . . ; he is willing to pronounce truths about the Middle Ages *in toto*, and to declare confidently this or that trait Renaissance or rococo" ("Leo Spitzer," 329). By 1983 Bellos's comments on the Racine essay simply echo Levy's 1949 worries about Spitzer's linguistic history. "One might say," Bellos offers, "that Spitzer's marriage of language and literature in his critical practice are achieved ultimately at the expense of linguistic and literary history" (*Essays*, xxiii). It is an expense that Bellos wishes Spitzer had not incurred: "It is obvious . . . that Spitzer not only needs but is constantly drawn towards the great schemas of intellectual and literary history, yet just as constantly draws back from any extended discussion of them. . . . This is, I think, a blemish in Spitzer's work, and one that is not a necessary blemish determined either by his cast of mind or by his in any case very flexible method" (xxiii).

Bellos's further view of "Die Klassische" as the "antipodes of most of what is called stylistic criticism in modern scholarship" (xvii) comments as much on the shifting concerns of critical theory as it does on Spitzer's article. Thirty years of critical thinking have passed, and Spitzer's "drawing back" from extended historical discussion can now be seen as the critical error it clearly was. But in 1950 aesthetic value is the first line of defense against a rampant literary and linguistic positivism, and Spitzer's analysis of Racine describes the artist under siege in a form that fits Spitzer's own vision of the critic as well. Théramène, Spitzer declares, "like Racine himself, is a humanistic historiographer who can teach only in a lengthy and ornate fashion, because history is a solemn and sad spectacle which can only be unveiled by a sage who steps beyond it and speaks of it from a higher, 'transposed' plane" (*Linguistics and Literary History*, 104). The historical and sociological features that Hytier urges upon Spitzer and his reading of Racine have no place on this higher, transposed plane. The value that Spitzer attaches to the stylistic reading is attached in turn to the value of the text in the larger aesthetic history that Spitzer creates for it. To include the more mundane is to yank the text into a different value framework, a different model of the relation between style, language, and epistemology.

The resolution of Spitzer's "desperate" methodological dilemma, to repeat Hatzfeld's words, thus continues to reside in his search for a new value system for literature that blends the historical and the epistemological. Spitzer rightly declares that language must not be seen simply as "a banal means of communication and self-expression, but also one of orientation in this world,"[10] noting that while language may be arbitrary in its structure, the structure nevertheless grows out of a cultural framework that is both dictating and dictated. The system undergoes change, and those changes are motivated. The science of language must concern itself with such motivation, and Spitzer reaches back once again to find a scientist of the mind who will support his arguments. Language changes "are not only mistakes or caprices of the language," Spitzer asserts, "but new categorizations due to shifts of attention: as we have learnt from Freud, no mistake is only a mistake; no single mistake or innovation that becomes generalized in a language is itself without meaning" (74).

The particular motives that Spitzer now supplies come from a wide and diverse cultural spectrum—ranging from "the restlessness of the musical guild" (74) to "the ambiguous attitude of man toward the future" (81)— but they remain more directly reminiscent of Humboldtian views of motive as *energeia,* to which Spitzer refers (93), than of Freudian needs and conflicts. Language provides a context for thought and behavior, "a ready-made *interpretation* of the world, truly a *Weltanschauung*" (83), but the basis of that framework is "the power of the collective subconscious as latent in the language," which originates in "the thinking of our ancestors" (83). In that Jungian vein, the concept of context reaches its ultimate spiritual range. The linguistic context becomes essentially that of Western intellectual culture, just as history has become Western literary history. Spitzer does rein in this claim and move on to discuss individual languages. But the replacement of the historical individual in favor of the cultural amanuensis remains. The goal of all linguistic activity becomes that ascribed to poetry: to produce "adumbrations of a metaphysical world" in which everyday laws are gone and "in which we vaguely come to visualize *other* laws" (87). No matter how far they range, however, Spitzer's metaphysical justifications cannot match the ideological power of scientific description now dominating mainstream work in linguistics and, by default, stylistics. The burgeoning interest in objective linguistic study virtually guarantees an increase in the emphasis on—and the stature of—formal descriptive procedures in stylistics, and the scientific stylistics proposed by Bruneau is preparing itself for twenty years of rule.

Appearing in the midst of these critical shifts, Michael Riffaterre's dissertation, published in 1957 as *Le Style des Pléiades de Gobineau, essai d'application d'une méthode stylistique*, provides both a literal and a figurative transition between the historically focused philological stylistics of Spitzer and the now popular acontextual stylistics of general linguistics.[11] As a student of Hytier, Riffaterre has undergone the Romance training that now allows him to pivot neatly between Spitzer's goals for stylistics and those of linguistic science at mid-century. Modern stylistics, in Riffaterre's view, has managed to disengage itself from grammar studies, rhetoric, and impressionistic aesthetics. What stylistics has not done yet is to follow that disengagement with a well-defined set of procedures for literary study. In light of this situation, Riffaterre's goal is "to reconcile Spitzerian views with methodical study, commonplace but sure" (17). It is a goal that ironically points to Spitzer's own early pursuit of a science of style.[12]

That pursuit, of course, is always more easily declared than attained. Riffaterre is attempting to resolve Spitzer's difficulties by combining a similar belief in the intellectual value of style with a contemporary model of linguistic description. But the difficulties to be faced in melding objective methods of linguistic description with an adequate concept of literary style are not minor, as Spitzer's own ongoing struggles demonstrate. Nor is Spitzer particularly eager to see his beliefs blended with contemporary linguistic procedures and purposes. Riffaterre's avowal of influence is destined to become one of those unfortunate bows to the fathers, and his initially declared alliance with the methods of Spitzer will eventually lead, not to cooperation, but to Spitzer's decidedly negative review of *Le Style des Pléiades*.[13]

The motives for that review are varied (Hytier's own review of Spitzer is not the least important), but the most immediate cause is Riffaterre's flawed assumption that the similar goals of his and Spitzer's stylistics can be adapted to the methodology of American structural linguistics. In the preface to *Le Style des Pléiades*, Riffaterre declares his intention to treat the literary text, not as a "pretext" for an exercise in linguistics, philology, or the history of literature or ideas, but as the primary source of meaning.

This view of the literariness of the text is combined with his further belief that the "primordial character" of the text lies in its style. Style thus rests at the center of the literary study, not only in terms of the material analyzed, but as the heart of authorial intention as well. Such views provide no difficulty for Spitzer, who can readily assent to their presentation of the proper place of stylistics within literary criticism, the location of meaning in the text itself, and the growth of style from the mental framework of the author.

It is the difference between Riffaterre's and Spitzer's methods that makes Riffaterre's projected combination difficult to achieve. The two most important words in Riffaterre's extension of the Spitzerian method are "methodical" and "commonplace." His study is to be literary, but it is also to be a scientific analysis of the mundane textual features at hand. And the literary impression will not be portrayed with the visionary tones of Spitzer, but will instead be presented more simply as the "choices" that Gobineau made from among the possibilities offered by the language as they were motivated by a stated intention or a certain mental disposition (15). In this move toward the measurable and the mundane, Riffaterre blends contemporary linguistic thought with Hytier's critical suggestions, thus moving beyond argument to a level of verifiability that Spitzer's philological circle does not pursue. Riffaterre will shift away from Spitzer's interpretive, "art-minded philology" and instead construct his model of style upon a descriptive structural linguistics. In short, the formal description of stylistic elements will be sufficient for Riffaterre; his analysis will not pursue Spitzer's historical and aesthetic ties between author and language. Its academic relevance instead will be achieved through the scientific quality of the analysis.[14]

To achieve that value Riffaterre must eliminate the possibility of *a priori* judgment that supposedly taints Spitzer's philological circle. The simplest means of doing so is to avoid entirely the use of personal intuition at the outset of the study. But the elimination of Spitzer's trained intuition leaves Riffaterre with a significant problem: how can the stylistician know that the element he finds so expressive in a work truly evidences a stylistic trait? Riffaterre's solution, well known by now, depends not upon an aesthetics of intention but upon a rhetoric of response. In contrast to the Spitzerian concern with the expressive text, Riffaterre introduces that of the receptive audience. In place of the piercing gaze of an authoritative critic like Spitzer, Riffaterre offers the more general glance of the common reader. If style is the attempt to produce a certain response in the reader, then the verification of stylistic traits must be based "precisely" on the reader, who is, after all, the "natural addressee" of the message (20).

The verification process, as described by Riffaterre, mimics the process followed by the field linguist concerned with analyzing the structure of a language. The first step involves finding helpful "native speakers" who are to be used, not for their ability to analyze the grammar of a language, but rather, as sounding boards. By eliciting responses to various possible forms and uses, both normal and deviant, the linguist slowly uncovers the particular traits of the language.[15] In similar fashion, by noting the responses of the general reader to a text, Riffaterre will uncover the stylistic traits of an author—here Gobineau. This method of collecting data (or stylistic units) aims to eliminate Spitzerian subjectivity from stylistics by ignoring any textual feature to which the ordinary reader would not respond (20).[16] At the same time, the value of the average reader's response will be weighted against two authorial features: the author's stated intentions about the writing and a "more sure" index, those unconsciously fashioned elements that are the core of an individual style (21). Like Spitzer, then, Riffaterre uses a mentalistic vision of creative activity to support his view of the value of style. By now, however, the Freudian model of the unconscious has become a cultural given, and no explicit reference to Freud or to any other psychological model, including the behavioral, is to be made.

Riffaterre's relative lack of concern with defining the specifics of authorial behavior is not surprising in light of his interest in audience. He does define style as a choice made according to a given intention or a certain psychic disposition (15). But Riffaterre's analytical procedures do not really require an authorial presence. It is the audience that must be well defined if we are to use their responses to describe a style. Unfortunately, "*la lecteur moyen*" (a concept that linguistics only loosely defines as the native speaker) is hardly more than a generalized idea at this stage of Riffaterre's methodology. The affective quality of stylistic devices cannot be described since Riffaterre offers no characterization of the audience that they affect, and a reference to such average readers as "you and me" (20) does little to solidify Riffaterre's method or to make it more objective than Spitzer's.[17] A huge gap exists, then, between Riffaterre's desire to replace Spitzer's authoritative reading and his method's need to satisfactorily define the average reader.[18]

That gap provides Spitzer with an obvious point of attack, but his review of *Le Style des Pléiades* takes an unexpected turn. Spitzer easily recognizes

Riffaterre's attempt to replace him with the average reader: "In place of the gaze of the [Spitzerian] eagle," Riffaterre intends to put "the moderately penetrating glance of you and me" (20). Yet rather than reject the generality of that moderate and only vaguely defined gaze, Spitzer inexplicably chooses to redefine himself, refusing to consider his reading as "anything more" than that of an average reader ("Review," 70). Such a claim obviously is not valid.[19] Spitzer has always assumed (at least in his role as critic) that there is a gradation of critical readings based on an equivalent gradation of talent and knowledge (a fact noted in his wry suggestion that if his method relies overmuch on talent, perhaps Riffaterre's can be put to use "*sans* talent" [70]).[20] The apparent paradox that Spitzer provides can only be understood in terms of his belief in an underlying spiritual quality in style, a quality that supposedly makes the text available to any adequate reader of the language—just as any sufficiently attuned author is free to make use of the possibilities offered by the culture's language.

In essence, Spitzer's sense of reading and writing, like that of the New Critics, proposes a text whose supposed general availability is really a mask for high aesthetics. Literary style is not simply the use of those possibilities present in *langue*. Nor is it everyday *parole*. The truly creative literary style responds to and refashions the communal language: "Anyone who has thought strongly or felt strongly in his language has reshaped language."[21] This division of style into the common style of a language and the personal, innovative style formalizes Spitzer's early (and now repeated) separation of Bally's stylistics from his own. The general stylistic patterns of a language are available to all; the creative artist develops a personal style. The obvious difficulty is to describe the division between the two kinds of style, a division later enshrined by the structuralists as the standard language/poetic language framework. Spitzer will not be any more successful than the structuralists in solving the exact nature of the opposition, but he uses this framework to question what it is that Riffaterre really seeks through his particular stylistic method.

For Spitzer, Riffaterre's study is limited primarily to the investigation of a language's style, and Spitzer equates that study with the noninterpretive linguistics of Bally. Does Riffaterre demonstrate that Gobineau really does have a personal style? "If one thinks in terms of that stylistic uniqueness that transforms the language," the answer is no. "In effect," Spitzer declares, "many of the expressive features that show up in Gob-

ineau are only stylistic features in the sense that Bally gives to that term
. . . 'style of the language' rather than individual *parole*" (71).

Riffaterre's quick response to Spitzer's review (June, 1958) underscores
his awareness of the source of stylistic validity at mid-century. Riffaterre
defends his approach by solidifying the relationship between his stylistics
and general linguistic theory, a relationship that once more points to the
difficulties in Spitzer's own Romantically weighted definition of language
and history. Riffaterre first refutes Spitzer's self-portrait as a common
reader. A judicious reference to Spitzer's own statement of the role that
"talent, experience, and faith" (*Linguistics and Literary History*, 27) play
in reading undercuts that claim. Riffaterre's response to Spitzer's standard
language/poetic language division is more complex, since it defines a core
difference of opinion between both critics over the cultural status of literary
language and the best means for describing it. To Spitzer's question of
the stylistic status of Gobineau, Riffaterre first offers the expected evaluative response; yes, Gobineau has a style of merit. More importantly,
Riffaterre also provides a methodological argument that denies the very
possibility of pursuing Spitzer's Humboldtian vision. Does the style discovered by Riffaterre in Gobineau constitute a personal style or only a
general style of the nineteenth-century French language? Riffaterre answers by stating that it is impossible to make the distinction. In order to
know what has been changed by, and within, the style, "it would be
necessary to know the state of the language in the period of the writer,
and also the total possible reader responses" (478–79). To call *Le Style
des Pléiades* a study of the nineteenth-century French language is to claim
a knowledge of the language which it is not possible to possess—once
the values of a philological approach to language are rejected. From within
a synchronic model of response, Riffaterre's study is necessarily a particular
study of the style of Gobineau.

Riffaterre's rejection is logical but not fully adequate. Historical knowledge obviously is a useful part of Spitzer's philological analyses. As a
historical linguist, Spitzer regularly claims the right to describe the cir-
cumstances of a change in language. As a stylistician, he likewise lays
claim to a capacity for describing the relation of that change to the consciousness of the age. To deny that possibility is to assume a temporal
prison, not unlike that hinted at by Cherniss, who painted himself into
an interpretive corner by rejecting the use of specific historical data. The
real difficulty in Spitzer's historical claims thus is bound up with Spitzer's

complex view of the writer as a leading intellectual figure within the age and of literary style as the leading form of expression. Spitzer needs this vision to justify the epistemological (and hence critical) value he ascribes to style, but because he cannot relate a style to the current issues of history (that would deny the Romantic hero's leading intellectual position), he must continually see style as extending beyond the particulars of its historical surroundings. Style is not simply the formal language of the text; it is a constant state of activity—not *ergon*, but *energeia*. Yet at the same time, it cannot be the simple activity of daily communication (too banal); it must be the activity of becoming or expressing something new. Riffaterre simply has no such developmental view of style in mind, and his definition of style is reduced to that which elicits a (synchronic) response, not that which changes the nature of the language. Thus, there is a profound shift in the basic definition of style—and literature—contained in Riffaterre's arguments. At the center of the concept of the average reader lies the sense that literature elicits certain responses to language and that style is a part of general linguistic behavior, whether that behavior is literary or not.

In arguing for a different intellectual validity for style, Spitzer had declared previously that Lovejoy's version of intellectual history was positivistic in its excessive concern with singular historical ideas. Spitzer countered that descriptive framework with his own view of a literary art founded upon a sensibility informed by, but beyond the deterministic reach of, simple historical events. Riffaterre can refuse this valorization of the literary text because the critical value of the new stylistics does not rest on an interpretive analysis of the context of production but on the universal appeal of the scientific study. "That which critics deny to Mr. Spitzer," Riffaterre declares, "is the right to confound intuition and science, talent and method, because the method must be universal, applicable by all" (478). Style's historical referentiality has been replaced by stylistics's universal analysis; the author's intention, by the reader's response. The scientific goals of general linguistics have become the intellectual validation of literary stylistics.

The origins of that shift are buried deep within the general trend toward scientific objectivity that has been going on within academia and within the culture as a whole. The belief in the importance of language to epistemological issues remains constant, while the values attached to the description of language and history vary according to the different descriptive frameworks used. And as the literary language becomes a part of language behavior as a whole, it also becomes subject to the methods used in describing that behavior. The exchange between Spitzer and Riffaterre dramatizes that moment as well as any argument in stylistics does. Riffaterre's response to Spitzer's review states at the outset that the goals of his new objective stylistics will differ from those of Spitzer's previous new stylistics, and he validates his goals by promising "an objective stylistic method" that is "free of all impressionism" ("Réponse à M. Leo Spitzer" (474–75). Riffaterre's choice of procedures defines these goals clearly enough. The critic defines as "marked," via average readers, all portions of a text that elicit any response. Such affective sections are not studied in terms of the readers' explanations of their responses, but only as signals of possible stylistic import within the body of the text. With a negative side-reference to Spitzer, Riffaterre describes all collected signals as the raw data that constitute the style of the text. A style, he notes, is not simply certain elements chosen by the critic as "a key to the rest, [style] is the combination of these elements with the rest," a combination that may even include "the *original combination* of entirely ordinary linguistic elements" (479).

The phrases are those of linguistic science, yet the final achievement of that scientific objectivity remains uncertain. In order to produce a universally applicable approach, Riffaterre must sterilize all responses. But Riffaterre's offhand stress on "original combination" has a decided effect on the scientific stature of the average reader. What level of reading ability is required if the average reader is to recognize that originality? The scientific quality of this new linguistic description of style thus returns to the average reader and the average reading, the point that Spitzer surprisingly accepted at face value. Without a proper definition of the average reader, the twin ideas of response and stylistic device remain equally ill-defined, and the subjectivity of the analyst always threatens to intrude itself into the gap. Should that occur, there would be little to differentiate between the subsequent analysis by Riffaterre and the analysis he ascribes to Spitzer. The only real difference would be that, for Riffaterre, the text with which he works is not the original but a compilation of numerous readings by undefined readers. The new machinery of stylistic objectivity has been proposed, but, for the moment, no working blueprints for the full construction of Riffaterre's revised stylistics can be said to exist.

Riffaterre's subsequent attempts to provide those blueprints are contained in two articles: "Criteria for Style Analysis," and "Stylistic Context."

They are linguistic with a vengeance and display, very clearly, the desire to root stylistics within the fertile soil of structural linguistics. Aggressively formalist, these essays reverberate with the belief that the academic value of stylistics lies not only in style's intimate ties to language, thought, and form but also in style's ability to fit neatly within formalist linguistic procedures. The cultural bias that leads to this pre-set evaluation is well entrenched. "We believe," Deborah Cameron observes ironically, "that science, distinguished from the arts by objectivity and from scholarship (e.g., history) by its power to explain things, will lead us to truth."[22] The opening sentences of Riffaterre's "Criteria for Style Analysis" are an accurate representation of that myth, as translated by Bloomfield, and of the power it wielded in stylistics from 1950 to 1970. And while the echoes of Spitzer's 1925 call for a scientific stylistics can still be heard in Riffaterre's own words, they are quickly drowned out by the larger overtones of differing ideas of style and science: "Subjective impressionism, normative rhetoric and premature aesthetic evaluation have long interfered with the development of stylistics as a science, especially as a science of literary styles. Because of the kinship between language and style, there is hope that linguistic methods can be used for the objective and exact description of the literary use of language" (154).

The strong gaze toward linguistic science is the hallmark of stylistics at mid-century, and Riffaterre's first step in this march toward the scientifically explicit analysis appears in a set of abbreviations that follow his title: "AR = 'average reader', as defined in 2.2.2 (never used in the ordinary sense); *poem* = 'literary work of art' (cf. 0.2); SD = 'stylistic device' " (154). To these efficient formulations will be added definitions of style, author, and context. In all of them, Riffaterre's purpose will be the elimination of any and all interpretive intrusions into the analytical process and the attainment of objective accuracy through a complete attention to linguistic features alone. To achieve that end the study of style will be divided into analytic and descriptive stages. The latter stage, which deals with the evaluation of style, is presented by Riffaterre as lying somewhat outside the realm of stylistics: "*Style* is understood as an emphasis . . . added to the information. . . . [B]ut the special values thus added to communication are not my concern; the consideration of these will come at the descriptive stage of stylistic research, or, rather, at a metastylistic (e.g. aesthetic) stage" (155).

Riffaterre's nonevaluative heuristic thus defines style in as empty a fashion as possible—in this case, by repeating the increasingly popular definition of style as a deviation from the norm, an escape from the expected (171). The obvious need is to provide some contextual boundaries for this norm, whether social, historical, or cultural. In Spitzer's model the new or the newly formed stylistic feature was to be defined against the backdrop of linguistic and literary history. But such large diachronic machinery does not match well with the tools available to Riffaterre's synchronic analysis, and he greatly foreshortens the general context of change. "The stylistic context," as Riffaterre defines it, "is a linguistic *pattern suddenly broken by an element which was unpredictable,* and the contrast resulting from this interference is the stylistic stimulus" (171). The move toward objectivity reduces the stylistic context to the linguistic material alone and lowers the psychological impact of the style to that of a behaviorally defined response.

Just as the critical environment led Spitzer to divorce style from any *Annales*-like history, so now the critical milieu leads Riffaterre to complete the process and to remove style from history altogether. The full discourse framework requires the description of writers ("encoders"), but they only enter as efficient causes, to ensure that there is a justification for the presence of style in the first place: "Since such a control of the decoding is what differentiates expressivity from ordinary writing (which is indifferent to the mode of decoding provided decoding takes place), and since this differentiation corresponds to the complex of the author's message, we can see in it the *specific mechanism of individual style*" (159). All other aspects of the author are ignored at this stage.[23] The author justifies the search for the style and then departs, leaving the critic to his real task: getting the style out of the text via the remaining third of this discourse exchange, the reader.

The importance of the average reader to Riffaterre's study thus is stressed once more, and he now takes the sorely needed step of defining that construct more precisely—in this case, by relying upon the native informant of linguistic theory. Riffaterre's definition draws the comparison directly, while he also makes clear the reduced role that the reader plays:

> It follows that stylistic investigation will have to use *informants*. These will provide us with reactions to the text: for instance, a native endowed with consciousness of the object language will read the text and the stylistician will draw from him his reactions. The segments of the text which cause his reactions, the informant will call in turn beautiful or unaesthetic, well or poorly written, expressive or flavorless; but the analyst will use these characterizations only as clues

to the elements of the relevant structure. . . . The simple reader is only one among many. A selected group of informants will be used, and the collected responses to a particular stimulus or to a "whole stylistic sequence will be called the *average reader*." [162, 165]

But this definition only creates a further need for methodological refinement, since it threatens to pulverize the new average reading into a collection of wide and unconnected responses, a possibility that Riffaterre recognizes and naturally rejects. He argues that conflicting readings are not predominant at the recognition stage, but usually are so at the secondary stage of interpretation (166). Such a separation of the reading into distinct stages saves the purity of the method, but only by increasing the gap between simple response and critical interpretation. The AR's temporal limitations clarify that separation—what was stylistic for one period may not be for another. Riffaterre accepts that fact, but in a final move toward freezing the text into an objective entity, he takes further aim at the previous bastion of linguistic methodology—historical description— and tries to reduce it to the relatively unimportant rubble of the "interesting consequences of the poem's extension in time" (167). Changes in usage will lead to what Riffaterre calls, in rather startling terms, "errors" of omission and addition. Omission occurs when the foregrounded element loses its effectiveness over time, a problem solved simply by declaring that no stylistic element exists since the response has faded. Should one *want* to know something of the original quality of the style, it can be uncovered by going to the literary historian or to the stylist studying the period, but that is clearly a recreation of the style and not its true—that is, contemporary—version.

Errors of addition (for example, misinterpreted archaisms) do show up as responses, however. Are these responses to be dealt with as stylistically important? Oddly enough, the answer is still no: "the informant who gives [an archaic term] this expressive value . . . is wrong, since then it was normal" (167). Clearly the average reading is to be reinterpreted by the analyst. The authoritative critic is to stand outside of the stimulus/response machine, culling the improper historical responses from the proper contemporary responses. Time, not history, becomes the yardstick of the correct response here, and even time has little role to play beyond that of duration of response. The context of the poem is reduced to the poem itself in order to confine the reader's response to the material at hand, and the historical situation eliminated as an unusable complexity of language. Riffaterre cannot expand the historical sensibility of his readers (beyond a general sense of what constitutes contemporary and archaic forms), so he must limit the range of the stylistic response to what is striking at the moment. This reduction of linguistic knowledge cannot be so readily applied to literary knowledge, however, since learning to read literature cannot be perfectly equated with learning a language. Riffaterre's stylistics, therefore, includes more than the informant's knowledge of language; it includes the informant's knowledge of the literary use of language. Riffaterre is struggling to unite the stylistics of Bally and Spitzer, and that union requires a melding of their equally divided sense of the science of linguistics.

It is at this point that Riffaterre suddenly points to differences in reading levels and offers his startling revision of Bloomfield's rules for the use of native informants. Bloomfield strives to obtain the simplest untutored response available; "educated or 'cultured' informants are by no means preferable and often inferior" in Bloomfield's field research because they damage the scientific neutrality that he seeks.[24] Riffaterre now intentionally alters this rule, arguing that it would be better "to have cultivated informants who are prone to use the text as a pretext for a show of learning. . . . Such secondary responses, misleading in linguistics, and possibly elicited by ephemeral fashions or prejudiced aesthetic beliefs, will not harm the objectivity of the inquiry because, once again, they will be recorded only as signals of what causes them" (163).

Riffaterre's use of the phrase "secondary response" is not innocent. These "prejudiced aesthetic beliefs" are exemplified in the readings of Spitzer, and they are to be dismissed as inherently fallacious, "[a]s Bloomfield showed during his controversy with Spitzer" (163n). The argument thus comes full circle, with the disagreements that began with Meyer-Lübke and Spitzer and then were recapitulated by Spitzer and Bloomfield now being addressed by Riffaterre. That Riffaterre should find Bloomfield's objective linguistics useful in countering Spitzer's arguments is not very surprising. And the satiric tone that Riffaterre adopts toward the idea of secondary responses is not all that exceptional, given the tone of Spitzer's review. Riffaterre undoubtedly derives a certain amount of satisfaction from renewing Bloomfield's and Hytier's charges against Spitzer, and from extending them even further by sarcastically granting a reduced quantitative value to the responses of "cultivated informants."

Yet no matter how much well-deserved fun is evident in Riffaterre's

quiet war with Spitzer, Riffaterre's debunking of the qualitative importance of cultivated responses cannot hide the fact that through them he
has introduced a significant revision into the construct of the native speaker/
average reader. He has shifted, and not in a minor way, the basic expectations surrounding the use of a native informant, and in doing so he
reintroduces Spitzer's factors of "experience" and "talent" into the stylistic
reading. Nor can Riffaterre save the objective purity of his procedures
by arguing that all metastylistic comments will be removed from these
cultivated responses. The admission of a hierarchy of readers necessarily
skews the gathering of stylistic responses. And because cultivated informants may well be preferable since they "will notice more facts" (163),
as Riffaterre states (making rather loose use of the term "facts"), their
presence obviously prejudges what constitutes the most useful body of
stylistic devices, if only on the basis of quantity.

The open-ended stylistic reading clearly is destroyed by this change.
Riffaterre's assumption that cultivated readers will recognize the greatest
number of stylistic devices (the primary characteristic of cultivated readers
is an "eagerness to make many comments"), grants greater value to the
educated reading. Worse still for a supposedly objective reading, Riffaterre's implication that the responses that occur in the largest number
will be the most useful to the critic stresses the critic's interpretive role,
which consists of picking through the data and deciding at yet another
stage what constitutes a useful response. The average reader disappears
in this secondary critical interpretation, and with it, the value-free reading.

Not surprisingly, that effect is not immediately apparent in the early
days of Riffaterre's theorizing, any more than the initial discussions of
reader-response criticism will reveal the hidden evaluations occurring in
that model. In fact, Riffaterre continues further in his pursuit of scientific
objectivity. His full adherence to linguistic principles becomes obvious
in the procedural refinements that he offers one year later in "Stylistic
Context," where the notion of historical context disappears completely.
Microcontexts are the relationships between the elements of any stylistic
device. Macrocontexts, contrary to their name, extend no further than
the borders of the literary work in question, rarely, it would seem, across
sentence boundaries. They are formed through the particular pattern of
expectations that any text builds within the reader as it is being read, and
a stylistic device is, for Riffaterre, any unexpected break in this pattern.
The macrocontext may therefore simply be defined as "that part of the

literary message which precedes the SD and which is exterior to it" (212). The context is thus the sentential structure within which the stylistic device is made apparent.

The theoretical reasoning behind this view is not hard to posit. If Riffaterre allows for any larger context, he takes the chance that subjective factors (the reader's knowledge of an exterior context, linguistic or literary) will enter and possibly skew the response. The same argument lies behind his rejection of Spitzer's distinction between personal style and the style of a language. He reiterates the claim here, stating that by limiting style and context to the work itself "we need not rely on an elusive and subjective *Sprachgefühl*" (207). The work becomes an object free in space whose linguistic components can be analyzed according to any responses they may elicit. Riffaterre's theoretical developments thus move in the direction of objectifying not only his methodology but the material to be analyzed as well. The vestiges of author and critic that existed at the time of his first arguments with Spitzer have been cleared away. He has struggled to make the "average reader" an objective construct, defining it so that it is useable as a sophisticated filtering agent—but no more. And the context of the work of art has been narrowed down to the work itself in order to make it a self-enclosed construct that can be analyzed without reference to any outside materials that might damage the objectivity of the analysis.

Whatever the subsequent judgment to be made concerning this phase of Riffaterre's work, it must be recognized that his pursuit is a logical function of the critical attitudes of the time, supplanting, as it unfortunately does, Spitzer's primary concern with historical interpretation. Indeed, Riffaterre now takes pains to announce that his method obviously differs from that of Spitzer, using behavioristic language to argue that his procedures "separate clearly the psychological processes and cultural conditioning of the perception from its stimulus."

> In the procedure I propose the analyst will scrupulously avoid hypotheses . . . and will wait, before building a structure, until all signals collected constrain him by their interplay and convergence to an interpretation taking them all into account. What is . . . alarming . . . in Spitzer's method, the purported control by other striking details may cause the analyst unconsciously to exclude clues which might have struck him were it not for his preconceived construction. Not only has the stylistic stimulus been confused with the value

judgment, but the control, applied to the judgment instead of its source, is exercised upon the coherence of the analyst's response rather than upon the text as it should be. [164]

In 1960 such arguments are considered unimpeachable within linguistic stylistics. Psychological and cultural subjectivity can and will be eliminated until stylistics can achieve a level of science comparable to that of general linguistics. Yet the scientific flavor of Riffaterre's studies is not achieved easily, and the control that he envisions remains not only costly but very tenuous—especially his control over the concepts of context and of the average reader.[25] The idea that each work develops an internal context is easy to accept, but the totally self-sufficient text is an empty myth, even from within a criticism that ignores history. All literature, especially poetry, is highly self-reflexive, and to ignore this generic reflexivity is to ignore an essential fact of literary language. Discussing Riffaterre's *Describing Poetic Structures*, Roger Fowler makes essentially the same point: "Riffaterre's 'lexical code' supplies a method for controlling the superreader and for ensuring a validity of the results of the analysis. . . . However, it could be argued that Riffaterre's lexical code is too cautious: certainly the reader possesses areas of coded knowledge, mediated through the structure of language, which are more abstract and of broader range than the lexical code."[26] There are, therefore, levels of stylistic recognition among readers, and it cannot be expected that the context can be emptied sufficiently enough to overcome these variations in reading. Riffaterre's postulation of the metastylistic level of analysis declares as much. Behind the collected responses of readers there is a hidden evaluation of the nature of literature and its audience, an evaluation formalized by Riffaterre's alteration of the native informant.

For all its concentration on style as an act of communicative behavior, Riffaterre's plan still acknowledges larger sociocultural determinants for style, both indirectly in the adjustment of the native reader and directly in the "metastylistic" stage added to the analysis. Nevertheless, the interpretive stylistic analysis of literary response is forced to become not the primary but the subsequent study. History fades before the reader, the reader becomes data collection, and data collection replaces interpretation. Yet for all its reductionism, Riffaterre's model catches the temper of the times. His stylistics fits the measurements of the critical mold, and the ideological weight of scientific procedures provides the critical validation. Spitzer's opposing approach during this ten-year period (beginning with his clash with Hytier, continuing through the person of

Riffaterre, and ending with Spitzer's death in Italy in 1960) finds no comparable argument for the value of history in stylistic criticism. But Spitzer's arguments during those ten years continue to lead us back to the importance of historical thinking. Today that viewpoint is once again beginning to take hold in the wider arena of literary criticism, if not in stylistics proper. The final question remaining for us is how to reintroduce historical interpretation into stylistics after decades of struggle by critics such as Spitzer.

NOTES

1. Frank Lentricchia dates the end of the New Criticism by the appearance of Northrop Frye's *Anatomy of Criticism:* "Northrop Frye published his monumental book in 1957, one year after Murray Krieger in *The New Apologists for Poetry* had summed up the position associated with the New Criticism, explored its theoretical contradictions and dead ends, and predicted—correctly, it turns out—that the New Criticism had done all that it could do for American literary critics (and the teaching of literature in the United States). . . ." (Lentricchia, *After the New Criticism* [Chicago: University of Chicago Press, 1980], 3). Another text also appeared in 1957, and it was to have an equally large, perhaps larger effect on stylistics: Noam Chomsky's *Syntactic Structures* (The Hague: Mouton, 1957).

2. Charles Bruneau, "La stylistique," *Romance Philology*, 5, no. 1 (1951), 1–14.

3. Michael Riffaterre, *Le Style des Pléiades de Gobineau, essai d'application d'une méthode stylistique* (New York: Columbia University Press, 1957); "Criteria for Style Analysis," *Word*, 15 (1959), 154–74; and "Stylistic Context," *Word*, 16 (1960).

4. The appearance in 1973 of Stanley Fish's "What Is Stylistics?" provides a useful date for the shift by stylistics toward a wider vision of the text. (In *Is There a Text in This Class?* [Cambridge, Mass.: Harvard University Press, 1980], 68–96).

5. Helmut Hatzfeld, "Stylistics as Art-Minded Philology," *Yale French Studies*, 2, no. 1 (1949), 62–70. See also his "Leo Spitzer and Stephen Ullmann's Stylistic Criticism," in *Language, Meaning, and Style: Essays in Memory of Stephen Ullmann*, ed. T. E. Hope (Leeds: University of Leeds, 1981), 39–54. The article is discussed briefly in this chapter.

6. Raphael Levy, "A New Credo of Stylistics," *Symposium*, 3 (1949), 321–34.

7. Jean Hytier, "La Méthode de M. Leo Spitzer," *Romanic Review,* 41 (1950), 42–59.

8. Hytier accepts Spitzer's statement that greater objectivity can be achieved through reference to the work of other critics: "The greater the objective certainty that a stylistic explanation can claim, the more we will have overcome that impressionism which, until recently, has seemed the only alternative to the positivistic treatment of literature" (38n). But Hytier also notes that Spitzer does not call as often as he might upon the readings of other critics in support of this objective reading (46).

9. Hytier concentrates on "The Récit de Théramène" in *Linguistics and Literary History.* His concern is with what he sees as the freewheeling way in which Spitzer labels whole historical periods, a problem further compounded by the notorious vagueness of the term. However, many of the arguments of "The Récit de Théramène" are contained within earlier work. The most thorough is the essay "Die Klassische Dämpfung in Racines Stil" (*Archivum Romanicum,* 12 [1928], 361–472, and 13 [1929], 398–99; rpt. with additions in *Romanische Stil- und Literaturstudien* [Marburg: Elwert, 1931]).

Spitzer argues that Racine's language is a language with a modulating "*piano* pedal" ("Racine's Classical *Piano,*" in *Leo Spitzer: Essays on Seventeenth-Century French Literature,* ed. and trans. David Bellos [Cambridge: Cambridge University Press, 1983], 4). The resulting variation in restraint and containment underwrites the idea of a progression from the baroque into the classical, and Spitzer wishes to place Racine along the continuum: "to my knowledge it has never been shown how these ornamental forms came to be calmed and controlled to produce classical style. I hope the present essay has provided some small preparatory sketch for the huge task that remains. A glance at the *sources* of the individual stylistic devices to Racine's classical *piano* shows in nearly every case a model from classical antiquity. . . . He modulates the overbaroque and exaggerated traits of the archaising imitators, he spiritualises classical formulae, but his forms of language and his formulaic language are classical" (107).

The major terms which Hytier finds ill-defined and poorly presented are thus established to a certain degree by this earlier article. Bellos is willing to declare today that Spitzer's study of Racine's style, while containing views not "universally shared," nevertheless "continues to be recognized as the best treatment of the subject yet written" (2).

10. Leo Spitzer, "Language—The Basis of Science, Philosophy, and Poetry," in *Studies in Intellectual History,* ed. George Boas (Baltimore, Md.: Johns Hopkins University Press, 1953), 93. The essay appears in a collection dedicated to A. O. Lovejoy and edited by George Boas, Spitzer's

fellow participants in the activities of the Johns Hopkins's History of Ideas Club.

11. Michael Riffaterre, *Le Style des Pléiades de Gobineau, essai d'application d'une méthode stylistique* (New York: Columbia University Press, 1957).

12. Daniel Delas declares that Spitzer's interest in an objective stylistics was one of the reasons for Riffaterre's interest in Spitzer's stylistics: "Leo Spitzer had been without a doubt the first to take notice of the necessity of elaborating a [stylistic] method that began with objective criteria. . ." (Daniel Delas, Préface, *Essais de Stylistique Structurale*, by Michael Riffaterre, ed. and trans. Daniel Delas [Paris: Flammarion, 1971], 6).

13. Leo Spitzer, "Review of *Le Style des Pléiades de Gobineau*," *Modern Language Notes*, 73 (1958), 68–74. The chief benefit of Spitzer's review might well have been Riffaterre's subsequent rebuttal ("Réponse à M. Leo Spitzer: sur la méthode stylistique," *Modern Language Notes*, 73 (1958), 474–80. In his reply Riffaterre would make direct mention of Hytier's review, connecting Spitzer's bad humor in reviewing his own work to Hytier (477). Spitzer's review undoubtedly had its own influence on the writing of the two later articles by Riffaterre that served to clarify his methodology further.

14. In Delas's discussion of Riffaterre's work, Delas's dismissal of Spitzer's method also relies upon the positive value attached to scientific verification: "To pass from a text to its author, from an author to his text is, in the state of our knowledge, to form unverifiable hypotheses, unless one has recourse to a certain idea of man, to a suitable humanism" (*Essais de Stylistique Structurale*, 7).

15. Leonard Bloomfield's *Language* (New York: Holt, 1933, 22–41) contains a general discussion of the linguist's use of a native informant. Riffaterre cites Bloomfield's more specific discussion found in *Outline Guide for the Practical Study of Foreign Languages* (Baltimore, Md.: Linguistic Society of America, 1942).

16. The general procedure is common to most modern linguistic methods, regardless of other methodological differences. Chomsky has the same intentions as Bloomfield on this score. Fredric Jameson, discussing Chomsky's version, notes its usefulness but adds context to the features that such speakers are expected to control: "Context is everything, and it is the feeling of the native speaker which remains in the last resort the test of the presence or absence of distinctive features" (*The Prison-House of Language* [Princeton, N.J.: Princeton University Press, 1972], 17). The addition is important, but how context is to be described or even delineated remains a key problem.

17. In a later French translation Riffaterre uses *architecteur* in order

to avoid what he claims were unwarranted assumptions regarding the notion of average. As opposed to the "average" reader, "*l'archilecteur* is the sum of the readings and not the average" (*Essais de Stylistique Structurale*, 46). This change, however, is more a change of the definition than of the procedure. In "Criteria for Style Analysis," for example, Riffaterre is obviously interested primarily in those responses that are common to all readers. He rejects the idea that a variety of readers would fracture the text, since "once the widely conflicting value judgments are weeded out, we find they all sprang from relatively few points in the text" (166). In fact, the whole purpose of the native-speaker analysis is to establish the features common to a language and to eliminate the particularities of an individual's speech.

18. Robert Scholes will make much the same point in his discussion of Riffaterre's rebuttal of Jakobson and Lévi-Strauss (see Scholes's *Structuralism in Literature* [New Haven, Conn.: Yale University Press, 1974], 32–40).

19. Riffaterre, in his own reply to this review, correctly directs Spitzer to his own words in *Linguistics and Literary History:* "But when I read that the 'click' is a 'divination' [19], that the sole guarantee of the click is that the reader/divinator has 'talent, experience, and faith' [26], I am forced to see in him a phoenix, if not an eagle" ("Réponse," 478).

20. Certain sections of this review are painful to read. There are valid points and specific problems to be addressed in Riffaterre's stylistic proposals. Does he, in fact, define the common or average reader well? Unfortunately, that question goes unanswered, along with the further question of what this construct reveals about the literary ideology of the time. The ideological power of science in 1958 probably accounts for the unpleasant aggression of Spitzer's review—Riffaterre's method points to core issues in Spitzer's own troubled methodology—but it does not excuse the sniping. For analysis, sometimes Spitzer has substituted attack; for critical reading, authoritarian judgment.

21. Leo Spitzer, *Linguistics and Literary History*, 15.

22. Deborah Cameron, *Feminism and Linguistic Theory* (New York: St. Martin's Press, 1985), 11.

23. Those features that Riffaterre eliminates from the stylistic analysis do have a chance of reentering the study at a "metastylistic" stage of analysis. The problem is when this stage will, if ever, be reached.

24. Leonard Bloomfield, *Outline Guide for the Practical Study of Foreign Languages*, 4.

25. My misgivings over Riffaterre's methods are a response to his work up to 1960, his strongest linguistic phase. It would be fairly easy to go to a later work, such as his *Semiotics of Poetry* (Bloomington: Indiana Uni-

7 Current Trends and Possible Options
Literary Style and Ideology

On September 3, 1960, Spitzer provided one last overview of the field of stylistics, as he saw it, in a paper delivered to the Congress of the International Federation of Modern Languages and Literatures. Thirteen days later he would die of a heart attack at the age of seventy-three. The paper, later published as "Les Études de style et les différent pays,"[1] offers Spitzer's most complete glance over the field as a whole, repeating the main themes of his stylistics while relating them to work both in Europe and the United States during the fifty years of his career. Two main currents run beneath Spitzer's discussion: (1) the desire to create a science of literary style, while separating himself from the ahistorical positivism that he sees as rampant in twentieth-century stylistics, and (2) the need to discuss style as a component of the author's psyche, while keeping free of an excessive determinism that he fears will reduce the aesthetic value of the literary text. The talk was delivered at a time when literary criticism was in fact beginning to move into areas that appeared to promise new possibilities for such interpretation. But while literary criticism was beginning to broaden its focus through structuralism, semiotics, and discourse analysis, the desire for a stylistics founded on the bedrock objectivity of descriptive linguistics would mark the general tenor of stylistic study for the next fifteen years. From 1960 to 1975 the scientific values sought by linguistic stylistics would dominate Anglo-American stylistics. The particular Bloomfieldian methods initially proposed by Riffaterre would be swept away almost immediately by the wave of interest that followed the presentation of Chomsky's transformational grammar in versity Press, 1978), and point to his own realization of the bias found in his early procedures: "the most profitable approach to an understanding of poetic discourse was semiotic rather than linguistic" (ix).

At the same time, there can be no quarrel with Riffaterre's attempts to eliminate the evaluative aspect of the standard-language/poetic-language dichotomy, nor with his attempt to make stylistic devices dependent on their particular situation of use, rather than on any essential quality of the device (a position also shared, as Riffaterre notes, with Spitzer): "Similarly, L. Spitzer, after comparing—with a very different approach— more styles than any stylistician ever had, concluded that the stylistic sign is 'empty'" ("Stylistic Context," 207n). The reference is to Spitzer's statement on Marvell: "But, believing as I do that any stylistic device is an empty form which may be filled by most diverse contents, I should prefer to treat each manifestation of wit, puns, etc., *in situ*, in the precise situation in which it appears" ("Marvell's 'Nymph Complaining for the Death of Her Fawn': Sources versus Meaning," *MLQ*, 19 [1958], 235n).

26. Roger Fowler, "Language and the Reader," *Style and Structure in Literature*, ed. Roger Fowler. (Ithaca, N.Y.: Cornell University Press, 1975), 93.

1957, but the key goal of descriptive efficiency would remain. The primary value of scientific linguistics was believed to lie within its objective efficiency, within its ability to display a descriptive power similar to that of most scientific disciplines and, thus, to complete the movement of linguistics into the arena of scientific study.

Yet the high status enjoyed by these scientific approaches has been undercut lately by critics who accuse them of a variety of errors, ranging from reducing the writer and reader of the text to nonentities to an inherent subjectivity that lies beneath their claims of analytic objectivity (as we have seen in Riffaterre). As we make headway through these attacks and counterattacks, several questions will occur and reoccur: (1) What was the basic attraction of the "new" new linguistic stylistics, especially that of 1960 to 1975?, (2) What were the effects on this approach of other issues, such as reader-response criticism with its movement outward from formal textual description to audience analysis?, and (3) How might stylistics make use of recent attempts to integrate history, sociology, and the analysis of ideology into critical interpretation—and how might that shift affect our contemporary reevaluation of Spitzer's work?

During the period immediately following Spitzer's death, the effect of newer linguistic methods on literary stylistics can only be described as immediate and massive, as attested to by the large number of critical editions dedicated to the "New Stylistics" (a description that quietly ignores Hatzfeld's stylistic bibliography of the same name).[2] These editions brandish the new tools of the trade: "Linguistic Approaches to Literary Style" regularly forms a part of their titles and subtitles. Roger Fowler's *Essays on Style and Language: Linguistic and Critical Approaches to Literary Style* (1966)[3] displays both the title and the unanimity of purpose (if not of method) that characterize the period. Among the declared interests of Fowler's authors, his own goal for "the development of methods and terms for describing [literary uses of language] with precision" (vii) best defines the heady eclecticism and sense of fruitful growth that characterize the period—even if that academic euphoria tended to mask what Fowler also wisely recognized as "the uncertain standing of 'linguistic stylistics'" (vii).[4]

By 1970 the linguistic framework that stylistics had achieved for itself can be encapsulated in Donald Freeman's succinct, if somewhat historically foreshortened, definition of "the new and emerging" field of stylistics.[5] Freeman's view of the new stylistics as "the application of linguistics to the study of literature" does not seem to make it particularly new, but when he says linguistics he means contemporary linguistics (and primarily American transformational-generative grammar).[6] What clearly is new, beyond the shift in types of linguistic method, is the relation of the method to the concept. Seen in Graham Hough's less enthusiastic terms, by 1970 style has not only been adapted to linguistic method, it has vanished into linguistic stylistics: "the term 'style' has tended to disappear from the main stream of modern criticism, while a quasi-independent study of 'stylistics' has simultaneously made its appearance."[7] In Hough's eyes, the methodological tail has begun to wag the dog.

While Hough may overstate the case somewhat, this singular attractiveness of objective methodology is real, and it encompasses both the hope that scientific linguistics can provide greater descriptive control over the mercurial nature of style and the simultaneous cultural belief that science possesses a particularly focused capacity for defining truth. The first hope is bolstered by the internal self-sufficiency offered by linguistic methodology. Anyone who undertakes a transformational analysis, for example, knows more about a text at the end of the analysis than at the beginning, no matter what might be the person's level of interpretive skill. At the same time, the attempt by stylistics to adapt this analytic framework involves more than adopting a new methodology; such a shift also engages the ideological power of scientific description itself. The qualities ascribed to science may be ideological myths, but as we noted in discussing Riffaterre, "the mythology of science," to repeat Cameron's argument, "is one that our culture worships. . . . there is a great deal to be gained, in terms of credibility and respect, from the use of the label *scientific.*"[8] The use of objective methods in stylistics thus offers a double reward: it promises to produce a particular knowledge of the linguistic material, and it offers an opportunity to participate in the social mythology that surrounds scientific description.

That attractiveness of method, and especially of the transformational-generative methods of Chomsky, is visible in Freeman's first text.[9] The initial essay in this 1970 collection is none other than Spitzer's "Linguistics and Literary History," and it serves as a display piece for the linguistic tradition upon which stylistics rests. The remaining studies, while demonstrating the influence of Russian formalism, Firthean linguistics, general structuralist attitudes, and other contemporary approaches, are nonetheless outnumbered by essays dealing with the transformational-generative grammar of Chomsky. The simplest reason for this rush to adopt and adapt the methods of Chomsky is the continuing attractiveness of scientific objectivity. But such objectivity was available from Bloomfield as well. Why the difference in acceptability? It comes from the sense that Chomsky's general linguistics, while possessing as its core purpose the efficient and logical description of language, also possesses a deeper affinity with the user than its linguistic predecessors. In the face of a Bloomfieldian stylistics that flattened both author and reader into stimulus/response fodder, Chomsky's concern with language and mind augurs well for the rebirth of both author and reader within literary stylistics.[10]

A good number of the early literary applications of Chomsky's model have at their core the belief that the grammar allows for the shadow-presence of the author, while still providing some measure of objectivity. Richard Ohmann's "Generative Grammars and the Concept of Literary Style" (1964) provides a convenient example of this assumption as it has been embraced by stylisticians.[11] Ohmann, one of the most influential and farsighted writers of this period, clearly hopes that a use of the grammar will help to display "the human action" (426) of style, by which he means the author's active creativity in forming the style. This sense of style as intentional literary activity appears throughout Ohmann's essay, predominantly in the link that he forges between the deep structure of Chomsky's model and the creative activity of the writer. And it is this implied link between language and logic, language and mind that dominates many of the earliest uses of Chomsky's methods.

Although Chomsky himself has always argued that his model of language description is not a model of mental activity, the easy analogy between deep structure and the deeper workings of the mind has proven irresistible to many critics of style. Transformational-generative grammar seems to provide a way to reintroduce the long-lost author to whom Spitzer dedicated a career and in whom many stylisticians continue to find the final argument for the critical relevance of stylistics. For Spitzer, the possibility for justifying an epistemological link between author and style had at first appeared to lie within a conjunction of the psychology of Freud and the goals of philology. By 1960 it seemed possible for stylisticians to establish a similar link through Chomsky. In fact, direct comparisons between Chomsky's initial theorizing about mental processes and the Freudian description of mind were often made. As we noted earlier, John R. Searle, a critic not given to rash theoretical statements, draws the comparison directly, linking Chomsky to Freud and other nonmechanistic theorists of the mind.[12] Searle does so in order to reject mechanistic science, and in the process he restates ideas repeatedly encountered in Spitzer's arguments. "Behaviorists," he declares, "have failed to see that the notion of human action must be a 'mentalistic' and 'introspective' notion since it essentially involves the notion of human intention" (31). But while the basic argument against mechanism is valid, comparisons such as Searle's have fallen upon more skeptical times of late, especially as Chomsky's own goals have become more objective. Searle's reference to "hidden" and "mysterious underlying laws" leans too heavily upon a metaphoric sense (regularly denied by Chomsky) of deep and surface structure.

The descriptive capacities of Chomsky's grammar are judged differently now, and the analogies with mental activity have been weakened. Morton Bloomfield hints at that weakening by referring to the "great if confused boost" that Ohmann's work gave to transformational stylistics, thus un-obtrusively removing one of the key components of the link between style and mind.[13] Elsewhere, Chomsky's attitudes have even been compared with those of Leonard Bloomfield. The idea is startling, but its arguments rest upon certain clear issues. While different theories of mind may lie at the bases of Bloomfield's behaviorist model and Chomsky's rationalist theory, both are equally concerned with that "given" of modern general linguistics—the creation of scientific linguistic systems. Significantly, these reevaluations of Chomsky come from other arenas besides that of literary stylistics. Jerrold J. Katz, discussing the place of meaning within trans-formational-generative grammar, readily links Chomsky and Bloomfield: "Given the philosophical sources of skepticism about meaning, one would expect C[homsky]—a strong opponent of empiricism in linguistics, phi-losophy, and psychology . . . to support meaning against its critics. But he has not done so. . . . [A]lthough C remains a nativist and a mentalist, his present position on meaning sides him with empiricists and behav-iorists."[14] Less than fifteen years after the appearance of Chomsky's *Lan-guage and Mind* (1968), the taint of empiricism thus reappears and rebuilds the wall between user and language that Chomsky seemed to have demol-ished; the issue of mentalism versus mechanism has become cloudier rather than clearer; and the desire of stylistics to reunite its analysis with the situation of use has been frustrated once again.

In the midst of this shifting and refocusing, a further critical problem has arisen as well. The drive for linguistic objectivity has continually displayed a rather blatant separation of linguistic methodology from critical interpretation, and as interpretation itself has become an issue for critical perusal, this clear separation has provided a ready target for some with-ering attacks. The most cogent and directed of these critiques can be found in the two versions of Stanley Fish's "What Is Stylistics?" (1973 and 1980).[15] Each article argues a similar point: objectively defined linguistic features can only be blended into stylistic interpretations through the subjective insights of the analysts, a list of whom includes such respected figures as Roger Fowler, Donald Freeman, and E. L. Epstein. Shorn of all incidentals, the arguments of Fish recapitulate the charge leveled by Spitzer against the objective philosophies of the mechanists: the analysis of formal linguistic features cannnot overcome the inherently interpretive nature of applied linguistics, stylistics, and science in general. The assumed objectivity of the linguistically centered study of style is both a myth and a false idol, and its supposed escape from subjectivity is undercut by a priori critical judgments, such as those found in Samuel Keyser's analysis of Stevens's "Anecdote of a Jar."[16] Keyser argues that the meaning and phonological shape of the word "round" serve as elemental structuring principles behind the form of the poem. But Fish points to the problematic relation between the two halves of the analysis: "The phonological shape of 'round' imposes an order on the poem only if you have already decided that the poem is about order. That is, the pattern emerges under the pressure of an interpretation and does not exist as independent evidence of it" (253).

Such arguments attack the core motivating assumption that has produced linguistics' dominant position in stylistic criticism, and their clear validity makes itself felt in Louis Milič's agreement that such a priori assumptions are part of any stylistic analysis.[17] That is a difficult admission for an objective study to make, but its honesty mollifies Fish not at all. He rejects Milič's declaration, calling it one of the "basic maneuvers of the stylistics game": Milič "acknowledges the dependence of his procedures on an unwarranted assumption, but then salvages both the assumption and the procedures by declaring that time and more data will give substance to one and authority to the other. It is a remarkable *non sequitur*" (73).

These arguments should sound familiar. They are very close to those used by Spitzer to attack Bloomfield's avoidance of meaning in linguistic analysis. Yet there is also an important difference between the arguments of Spitzer and those of Fish. Spitzer sought to validate his own opposing critical interpretations via the historical situation of their production; Fish seeks to do so through the reader and the context of interpretation. In making this shift Fish displays the current desire to make literary criticism answerable to some criteria of interpretative strength by placing meaning not in the inviolate text but in the act of reading. That attempt is not only laudable, but in most cases it is also theoretically acute. But these arguments, while important in themselves, do not preclude Spitzer's argument that history and the context of production also play a role in critical interpretation. In fact, as critics such as Mary Pratt have shown, Fish's idea of an interpretive community actually underwrites the notion of historical analysis in stylistic criticism. But the immediate impact of Fish's arguments has masked that implication, even as his discussions have hidden the fact that Fish's own model contains the same difficulties raised by Riffaterre's average reader. In the days following Fish's blast, stylistics spent most of its time trying to defend itself.

The influence of Fish's arguments is evident in Timothy Austin's *Language Crafted: A Linguistic Theory of Poetic Syntax*, one of the most thorough and recent of those stylistic models built around transformational-generative grammar.[18] Like the work of Chomsky, to which it is indebted, the text argues for the regular, logical development of formal description. The basic thesis—that stylistics depends upon linguistics and that the best linguistic methodology is transformational grammar—is laid out early in the text. From that point on the text displays Austin's three-staged stylistic analysis: a technical phase (formally capturing "purely syntactic processes that contribute to a given text's linguistic identity"); an aesthetic phase ("examining the interaction between the syntactic features of a text and certain independent aesthetic forms"); and an interpretive phase (correlating content with "both technical and perceptual observations" [13–14]). Each successive stage of the analysis thus moves further away from strict linguistic description toward the larger arena of interpretation. That sequential movement reenacts Riffattere's earlier two-part proposal: an initial description of affective stylistic devices followed by a metastylistic stage of interpretation. But Austin wisely attempts to avoid the clear separation of levels that Riffaterre proposed. The problem of moving from formal description to interpretive analysis has been made only too apparent by recent arguments, and Austin is quick to respond to them. He reviews Fish's attack and agrees with the benefits to be gained by adding "reader-oriented factors" to the stylistic reading (6). But while Austin accepts Fish's theoretical arguments, acquiescing to his practical solutions is more difficult. For Austin, Fish's interpretive community cannot be used as a component of the study unless and until it can be more rigorously defined. As was true for Riffaterre's work, if Austin's stylistics is to maintain some measure of objectivity, it needs a more sophisticated definition of the reader. To that end, Austin declares the function of stylistic analysis to be that of "explicating the relationship between readers' shared syntactic competence and their similarly shared experience of a given text" (11).

Austin thus agrees to define a receptive, rather than a productive, stylistics, while he also severely restricts his primary analysis to the discovery and description of important syntactic features. In doing so, Austin demonstrates his desire to remain with that objective stylistics that so heavily influenced Riffaterre's stance in 1959 and 1960, even as he adds the overtones of reader and context made necessary by Fish's arguments. Final success for this kind of analysis thus depends upon maintaining a clear hold over the reader, native and otherwise, to whom Riffaterre devoted so much effort. But a hesitation similar to Riffaterre's is apparent in the various psychological interpolations to which Austin is led in describing his reader. He notes, for example, that "a poet's decision to violate a given condition *necessarily* puts the reader's mind under a certain kind of cognitive pressure" (44), and he cites experiments by Clark and Clark as experimental evidence for this claim (147n).[19] But that "certain kind of cognitive pressure" is then relegated to the level of interpretation rather than technical analysis. In like fashion Austin states, concerning aesthetic response, that "patterns of various sorts, I take it, form part of mankind's general aesthetic code" (66). But the specifics (or the usefulness) of that postulated code are not immediately available.

The portraits are rather abstract, but the motives for presenting them are very clear. Austin's willingness to make claims about cognitive functioning and reader response is proof of a methodological need and a critical desire. Austin needs the native reader as a methodological ideal that validates a postulated stylistic response. At the same time, the reader is used to satisfy the critical desire to move out of the isolated text and into the realm of literary reception—from linguistic matter to literary response, as it were. The native reader is thus both an abstract, unrealizable linguistic construct and a way of discussing style as a form of literary activity, an admitted "creature of th[e] theory" (133). The internally defined reader rests upon "a series of abstractions and simplifications of individual events inescapable if one wishes stylistic theory to achieve a high level of what Noam Chomsky would term 'descriptive power'" (133).

The methodological pressures on Austin's system—and its resulting restrictions—loom large in this declaration. The academic value attached to scientific description (the guarantee of a chance to wield efficient power) offers an attraction not available with the less efficient models tied to sociological, psychological, or other external interpretive frameworks. The stability offered by the retreat into linguistic objectivity is shaken, however, by the clear validity of reader-response theorizing (and by Fish's arguments against linguistic objectivity)—hence the Riffaterre-like need for a reader to validate the presence of the style. But unlike Riffaterre, who attempted to blend the two through a reliance upon a behavioristic compilation of textual responses, or Fish, who creates interpretive communities, Austin relies upon a neo-rationalist concept of linguistic competence. The reader of a text becomes not just the average reader but the abstraction—"reader." The descriptive strength of the linguistic system is maintained by avoiding actual performance, and Austin quietly halts his movement into the realm of actual disourse activity while he reestablishes Riffaterre's separation between critical interpretation and untutored response. Even interpretation must be redefined into a watched subfield of the discipline. The task of interpretation is only to be that of "characterizing and categorizing the wide variety of relations that may from time to time obtain between *technical* and *perceptual* aspects of poetic syntax, on the one hand, and the *meanings* of the poetic texts in which they occur, on the other" (98).

The similarity to the metastylistic stage of Riffaterre is unmistakable, as are the results. The search for a rigorous scientific methodology, together with the abstract definition of reading and writing that results, produces a critical paradox in which an admitted goal of stylistics comes to be seen as a dangerous risk. "It is ironic," Austin tells us, "that this treacherous domain of interpretation should represent both the goal of most stylists' work that carries the greatest popular appeal and that area in which they venture furthest from their roots, furthest from the relatively 'safe' territory of technical description" (130–31). In fact, Austin's critical interpretation apparently occurs prior to the stage of linguistic analysis. "[T]he actual process of achieving for oneself a satisfactory interpretation of th[e] text," Austin states, "is wholly independent of, and will generally *precede* (theoretically if not practically), even the earliest stages of an interpretive stylistic discussion of its technique" (98). If this sequence were actually followed, however, the critical purpose of a posterior stylistic analysis becomes somewhat suspect—at least as far as literary criticism is concerned.

Austin's qualifying phrase—"theoretically if not practically"—hints at his later claim that the actual progress of any interpretation is not linear but cyclic. Interpretation is a cycle of analysis and insight, he notes, and he supports that generalization with references to Leech, Short, and Leo Spitzer (154n). But that last reference seems out of place, given the separation of linguistics and critical interpretation that Austin still proposes for stylistics. In fact, these arguments over the best procedures for literary stylistics now appear to proceed just as Hough has described them— remarkably free of any complex discussion of the nature of style and literature. Just what style might be is only implied through the various references to writer and intention, along with certain statements about response. And the results for stylistics are clearly damaging. The close of Austin's text, as forthright as the rest, stresses that the "New Stylistics" of 1960 and 1970 now stands at an intellectual crossroads in 1985. Stylistics is in "disarray," Austin candidly admits, "in need of considerable repair . . . exhausted by the rapid progress of the sixties and seventies yet uncertain of where the eighties will lead" (139). That disarray is due, in large measure, to stylistics's concern with objectivity at the cost of complexity, an objectivity that makes itself ripe for criticism, such as that from Fish. And while Austin still resists a fuller movement outward into the realm of context and interpretation, the pressures to make that move have been building all along during this period.

The presence of reader-response criticism is one indication of that pressure; the arguments for a new historicism are another. Thirteen years before the appearance of Austin's text, Karl Uitti already was arguing for the importance of a revitalized philology to contemporary critical issues and to what he significantly stressed as the *"sciences humaines."*[20] Although left to one side in the rush from philology to general linguistics, Spitzer's methods thus reassert their own particular strength as an argument for the role of history in style. The philological circle, redefined into *explication de texte,* may lack the general efficiency and power of contemporary linguistic grammars. But Spitzer's work displays a particular critical relevance by insisting upon seeing the literary text as more than its verbal material and choosing instead to define the basic goal of stylistics as the uncovering of the historical and cultural relations that are caught in the formal and semantic webbing of the work.

In "Les Études," Spitzer appears to have sensed the beginnings of the shift back to context, once more asserting that a science of style must blend author, culture, and literary expression. In one last attempt to merge style and intent, he agrees to the pursuit of any interpretation that initially arises from a concern with the text's meaning, whether the analysis is based upon an observation of word, structure, genre, or history of ideas. This orientation allows Spitzer to testify to the similarities—and differences—between his stylistics of "beauty," Auerbach's sociohistorical concerns, Hatzfeld's and Spoerri's historical typologies, and Alonso's poetics. The *explication* undertaken by all of them differs from that of New Criticism or Russian formalism by insisting upon a link between the context and the text. Among the possible figures and frames for providing that link, Freud is still described in "Les Études" as "the great Viennese" and also as the greatest influence on Spitzer's early career, but he remains a problematic figure. The reasons that Spitzer gives—psychoanalytic techniques do not apply to pre-Romantic writers and risk embracing the biographical fallacy anyway—are familiar enough, as is the absence of a clear dividing line in Spitzer's actual analyses between a correct and an incorrect recourse to the author's psyche. As recently as 1957, Spitzer finds himself correcting Stephen Ullmann for still describing his stylistics as psychoanalytic: "I admit the applicability of psychological stylistics only to writers who think in terms of the 'individual genius,' of an individual manner of writing, that is to writers of the eighteenth and later centuries."[21]

This vision of psychoanalytic criticism—which views it as rooted in the analysis of individual pathology and sees it as ignoring larger historical issues—asserts itself in Spitzer's "negative reading list," also produced in 1957, which urges young critics to avoid certain theoretical (and predominantly nonliterary) texts: "I should like to establish once and for ever a 'negative reading-list' (that is a list of books *not* to be read) for our younger scholars who deal with older literature: Buber, Bergson, Dilthey, Freud, Heidegger, Ortega, Sartre, Scheler, Spengler, Unamuno."[22] But the list is not drawn up solely for prescriptive purposes. Spitzer produces it because he feels the ten authors named are regularly misread, regularly interpreted outside of their historical context. It is the critics' readiness to apply a contemporary interpretation to an historically defined text that produces Spitzer's advice, advice provided for "young" (i.e., naive) scholars. "If Mr. Gilman had consulted here the philologian Curtius instead of the mystic Martin Buber (whose term does not apply to the *Celestina*)," Spitzer suggests, "he would have been able to judge *historically* the invasion in the *Celestina*, of rhetoric into theatre dialogue"; or again: "We shall find throughout Mr. Gilman's book as ever recurrent terms (whose evocative power, without their content, seems to have overwhelmed him) the words 'vital' and 'living' borrowed from Dilthey and Ortega, but misapplied to historical or literary phenomena which were 'alive' at their time, but are not necessarily alive today" (6).[23] The problem is not only one of historical determinism but one of ahistoricism.

The vigilant protection of the text from any contextual misreading also dominates Spitzer's argument with George Boas over the place of biography in reading.[24] The use of biographical details in literary criticism is not the only subject of this self-proclaimed "polemic" (116) against Boas's literary hermeneutics, but it is a key component of its overall assault. Spitzer's primary goal is to discredit Boas's approach to language in general (and to Milton's "Methought I saw" in particular), an approach that he finds destructive to both philology and literary understanding. Spitzer's own decidedly Romantic position—"all philology rests on the assumption that all men on earth are basically alike" (116)—serves as the marker of his divided humanism: the individual style is historical, but the historical individual lies outside of the stylistic analysis.

True to his critical goals, Spitzer counters Boas's argument with an interpretive method that elevates the merely biographical upward into the literary and the cultural. His interpretation of the poem is not based on the biographical elements of Milton's life, which Boas argues are a necessary adjunct to the text, but upon the varied motifs of dream and blindness available throughout literature. As a motif, blindness is assumed to display a level of meaning far beyond that provided by the simple biographical facts, and Spitzer's compilation of equivalent texts and related materials in proof of that assumption displays his reading knowledge at its widest range. Supported by his tropic evidence, Spitzer argues that the reference to blindness in the poem is to be read metaphorically, and only metaphorically: "In view of this grandiose picture of man between two separate worlds how irrelevant would be the personal detail that Milton was blind at the time of his second marriage and hence has never seen his wife" (126)! The detail of Milton's blindness serves "only a 'metaphorical' function, suggesting, as it does, our actual world deprived of the Ideal" (127).

The difficulty with this reading lies not in what it discovers but in what it refuses to see. Spitzer continues in the last decade of his career to draw comparisons between the literary and the historical, but he finds a broad cultural aesthetics to be the only useful bridge between the two. Freud, psychology, biography, and literary history continue to enter the stylistic model when they serve to substantiate not the particulars of the individual, the society, and the culture, but the general expression of the literary text.[25] In 1960, as Spitzer closes a career dedicated to the union of history and literature, he has found no interpretive framework (philosophical, psychological, linguistic, or literary) adequate to his goal of an epistemological union between the historical and the literary.

The difficulties surrounding the struggle to find that missing epistemological frame are not exclusive to Anglo-American criticism. As we look back to the Continent where Spitzer began his search, we can pick up the trail of Spitzer's American career in the trajectory that Peter Uwe Hohendahl plots for West German criticism, which avoids the self-serving historicism of the Nazis by adopting some of the basic features of American New Criticism.[26] The approach "focuse[s] its attention on the aesthetic structure of the work of art, thus displacing the historical context in such a way that the political problematic disappear[s]" (28). But that stance eventually unravels in West Germany, as it does in the United States. By 1960 it is being replaced by structural and semiotic approaches and, later, by Wolfgang Iser's and Hans Robert Jauss's reception theories. Given this trajectory, it is exceedingly fitting to find Bellos stressing the influence of Spitzer on postwar Germanic linguistics in general and on Jauss in particular (xxiv). The movements of Germanic criticism thus mirror those of Spitzer's later career in significant ways, with the thinking of Jauss and Iser serving as the major indication of criticism's break with the acontextual text. But the desire to legitimize academic literary criticism by making it an aspect of newer social and historical theories carries Continental criticism further than the boundaries of Spitzer's work or even those of reader-response criticism, and it is in the new concern with social and historical frames of interpretation that the epistemological model sought by Spitzer for language and style is finally being formed, in the United States as well as in Germany.

As Mary Louise Pratt has demonstrated, neither the lone individual author of Romanticism nor the amorphous interpretive community of Fish provides a full epistemological argument for the acts of writing and reading. Instead, Pratt redefines Fish's community in order to include within it those social and historical issues that are recognizable as the ideological constructs which constitute the community. The social group is not a strangely connected (or strangely unconnected) literary entity: "interpretive communities are bound to be communities on other grounds as well, bound to have common interests besides the production of interpretations, bound to correspond to other social differentiations."[27] This expanded view of community/context answers two difficulties found in an author-oriented stylistics such as Spitzer's, and in stylistics in general. First, it

provides an epistemologically valid portrait of the interplay between society and the individual. Second, it overcomes the bias against the historical origin of the text by noting that the logical companion of an
interpretive context is a productive context.

Pratt's arguments solve the first issue by relying, at least obliquely, on
the psychoanalytic framework that Spitzer always knew to be valuable
but could not revise in order to make it fit into his own approach. She
neither romanticizes the role of the text and/or its author (Spitzer's final
resolution) nor reduces them to the flat presentation of biographical facts
(Spitzer's ultimate fear). "[T]he literary speech situation," Pratt tells us,
"tends to be viewed as a one-to-one private interaction between THE
reader and THE text (with the text substituting for THE author because
she or he is not actually there)."[28] The existence of this critical myth
depends on another myth, that of the unified subject, the individual as
definable outside of a social or historical framework. The rejection of this
false apotheosis of the individual provides for the expanded view of author
and context that escapes from the merely factual or the merely aesthetic.
The result is a view of the "non-essential, socially constituted subject,"
for whom the context is more than just "the backdrop against which a
person speaks—we've always known that was too schematic. Rather the
context and the subject continually and mutually determine each other"
(9). The portrait of both reader and writer as socially constituted, yet
socially constituting, allows a portrayal of author and context that is neither
romantically individualistic nor psychologically deterministic, and it provides a descriptive power more inclusive than that belonging to a scientific
methodology.

This resurrection of the writer undoubtedly has been aided by the shift
out of the critical text effected by reception criticism. Reader-response
criticism has been led by its own logic to recognize that factors beyond
the boundaries of the text contribute to a particular reader's response.
Admitting those factors in literary interpretation is logically followed by
admitting the same factors as components of literary production. Their
presence further entails, "among other things," Pratt tells us, "exploring
the specifics of reception as a socially and ideologically determined process, and coming to grips with the question of artistic *production*" (205).
The interpretive community is free to open up to social description and,
at the same time, to reintroduce the text's productive community and,
with it, the author.

Pratt's ability to use the implications of the interpretive community in this way is not all that startling. The author has never been far removed from any stylistic argument, linguistic or otherwise. Austin, recognizing the appeal of extended interpretation, readily suggests that stylists should "share their temerity with critics of many other persuasions— biographers, historians, and psychoanalysts, for example, all of whom eventually find themselves forced to lay aside their respective specializations and to make unambiguous *critical* claims about a specific literary text" (131). Indeed, Austin is willing to recognize a writing figure at almost every stage of his analysis, even though he hesitates under the pressure of linguistic methodology and grants the poet only the "correct degree of prominence in stylistic theory" that will make the poet an "intriguing but by no means integral aspect of the stylist's work" (137). Critical theory thus continues to offer evidence of its repressed desire to discuss the author, whether in terms of formalist or antiformalist doctrines. Austin, for all his objective rigor, admits as much. "Only if we deliberately broaden our view to include the speaker/writer's communicative *intent*," he writes in discussing Dryden, "can we make any sense of the structural frames that he has chosen" (118). At the same time, he cautiously admits to having "toyed with psychoanalytical reconstruction" (137) in a paper on Wordsworth. Nor is Austin alone in his admission. Many of those critics instrumental in the reevaluation of linguistic stylistics, such as Barbara Herrnstein Smith, E. D. Hirsch, and Morton Bloomfield, also have hinted at the importance of the author to the critical interpretation.

The success of fictive discourse, as defined by Herrnstein Smith, depends upon the reader's awareness of the poet, and intention is a part of her definition of interpretation: "[A]mong the meanings we seek for and infer from a poem are those that, in Aristotelian terms, might be called its *final* causes: that is, the motives or intentions, the governing design, of the poet as artist, distinct from either a natural speaker or the fictive speaker of a poem" (39). The qualifying phrase "the poet as artist" is a common signal in criticism that this "poet" is Booth's implied author, a theoretical construct used only for the purpose of literary interpretation. But that qualification no longer serves to validate a context-free analysis. Intention, or the poet as artist, serves not only as a marker of fictive discourse but as a marker of a particular critical desire to find some role for the writer. The greatest difficulty is not in readmitting some level of authorial presence but in defining that presence in terms of an adequate historical frame.

E. D. Hirsch demonstrates the difficulties of that struggle as he tries to provide some separation between poet and person, art and writing. "The speaking subject is not," he corrects us, "identical with the subjectivity of the author as an actual historical person; it corresponds, rather, to a very limited and special aspect of the author's total subjectivity; it is, so to speak, that 'part' of the author which specifies or determines verbal meaning" (*Validity*, 242–43). The opacity of this description makes for its own problems, but the questions that it begs are even more important. What, for example, is "an actual historical person"? The answer in criticism would appear to be those biographical facts that accumulate around an individual. But the assumption of an easily defined space between writer and creative author, or individual and society, or biography and history has little substantive basis. The argument exists primarily to attack any taint of determinism in the description of the creative act.

Morton Bloomfield's "Stylistics and the Theory of Literature" demonstrates the dangers of this argument. Bloomfield attempts to avoid mixing linguistic analysis and authorial intention through the use of a standard language/poetic language framework. Style is to be found in the individual features particular to each literary work. The definition of these features is to depend upon the establishment of a background or generic text, since without such a zero degree of genres and types, there is no means for establishing the unique variations or repetitions that constitute style. Yet Bloomfield states openly that this undertaking has few guarantees of success. He refers to the search for neutral genres as "utopian" and "daunting," admitting that "the pursuit of a zero degree definition of a complex genre seems a will-o-the-wisp" (291). In the face of such formal difficulties, Bloomfield provides a way out, but only by falling on the very sword that could cut through his theoretical difficulties. If a zero-degree text is not possible, he admits, "we shall have to settle for a different kind of stylistics—with emphasis on the psychology of the author or a descriptive stylistics on the surface level" (285). A descriptive stylistics can be dismissed as mere formalism. The remaining option, which Bloomfield intentionally burdens with the supposed albatross of psychological determinism, is really only the figure of the productive author. We will not "have to settle" for any lowering of stylistics at all, provided we choose a sophisticated model of literary production.

Such a model must address the aesthetic, sociological, and historical dimensions of discourse, and it must do so in such a way as to resolve the major questions gathered around Spitzer's stylistic goals. Spitzer's theory remains weakest in its singularly Romantic definition of the author's role, a weakness that steadily increased with his movement away from two key explanatory models—psychoanalysis and the specifics of history. Spitzer's general reasoning in both cases is valid: an overly intense focus on the author can result in a deterministic reading of the text, amounting to no more than Romantic individualism. Unfortunately, his own resolution of this problem is based upon a weakened image of the writer that is lightly washed by those very tints of Romanticism. His argument relies too heavily upon authorial intention as a higher, aesthetic mode of existence, thus providing an epistemological model lacking ties to social behavior.

Pratt's arguments for an epistemology rooted in the study of the social and ideological determinants of style offers a refining framework rooted in a wider view of the issues surrounding individuality, society, and literary activity than the one offered either by biography or the implied author.[29]

> [T]heoreticians have invented an entity called the implied author, a voice or position abstracted away from the "real" author who produced the text but who cannot exist personally for recipients of the text. I believe this mediation is the only motive there is for postulating an implied author, and if you abandon the notion of an authentic, essential "real author" out there somewhere, the category of implied author becomes unnecessary. With respect to a given text, in this view, "authorship" is a certain, socially constituted position occupied by a speaking subject . . . no more, and no less, than another of the many ways a subject realizes itself through speech acts. ["Ideology," 10]

Stylisticians may desire a more staid discourse model, but all models vary in their level of applicability to literary critical interpretation, and many of them miss the opportunity provided by the study of ideology to reintroduce important contextual issues to to the study of style. And the question facing the discipline today is not one of descriptive power (i.e., universal applicability) but of descriptive adequacy. Working along these lines, Mary Poovey has produced a model that, in addressing the need for descriptive adequacy and complexity, also produces its own form of descriptive power.[30]

The three features that Poovey uses to define literary style—author, behavior, and ideology—are all problematic in terms of previous work because they run counter to linguistic and critical methods that pursue the context-independent literary text. Poovey, on the other hand, chooses to begin precisely at that point, seeing style as a specific part of writing behavior and behavior as a function of social and cultural ideology: " 'style,' understood in the largest sense of this term, represents ideology as it has been internalized and articulated by the individual" (xiii). With such a model, we reintroduce the issues of history and psychoanalysis with which Spitzer began his own search.

Poovey's work does remain open to the charge that it inadequately addresses the linguistic aspects of style, although an argument can be made that studying style through linguistic methodology has yet to resolve the problems created by the discipline's agenda of hidden formalism. That weakness remains a part of stylistics, but the ties between language study and stylistics run so deep in western tradition that the field probably should not be pursued without embracing some serious linguistic methodology. Pratt's modified speech-act theory thus appears to provide the best procedures for satisfying the large, contextually focused goals that stylistics must set for itself. These goals are clear enough. First, the general view of a one-to-one exchange as the normal discourse situation will have to be altered in order to address the larger complexities of literary and, indeed, most written discourse. Second, the idea of a unified subject will obviously have to fade before the more complex conception of the dynamic tension between individual and ideology. Finally, the discourse situation will have to be defined in terms of socially realistic dynamics. These criteria allow for a reformation of stylistics, not into a radically new form, but into a form that addresses those historical, linguistic, and epistemological issues that Spitzer struggled to resolve throughout his career.

These resolutions of stylistics' problems may not be exactly those that Spitzer would have chosen, but they follow the directions that his efforts first mapped out. The stylistic model we seek thus raises itself around the framework that Spitzer first envisioned when he attempted in 1910 to devise a "more scientific" definition of literary style. It is scientific in Spitzer's sense of that term, that is, the model attempts to rest itself upon the foundation provided by a clearly elaborated study of language and its role in epistemology. Yet the way that methodology is constructed allows it to escape from the reductionism that accompanies the ideological appeal of efficiency and descriptive power. The escape is simple enough. It begins with a refusal to accept anything less than a complex definition of discourse rooted in an equally complex definition of user and context. That entire definition, supported by a willing description of the psychological, sociological, and historical contexts that surround literary production, will provide the academic validity for stylistics that Spitzer sought. In his attempt to realize a full epistemological role for style, Spitzer's Romanticism led him to eliminate any and all features that smacked of positivism. This elimination, unfortunately, was equated with the removal of the social and historical issues that formed a part of the literary context, leaving Spitzer to define style in terms of a spiritualized aesthetic. Contemporary stylistics seeks instead to recapture the full productive context and make it primary in any discussion of style, thus returning, newly outfitted, to the search for those "sensuous, witty, disciplined" authors and their surroundings whose absence from linguistic analysis first led Spitzer to the kind of interpretive literary stylistics we are pursuing today.

NOTES

1. Leo Spitzer, "Les Études de Style et les Différent Pays," *Langue et Littérature, Actes du VIII Congrès de la Fédération Internationale des Langues et Littératures Modernes* (Paris: Société d'Édition « Les Belles Lettres », 1961), 23–39.

2. Great Britain offered several models, each providing its own level of formalism, although all were about equally dedicated to the systematic descriptions of this period. The works of Firth and Halliday are the most important, although these never achieved the immediate popularity in the United States that Chomsky's work enjoyed. See Halliday's articles in Freeman (note 5) for a view of the better-known examples of these particular stylistic approaches.

3. Roger Fowler, *Essays on Style and Language: Linguistic and Critical Approaches to Literary Style* (London: Routledge & Kegan Paul, 1966).

4. Perhaps no book displays the procedural eclecticism of the period better than Geoffrey Leech's *Introduction to English Poetry*, a text that encompasses stylistic methods ranging from classical rhetoric to contemporary linguistics. But even in the midst of this variety the core importance of formal linguistic description predominates (Geoffrey Leech, *A Linguistic Guide to English Poetry* [London: Longman, 1969]).

5. Donald Freeman, ed., *Essays in Modern Stylistics* (New York: Methuen, 1981), 3.

6. Helmut Hatzfeld's *A Critical Bibliography of the New Stylistics Applied to the Romance Literatures: 1900–1952* provides an earlier beginning point for it all. A quick comparison of Hatzfeld's bibliography of the "New Stylistics" (Helmut Hatzfeld, *A Critical Bibliography of the New Stylistics Applied to the Romance Literatures: 1900–1952, University of North Carolina Studies in Comparative Literature*, 5 [Chapel Hill: University of North Carolina Press, 1953]) and bibliographies of English-

language stylistics for these same years (see, for example, Milič and Bailey and Burton) demonstrates a difference in the sheer quantity of work being done on the Continent.

7. Graham Hough, *Style and Stylistics* (London: Routledge & Kegan Paul, 1969), 11.

8. Deborah Cameron, *Femininism and Linguistic Theory* (New York: St. Martin's Press, 1985), 11.

9. Donald Freeman, *Linguistics and Literary Style* (New York: Holt, Rinehart & Winston, 1970). Ten years later, inside his collection, *Essays in Modern Stylistics* (see note 5), Freeman would glance back at the first volume and note that one reviewer described it as "old hat" (3). The new volume would avoid that difficulty, reprinting only those essays that Freeman sees as "the most promising . . . for further practical work, and . . . of the greatest potential use." All of them center, with one exception, on modern transformation-generative grammar and its ramifications (4).

10. Chomsky also generated a great deal of political interest during the Vietnam War. His linguistics and politics may both have suffered some misreadings at the time. But it remains difficult (and undesirable) to read Chomsky's writing without including and admiring his political activity.

11. Richard Ohmann, "Generative Grammars and the Concept of Literary Style," *Word*, 20 (1964), 423–39. Ohmann's work can be used to track the changing shifts in stylistics throughout this period, and his later articles provide a short history of thinking about literary language in terms of speech-acts: "Speech, Action, Style," *Literary Style: A Symposium*, ed. Seymour Chatman (New York: Oxford University Press, 1971), 241–59; "Speech Acts and The Definition of Literature," *Philosophy and Rhetoric*, 4 (1971), 1–19; "Literature as Act," *Approaches to Poetics*, ed. Seymour Chatman (New York: Columbia University Press, 1973); and "Speech, Literature, and the Space Between," *Essays in Modern Stylistics*, ed. Donald Freeman (New York: Methuen, 1981), 361–76.

12. John R. Searle, "Chomsky's Revolution in Linguistics," in *On Noam Chomsky*, ed. Gilbert Harman (Garden City, N.Y.: Anchor Press/Doubleday, 1974) 2. See chapter 2 for the full statement.

13. Morton Bloomfield, "Stylistics and the Theory of Literature," *New Literary History*, 7 (1976), 272.

14. Jerrold J. Katz, "Chomsky on Meaning," *Language*, 56 (1980), 2–3.

15. The articles are reprinted in Stanley Fish, *Is There a Text in This Class?* (Cambridge, Mass.: Harvard University Press, 1980). The text also provides Fish's added commentaries, which are as useful as the reprinted articles. The essays appear on pages 68–96 and 246–67, respectively. Barbara Herrnstein Smith's "Surfacing from the Deep" (1978) provides

another good example of the basic argument. Originally appearing as a review article in 1977 (*PTL: A Journal for Descriptive Poetics and Theory of Literature*, 2 [1977], 151–82), the essay reappears in her *On the Margins of Discourse* [Chicago: University of Chicago Press, 1978]).

16. Samuel J. Keyser, "Wallace Stevens: Form and Meaning in Four Poems," *College English*, 37, no. 6 (1976), 575–98.

17. Louis Milič, "Unconscious Ordering in the Prose of Swift," in *The Computer and Literary Style*, ed. Jacob Leed (Kent, Oh.: Kent State University Press, 1966), 79–106.

18. Timothy R. Austin, *Language Crafted: A Linguistic Theory of Poetic Syntax* (Bloomington: Indiana University Press, 1984).

19. Herbert H. Clark and Eve V. Clark, *Psychology and Language: An Introduction to Psycholinguistics* (New York: Harcourt Brace Jovanovich, 1977). Austin's reference is on page 147n.

20. Karl Uitti, "Philology: Factualness and History," in *Literary Style: A Symposium*, ed. Seymour Chatman (Oxford: Oxford University Press, 1971), 112. Intentionally contrasting the "more 'humane'—or humanistic—science" of philology with that of descriptive linguistics, Uitti argues that "the characteristic historicity of philological approaches . . . suggests that they offer a context in which our contemporary fascination with sign patterning might once again be reconciled with some of the traditional values associated with literary study" (127–28).

21. Leo Spitzer, "Review of Stephen Ullmann," *Style in the French Novel, Comparative Literature*, 10 (1958), 371. Ullmann is congratulated for having avoided the segmentation of Sayce's work by studying the complete novels. The review is exceptionally positive, perhaps because Spitzer recognizes a fellow Continental Romance scholar in Ullmann's work. " 'Stylistic studies,' " Spitzer declares, "in the sense in which continental European and American scholars have used the term since approximately the year 1900, seem to be gaining vogue in England—which had, in this field, remained behind French and German and also Spanish and Italian scholarship" (368).

22. Leo Spitzer, "A New Book on the Art of *The Celestina*," review of *The Art of "The Celestina*," by Stephen Gilman, *Hispanic Review*, 25 (January, 1957), 1–25. This list provides "pedagogical advice that Spitzer happily did not follow himself as a young man," Wellek tells us. "What would he have become," he asks, "without, at least three names on the list: Freud, Dilthey, and Bergson?" ("Leo Spitzer," 324).

23. Mention is made of the other figures on the following pages (among others): Bergson, 19; Freud, 15; Heidegger, 19; Scheler, 19; and Unamuno, 22.

24. Leo Spitzer, "Understanding Milton," *Essays on British and Amer-*

ican Literature, ed. Anna Hatcher (Princeton, N.J.: Princeton University Press, 1962), 116–31.

25. There are other examples of this sensibility at work. Spitzer strongly attacks Boas's introduction of Katherine Woodcock's name into the poem, viewing it as "a regression to the positivistic ideals of past generations" (128n) and "as shocking as the whole proposition of making the poem more empirically concrete than it has been conceived" (129). Spitzer would have known, of course, that Cherniss opens his own attack on the biographical fallacy with a derogatory remark about the value of the discovery of the bill-of-sale for Milton's house.

26. Peter Uwe Hohendahl, *The Institution of Criticism* (Ithaca, N.Y.: Cornell University Press, 1982).

27. Mary Louise Pratt, "Interpretive Strategies/Strategic Interpretations: On Anglo-American Reader Response Criticism," *Boundary* 2, 11, nos. 1 and 2 (1982/83), 201–31. The quotation appears on page 228.

28. Mary Louise Pratt, "The Ideology of Speech-Act Theory," *Centrum,* 1, no. 1 (1981), 5–18. The statement appears on pages 7–8.

29. Pratt's usefulness to this study is supported by her early (if brief) use of Spitzer, in *Towards a Speech-Act Theory of Literary Discourse,* in order to deny the choice of form over intention: "The poetic text, which 'forms itself' . . . is every bit as mechanistic, as divorced from the reality of human communication as the 'ordinary' utterance that 'transmits merely information about the outside world.' Spitzer, by contrast, simply declares, 'Whoever has thought strongly or felt strongly has innovated in his language' " (*Towards a Speech-Act Theory of Literary Discourse* [Bloomington: Indiana University Press, 1977], 5).

30. Mary Poovey, *The Proper Lady and the Woman Writer: Ideology as Style in the Works of Mary Wollstonecraft, Mary Shelley, and Jane Austen* (Chicago: University of Chicago Press, 1984).

Index

Note on the Author

James V. Catano is currently an associate professor with the Department of English at Louisiana State University, Baton Rouge. His previous publications include "The Place of Leo Spitzer's Intentional Stylist in Contemporary Stylistics," which appeared in the journal *Language and Style*, and, more recently, his "Style and Stylistics," which was published by the journal *Style*.